The Railways and Locomotives of The Lilleshall Company

By Bob Yate

IRWELL PRESS Ltd.

Copyright IRWELL PRESS LIMITED
ISBN 10-1-903266-86-6
ISBN 13-978-1-903266-86-1

ACKNOWLEDGEMENTS

Many of the sources were, as indicated, accessed through various local and national libraries and archives. I should like to record my thanks to the staffs of the following for their help and guidance: Madeley Library, Newport Library, Telford Library, Wellington Library, Flintshire Records Office, Hawarden, Shropshire Records and Research, Shrewsbury, Ironbridge Gorge Museum Trust, Coalbrookdale, National Railway Museum Library and Archives, York, Public Record Office, Kew.

In particular, I am particularly grateful to John Powell and Jo Smith (Ironbridge Gorge Museum Trust) for their help and forebearance in locating the Lilleshall Company records, and to Jim Cooper, local historian, for his assistance in interpreting much of these records and his expert local knowledge. Members of the Industrial Railway Society and Industrial Locomotive Society also provided a great deal of useful information, especially regarding the locomotives, and often when the prospect of uncovering further clues seemed daunting, as follows: Allan Baker, Alex Betteney, Vic Bradley, The late Alan Bridges, Bob Darvill, John Fletcher, Peter Holmes, Colin Mountford, Martin Potts, Peter Rowbotham, Russell Wear, Mike Wood.

Local knowledge and anecdotes were contributed by former employees of both the Lilleshall Company and the NCB and local business people: Peter Bushell, Peter Harris, Len Jones, Arthur Leek, Edgar Meeson, Alan Minor, Jim Rollason, Ernie Wood.

Photographs were kindly supplied by Allan Baker, Mike Dodd, Frank Jones, Tim Shuttleworth, the late Jim Peden, Tony Carr at Shropshire Records and Research, Shrewsbury and by John Powell on behalf of the Ironbridge Gorge Museum Trust.

Additional information and direction was gratefully received from Angus Breton (Group Secretary of the erstwhile Lilleshall plc), and from the Telford Horsehay Steam Trust, Paul Hughes and Reg Stanley.

Finally, this work could not have been completed without the support and patience of my wife, Sandra.

**First published in the United Kingdom in 2008
by Irwell Press Limited, 59A, High Street, Clophill,
Bedfordshire MK45 4BE
Printed by Konway Printhouse**

CONTENTS

Beginnings	Page	5
Chapter One – Establishment of the Company	Page	7
Chapter Two – Growth of the Company	Page	11
Chapter Three – Development of the Transport Needs	Page	35
Chapter Four – The Lilleshall Company Railway	Page	37
Chapter Five – The Humber Arm Railway	Page	41
Chapter Six – The Narrow Gauge Railways	Page	45
Chapter Seven – Locomotives built by the Lilleshall Company	Page	47
Chapter Eight – Locomotives of the Lilleshall System	Page	67
Chapter Nine – Operating the Railway	Page	79
Chapter Ten – Limestone Quarries	Page	96
Chapter Eleven – The Collieries under NCB Ownership	Page	100
Appendix 1 – Lilleshall Company Mines	Page	120
Appendix 2 – The 1862 built locomotive	Page	121
Appendix 3 – The Identity of 'Phoenix'	Page	122
Appendix 4 – Lilleshall's 'Express Locomotive'	Page	123
Appendix 5 – Lilleshall Company Wagons	Page	126
Appendix 6 – Code of Signals	Page	127
Appendix 7 – Private Sidings Agreements	Page	128
Appendix 8 – Comparison of Locomotive Data – Lilleshall Fleet Locos	Page	129
Sources	Page	131
Index	Page	133

Lilleshall 0-6-0ST No.6 (90 of 1869) in fine condition, around 1910.

Beginnings

The area around today's Telford, and specifically that of Coalbrookdale, is well known as the cradle of the industrial revolution. However, the story goes much further back than Abraham Darby. The Roman settlement of 'Uscocona' became that latterly known as Oakengates. The Romans are known to have worked outcrops of coal in this part of East Shropshire, and this mining continued on right through the Middle Ages. Locally, the 'longwall' technique of mining was developed, which involved excavating along the lateral face of the coal seam, rather than 'head first' into the seam. Such small pits were typically only 60 to 100 feet deep at the start of the industrial revolution, and many of this depth continued, even into the 20th century.

Not surprisingly, such mining activities revealed other minerals for which uses were either initially apparent, or for which the resourcefulness of the miners found a new use. The deposits of ironstone and fireclay were exploited in this way, and thus new products were developed and new markets opened throughout Britain, and eventually exported. As an example, one early blast furnace was opened in Lilleshall village in 1591. Later, and nearby, the well established Coalbrookdale Company built blast furnaces on land leased from Earl Gower at Donnington Wood in 1783.

This area was one of the most heavily industrialised in the country for many decades, and its contribution to the nation's wealth is often under appreciated. For example, it is recorded that around one quarter of the iron produced in Britain in 1806 came from here.

The Lilleshall Company came to be the largest employer in the region, utilising the local iron, coal and limestone reserves and developing these heavy industries by the application of the accumulated skills in the area, and drawing on new technology from further afield.

The former GWR '2721' class 0-6-0PT No.2794 and Lilleshall No.12 stand in the sunshine outside the engine shed at the New Yard Works in 1951. [C. R. Nicholls / Ironbridge Gorge Museum Trust]

A beautifully posed photograph, full of character from an early date, possibly around 1900. The locomotive is Lilleshall 0-6-0ST No.7 (135 of 1870) though the location of the crossing is not known. [Ironbridge Gorge Museum Trust]

An excellent engraving from 'The National Portrait Gallery', depicting the 2nd Earl Granville, Granville Leveson-Gower.

CHAPTER ONE
ESTABLISHMENT OF THE COMPANY

The origins of the company lay with the Leveson-Gower family, who had made their fortune from the wool trade in Wolverhampton in the 15th and 16th centuries. One ancestor, James Leveson, purchased the Lilleshall estates from Henry VIII in 1539, following the forfeiture of Lilleshall Abbey and its surrounding lands to the Crown during the Dissolution of the Monasteries. The 1st. Baron Gower (1675-1709) and his son, the 1st. Earl Gower (1694-1754), enlarged their properties through acquisition and marriage. Granville Leveson-Gower, the 2nd. Earl Gower (1721-1803), continued this tradition in 1748 by marrying Lady Louisa Egerton, the daughter of the Duke of Bridgwater.

The 2nd. Earl Gower was an astute businessman, always looking to make the best use of his considerable properties. Looking at the various new industries prospering nearby, it was a logical step to join these and to similarly profit by them. However, lacking the necessary technical knowledge and industrial experience, he wisely formed a partnership on 8 September 1764 with two brothers, John Gilbert and Thomas Gilbert, to develop the minerals on the Earl's estate. John Gilbert had initially been apprenticed to Matthew Boulton before joining his father's metalworking firm in Birmingham. However, he moved on to become agent to the Duke of Bridgwater and thus gained valuable knowledge of canal construction and operation. His brother, Thomas had been educated more formally and qualified as a barrister. This partnership, trading as Earl Gower and Company, lasted until 1786 when he became the Marquis of Stafford. Thereafter, the partnership continued, logically as Marquis of Stafford and Company, until 1802. During this 38 year period, the coal, iron and limestone deposits were developed, and canals built both within the Earl's estate and connecting to others outside. One of the earliest examples was the Donnington Wood Canal opening in 1768 to run for 5½ miles from Donnington Wood to Pave Lane (near Newport, and on the Chester trunk road).

The titles and estates of the 2nd. Earl Gower would pass on his death to his eldest son, George Granville Leveson-Gower (1758-1833), who married the Countess of Sutherland in 1785, and was created Duke of Sutherland shortly before his death in 1833. However, the second son, confusingly named Granville Leveson-Gower (from the 2nd. Earl Gower's second marriage) was more active in the management of the company. In February and March, 1802 he acquired the partnership holdings of the Gilbert brothers who had died in 1795 (John) and 1798 (Thomas). His father passed to him his partnership holdings in April, 1802. Very shortly afterwards, Granville completed his reorganisation of the company by dissolving the existing partnership. This was replaced by a new partnership agreement coming into force on 24 June 1802 as the Lilleshall Company, being so named after the family seat and estates. New partners were admitted, who mostly brought in their capital in the form of their existing local mines and ironworks at Snedshill, Wrockwardine Wood and Donnington Wood. The new partners were James Bishton (managing partner, with 5/16 share), John Onions, James Birch and William Phillips (these three with 1/16 share each),

An engraving of the 2nd Duke of Sutherland, George Granville Leveson-Gower from a book titled 'The National Portrait Gallery', published around 1900.

7

and the new capital of the partnership was fixed at £160,800. Granville, having the remaining half of the shares, was appointed Chairman. Later, in 1833, he was created the 1st Earl Granville.

In 1807, the notable local ironmaster William Horton joined the partnership, and during 1830 William Blount and J. Hombersley joined as further partners with their Snedshill businesses. As time went on it became necessary for the new company to acquire further land rights for mining and manufacturing. These, of course had to be leased by the Company from the successive Dukes of Sutherland and another neighbour, the Jerningham family, headed by Baron Stafford. This family was quite separate from the Leveson-Gower family who, as indicated above, had inherited the title to *Marquis* of Stafford. As examples of the respective mining rights, the 1915 Valuation records that the 60 year lease with Baron Stafford dated 1 January 1878 for mining coal, ironstone, fireclay, brick clays, limestone, etc. and covering the Woodhouse, Stafford, Lawn and fire clay pits was estimated to contain unworked coal totalling 17,093,500 tons. The 50 year lease dated 25 December 1908 with the Duke of Sutherland covered the northern pits and at the same date was estimated to contain 49,167,000 tons of unworked coal.

Under the 2nd. Earl Granville, the company took advantage of new legislation, and was incorporated with limited liability as from 1 January, 1862. However, the name was not changed to the Lilleshall Company Limited until 31 December, 1880 The authorised share capital was £600,000 and the issued share capital was allocated as follows:

Granville Leveson-Gower, 2nd. Earl Granville, 18 Carlton House Terrace, London £85,000

Henry Valentine Stafford, Baron Stafford, Costessey Hall, near Norwich £108,000

Hon. Edward Frederick Leveson-Gower, MP, 14 South Audley Street, London £75,000

T.D. Gilbert 16 Old Burlington Street, London £22,000

W Blount Gerards Cross, Buckinghamshire £43,000

T. E Horton Shifnal, Shropshire £22,000

Charles Lucena, Englefield, Staines, Berkshire £22,000

Total £377,000

Chairmanship of the company passed through the side of the family shown on the accompanying family tree as inheriting the title of Earl Granville. The 1st. Earl Granville also established the well known Shelton Bar Iron Company at Etruria, Stoke-on-Trent. The 2nd. Earl Granville was notable for pursuing a successful political career, during which he was twice appointed as Foreign Secretary under Gladstone. The foreign contacts that he made in this position proved of considerable use to the Company. Meanwhile, the Duke of Sutherland's lineage continued to own the substantial estates in Shropshire. It is worthy of note that the 3rd. Duke was apprenticed to James McConnell at the LNWR Wolverton Works, and later went on to play a leading role in the fortunes of the Highland Railway. There is no doubt that he influenced the Lilleshall Company in its inclination towards production of locomotives.

As we shall see later, the company's remaining coal mines were nationalised with effect from 1 January 1947. The Labour government of the day also indicated its intention to nationalise the British iron and steel industry, and the necessary powers were enshrined in the Iron and Steel Act, 1949. This required all companies producing more than 20,000 tons of steel or pig iron per annum to be brought

Share certificate recording the effective nationalisation of the Lilleshall Iron & Steel Co. Ltd. in 1951 [Courtesy: Ironbridge Gorge Museum trust]

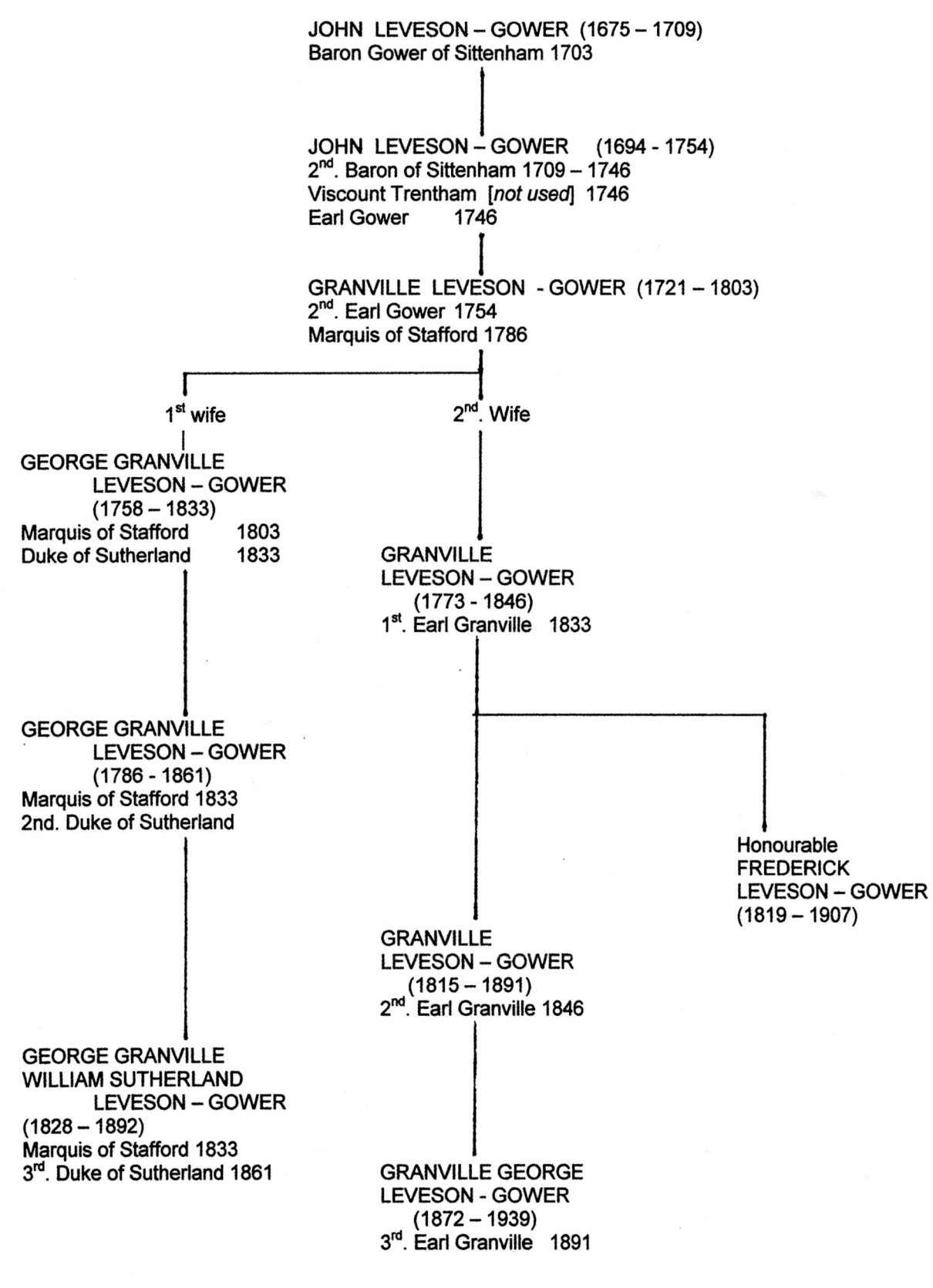

Six portraits of former Chairmen of the Lilleshall Company, reading from top left:
Sir George Granville Leveson-Gower, KBE, MA (Chairman 1903-1908 and 1940-1945).
2nd Earl Granville, KG, PC, DCL (Chairman 1846-1891).
Hon. Frederick Leveson-Gower, MP, DL, JP, MG (Chairman 1891-1902).
3rd Earl Granville, PC, GCMG, GCVO (Chairman 1908-1939).
4th Earl Granville, KG, KCVO, CB, DSO (Chairman 1945-1953).
1st Earl Granville, GCB (Chairman 1803-1846).
[Ironbridge Gorge Museum Trust]

into public ownership under the Iron and Steel Corporation of Great Britain (ISCGB). This eventually comprised 298 former private companies, with over 300,000 employees and a total annual turnover exceeding £500 million. In anticipation of this requirement, the Company had transferred the 'assets and goodwill of its iron and steel branches' to a new subsidiary – Lilleshall Iron and Steel Co Ltd as from 31 December 1947. This subsidiary was vested in the ISCGB as from 15 February 1951 when it acquired the entire share capital of the subsidiary (184,831 shares of £1 each) for a net value of £129,382. However, the nationalisation act was deeply flawed and was repealed by the Iron and Steel Act 1953. Consequently, the ISCGB businesses were first transferred to the Iron and Steel Holding and Realisation Agency, from which they were returned to private ownership. The Company reacquired its subsidiary for a net consideration of £95,000 with effect from 2 October 1954 and this subsidiary continued in operation until after the complete cessation of the iron and steel business.

The business was subsequently floated as a public company on the London Stock Exchange, and changed its name to Lilleshall plc as from 23 May 1988. By this time, the Company had moved its operations away from the area, the registered office being transferred to Gloucester in 1984. In January, 2001 the Company finally lost its independence, becoming part of the private group of Wyko plc. As indicated, for many years the Company has not been based in Shropshire, nor in its traditional businesses, which as we shall see have all disappeared.

In the remainder of this work, for reasons of brevity and clarity, the business in its various forms, will be simply referred to as 'the Company'.

An explanation is required to clarify the events of 1833. In this year, George Granville Leveson – Gower was created the 1st. Duke of Sutherland; consequently, the title 'Marquis of Stafford' was henceforth deemed to pass to the eldest son of the Duke. So this title passed at that time to his son of the same name. However, the new Duke died in the same year, so his dukedom passed again to his son, whose 'Marquis of Stafford' title correspondingly passed at the same time to his son, George Granville William Sutherland Leveson - Gower.

Note also that the name Leveson – Gower is pronounced 'Looson – Gore'.

One final note of caution is inserted here, to warn readers not familiar with the intricacies of the nobility. It was mentioned earlier that the Jerningham family had (and still have) the title of Baron Stafford, whilst the Leveson – Gower family have the title Marquis of Stafford. The use of the word 'Lord' is simply a form of address to any member of the nobility, regardless of their actual title, which may be Baron, Earl, Marquis or Duke. Thus, it is quite proper to address either Baron Stafford or the Marquis of Stafford as 'Lord Stafford'. In researching for this book, this latter form of address has been found in much correspondence, and in many cases it has taken considerable effort to identify the person being referred to.

The Honourable Frederick Leveson-Gower, MP, DL, JP, MG (Chairman 1891-1902). [Author's Collection]

The First Earl Granville, Granville Leveson-Gower, GCB (Chairman 1803-1846). [Author's Collection]

The 2nd Earl Granville, Granville Leveson-Gower, KG, PC, DCL (Chairman 1846-1891). [Author's Collection]

CHAPTER TWO
GROWTH OF THE COMPANY

The company grew at a prodigious rate during the 19th century and the early part of the 20th century, so much so that to explain in date order the various works that were opened, expanded, reduced and closed during these periods would be very taxing to the reader. Therefore, for clarity, each of these works are listed separately along with a brief history of their development and subsequent disposition. Most of these will be found on the accompanying plan of the railway system, but a few were either not connected to the system or were closed before the internal railway was opened.

Wrockwardine Wood Brickworks and **Donnington Wood Brickworks.** These were originally two very early brickworks being based at small mines where fireclay was produced as a by product. They were in the vicinity of The Nabb, and the one at Wrockwardine Wood is known to have expanded into a separate works by 1793. However, it is not clear when it finally went out of use.

Meanwhile, the one at Donnington Wood continued in use until the 1850s when the new Donnington Brickworks replaced it, although it is believed that at least some of its facilities continued in use after that date.

Snedshill Brickworks was originally supplied with clay from the quarry on its north-eastern side, as well as fireclay from the company's mines to make tiles, quarries, white bricks, firebricks and land drainage pipes. It is uncertain when the works opened, but it was in operation by 1850. As the original quarry became worked out, the brickworks itself expanded into this area. A second kiln was added in 1936, and the range of products expanded to include the famous Belfast sink, salt glazed pipes, refractories, glazed bricks, urinals, and wash basins. As the supply of fireclay from the company's mines dwindled, it was sourced instead from the nearby Wrekin Coal Company, of Dawley and delivered by road. Ball clay for glazing of the various products was delivered by rail from Cornwall. During World War II, the kilns were converted for use as annealing furnaces for special steel products. This was the last of the Lilleshall brick works to continue in production, closing in 1977. Most of the buildings remain, in use as a small industrial estate.

Donnington Wood Brickworks were opened in 1850, consisting of 12 rectangular side kilns and a machine house supplied with red marl from a nearby clay pit estimated at containing 1 million tons of clay. This brickworks replaced earlier ones at Wrockwardine Wood and the nearby works at Donnington Wood. In 1875 the brickworks was entirely reorganised and was equipped with a circular 13 compartment Hoffmann Kiln. The works continued in this way manufacturing building bricks until final closure in 1971, and was subsequently demolished.

Wrockwardine Wood Furnaces consisted of two blast furnaces dating from 1801, which were finally blown out in 1824 and subsequently demolished.

Donnington Wood Furnaces comprised three blast furnaces, two of which dated back to 1783 and one from 1802. Two were blown out in 1846 and the last one in 1859.

Lodge or Old Lodge Furnaces. This site was named after a medieval hunting lodge, built by the Abbot of nearby Lilleshall Abbey, although no trace now remains of this building. Two furnaces were built here during 1824, being blown in during the following year to replace the Wrockwardine Wood furnaces. Another furnace was added in 1846, and two further during 1859. These latter replaced the furnaces at Donnington Wood. In 1870 two calcining kilns (to roast the iron ore before adding it to the furnace) were added to the top of the furnace bank. These furnaces produced 'cold blast' pig iron, which was much favoured over more modern 'hot blast' iron for many years. At this time, output was given as around 7,000 tons of pig iron per year. The Old Lodge Furnaces were finally blown out in 1888, but were not demolished until 1905, under a contract awarded to Thos. Molineux Jnr. A tall chimney, measuring some 140 feet high by 13 feet diameter, and known locally as 'The Lodge Stack', was demolished on 8 May of that year. Even so, parts of the bases and a retaining wall can be seen today as part of the Granville Country Park. The Coking Department (see below) continued for a few years more at this site. After World War II, this 7½ acre site was used for dismantling surplus war equipment (for example: vehicles, cranes and machine tools) for scrap recovery between 1945 and 1949, utilising as labour around 600 Italian prisoners of war from the nearby Sherriffhales camp.

Lodge Bank Coke Ovens were opened at the Lodge Furnaces site in 1842 with 42 beehive ovens. A further 10 ovens were added in 1901. Coal was supplied from Freehold, Muxton Bridge, Meadow

An extract from the 'London Iron Trade Exchange' of 2 January 1875 with an excellent engraving depicting the Lodge Furnaces. Some of the tramways are visible, as are the coke ovens in the distance, and the engine house on the right although, as the caption indicates, the illustrator has omitted the chimney by the engine house.

Extract from the 'London Iron Trade Exchange' of 2 January 1875, this time depicting the Priorslee Furnaces from the north-east, with the engine house on the right.

Illustration from the 'London Iron Trade Exchange' of 2 January 1875, this time recording the New Yard Engineering Works, viewed from the east, across Gower Street. Although the works were significantly extended around 1900, the distinctive clock tower was retained, and removed around 2006.

Donnington Brickworks from the air, some time in the 1930s. This gives a good impression of the circular Hoffmann Kiln, while the plateway from the clay quarry can be seen running in from the top right of the picture. [Ironbridge Gorge Museum Trust]

and Cockshutts mines for which screening and washing was also performed here. Coke was supplied to the Old Lodge furnaces initially, and later to the Priorslee furnaces, as well as to the Madeley Wood Company's ironworks at Madeley Court (closed in 1902) and Blists Hill (closed in 1912). The coke ovens continued after the closure of the Lodge Furnaces, but eventually closed in 1908, although coal screening continued in operation until 1910.

Snedshill Furnaces. Three blast furnaces were built here in 1780 by the well known ironmaster, John Wilkinson, and was producing 3,400 tons of iron in 1796, although this was down to 2,830 tons in 1823. Pig iron production ceased here in 1830, when the furnaces were closed, but the forge for wrought iron and the wire rod mill continued in operation as a separate business, known as Snedshill Iron Works. This business was begun with three partners: Horton, Simms and Bull. However, Robert Horton subsequently died and his son Samuel inherited his share. The partnership was dissolved in 1854, and Samuel Horton bought out his partners' shares. In 1855 a new company was formed (the Snedshill Bar Iron Company) comprising the following partners: The 2nd. Earl Granville, The Honourable Frederick Leveson-Gower, W. Loftus Lowndes, Samuel Horton, William Blount, Charles Pugh, W. Ellwood Horton, Samuel Lewis Horton, and W. H. Phillips. This company was not initially a subsidiary of the Lilleshall Company, but was effectively under the same management. However, this situation was regularised as from 31 December, 1887 when the company was purchased by the Lilleshall Company at a value of £65,000 for assets, liabilities and goodwill, with stocks at an additional valuation.

By the second half of the 19th century the works included six rolling mills and rod mills, and was producing round and square bar, flats, cable, rivets, boiler plates, sheets, wire rods and angles. Thus the company had now principally become a rolling mill, whose production of wrought iron declined markedly until ceasing in 1924. Nonetheless, this works was locally referred to as either **Snedshill Steelworks, Snedshill Ironworks or Snedshill Forge**, even after World War II. However, one rolling mill was moved to the Priorslee steelworks in 1900 and the wire rod mill closed in 1902, although a new Guide Mill was installed at this time. Shortly

Snedshill Brick & Tile Works in the 1930s, illustrating the sidings that served them and the Company's 'main line'; this runs across the picture and over the Holyhead Road. [Ironbridge Gorge Museum Trust]

after, land to the west of the works was sold to John Maddock & Son Ltd. for the creation of a general iron foundry, later known as their 'Old Works'. After closure of the forge in 1924, the remaining plant was sold for scrap to J. Cashmore of West Bromwich for £8,150. Their tender for this contract was accepted at a Board Meeting dated 2 January 1925. One rolling mill continued in use, but the buildings were mainly used as a machine shop and engineering works. Just before World War II the building was also sold to Maddock who expanded their foundry here, this becoming known as their 'New Works'.

Nearby, a landsale yard was located on the opposite (northern) side of Canongate until nationalisation, for the local sale from the company's collieries in the Priorslee district.

Priorslee Furnaces or Ironworks were opened in 1851, with the blowing engines being built in that year by Murdoch, Aitken & Co. of Glasgow, and named DAVID and SAMPSON *(sic)*.

These two fine engines are preserved at the Blists Hill Open Air Museum. In 1862, the works were producing 230 tons of iron per week, and by 1870 there were 40 beehive ovens in use. In 1881 four furnaces, each 90 feet high, were introduced. These were, in turn, replaced by three iron cased 70 feet furnaces around 1908. Two of these furnaces were regularly in operation producing pig iron for the associated steelworks, until that closed in 1925. Thereafter, with the exception of a short period during World War II, only one furnace was in regular use. However, the rolling mills were still in use, and the ironworks gradually became part of the steelworks site.

Priorslee Steelworks were opened in 1882, and by 1890 were producing 700 tons of steel per week. Three Bessemer Converters, each of 7 tons capacity, were supplied as part of the original plant and one Siemens Open Hearth furnace was added in 1900. However, steel making ceased in 1925, so that the plant then concentrated on making pig iron (as above), and on its rolling activities. Nevertheless, it was still referred to as the 'steelworks'. Coal crushing and washing plants were also installed here, along with a battery of 54 coke ovens to replace earlier beehive ovens around 1912. These continued in operation until 1929, after which time coke was supplied from North Staffordshire and South Yorkshire.

An unfortunate explosion in one of the furnaces in 1896 caused considerable damage, and left much of

Snedshill Brick and Tile Works in 2002, now divided into units to form an industrial estate. A large fire engulfed much of these buildings in January 2006 which still await redevelopment in 2008. The main road is the Holyhead Road, long since by-passed for through traffic. [Author]

The New Yard Works around 1950. The offices were located at the front of the works, and the sawmill on the right. The locomotive shed and repair shop are in the top right corner, with the smaller, separate building used for permanent way purposes. [Ironbridge Gorge Museum Trust]

The New Yard Engineering Works, still extant in 2002; like Snedshill, it was divided into units as an industrial estate. The ornate clock tower was a particularly pleasing survivor, but since this date it has been removed. Only the buildings in the foreground remain in 2008. The rest of the area has been redeveloped as a housing estate. Compare this to the earlier photograph. [Author]

the plant in a dangerous condition. Normal demolition techniques failed to dismantle the affected area, which was finally felled by the judicious use of a cannon!

By 1959, there were severe price problems in the market place, and the works were pretty well worn out, with only one furnace in operation. The decision was taken to cease production, and this last furnace was blown out on Good Friday, 1959. The iron making plant was promptly demolished, but the rolling mills were converted to electricity and continued in operation, finally closing in 1982. The site was cleared and sold to Telford Development Corporation, along with much of the Company's other freehold property from 1970 onwards.

Old Yard (Donnington Wood). This was a general engineering works, which also built boats for canals, but was closed in 1861.

New Yard Engineering Works (or Phoenix Foundry), St. Georges. Opened in 1861 upon the closure of the Old Yard Works, covering a site totalling 10.88 acres of which 600 sq. ft. was under cover. The main products were colliery winding engines, blowing engines, steam hammers, presses, water equipment, gas engines, and of course, railway locomotives. The foundry was built with a capacity of 60 tons of castings per week. The original smiths shop had one steam hammer and 15 fires. In 1900 the works were expanded with new machine shops, and a new fitting shop and erecting shop. An independent generating station was also installed. In 1902, the wagon shop was opened using wood from the sawmill on the site, for the manufacture and repair of the company's extensive fleet of wagons. It is not known if such work was undertaken for outside concerns.

The works were closed in 1931, making over 1,000 persons redundant. The plant was subsequently sold off piecemeal, but there was much in the way of surplus, unwanted industrial machinery at the time, and the total realised was only £20,000. The land lay mostly derelict thereafter, but in 1937 some of it was let out to other companies, and at the same time some production of engineering was restarted, but on a much reduced basis. New machinery was installed in World War II for the production of ammunition for the Middle East, bullet proof rivets for tanks, and tank track links. During the 1950s the output from the revived engineering business included agricultural machinery, bottle packing machinery, and modular steel buildings. The works were finally sold in 1984, having lain empty for several years.

Concrete Works, Snedshill. Established in 1903 on the northern side of Canongate, across the road from Snedshill Furnaces. It initially produced concrete blocks, fenceposts, and slabs. From 1917 pit props were added to the product range. This works was demolished after World War II, and new works, incorporating revised production methods, built on the site of the former coke ovens at Priorslee, adjacent to the Holyhead Road. Both works were most successful, and saw continual development and expansion right to the end of the company's operations in this area in 1979.

Distillation Plant, Priorslee. Opened by the German firm of AG fuer Kohlendestillation, of Duesseldorf in 1912, this consisted of a coal washery, 50 coke ovens, by-products plant and benzole plant on an integrated site at the northern edge of Priorslee Steelworks, south of the Holyhead Road. Initially used 1,500 tons of coal per week from the Lilleshall collieries, but this was much reduced during the 1920s when only one furnace was in operation at the steelworks thus limiting the demand for coke. This firm was taken over by the government during World War I being classified as the assets of an enemy power, and sold to Lilleshall Company for £19,000 in 1920. A separate company, The Lilleshall Coal Distillation Co. Ltd. was established for this business. The distillation plant

An aerial view of the Priorslee Furnaces, probably dating from around 1950. The ironworks and rolling mills can be seen top left, with the concrete plant behind, on the former site of the steelworks. The asphalt works are in the bottom right corner, with the remains of the slag heaps bottom left. The connection to the GWR Hollinswood sidings is to the left of the asphalt works. The locomotive hauling a rake of mineral wagons is almost certainly Barclay 0-6-0T No.11, on the line which formerly ran to the Stafford pit. [Ironbridge Gorge Museum Trust]

A 1920s postcard of the coal distillation plant, looking westwards, with the ironworks and rolling mills on the left. The prominent building centre right is the 98ft coal bunker, demolished in 1936. [Ironbridge Gorge Museum Trust]

A wintry scene at Woodhouse Colliery, probably dating from the 1920s. [Ironbridge Gorge Museum Trust]

Priorslee Hall, around 1900. [Ironbridge Gorge Museum Trust]

was finally closed in 1928, the site being later used for the construction of an entirely new Concrete Works. However, the washery continued well into the 1950s, washing coal for nearby power stations, notably that at Ironbridge.

Asphalt Plant, Priorslee. Built by the German firm of H. & E. Albert in 1912. This plant used slag from Priorslee Furnaces which was processed via a crushing and screening plant and covered with tar from the Distillation Plant to produce road making materials. Later, fertiliser was also produced, which found a ready market in the nearby Shropshire agricultural industry. This plant was also acquired from the government in 1920, having similarly been sequestered during the First World War. It closed along with the Priorslee Furnaces in 1959.

MINES

Such was the geology of the region, that most of the pits mined ironstone and fireclay as well as coal. In some cases the mines were originally specifically sunk for ironstone, but when those reserves were exhausted, the shafts were deepened to reach coal seams. In other cases, the coal and ironstone were mined alongside each other for several decades. Note that the Madeley Wood Company also operated pits named 'Lawn' and 'Dark Lane', which were quite close to the Company pits of the same names.

The Lawn (Priorslee)
The shaft was sunk in 1818, production starting soon afterwards. In 1896, there were 19 underground and 13 surface workers. This pit finally closed in 1906.

Waxhill Barracks
Sinking of the shaft was begun in 1818 and eventually exceeded a depth of 300 yards, but the pit did not open until 1828, and was named after the nearby company housing scheme. In 1896, there were 40 underground and 25 surface workers. The pit closed in 1900, although pumping continued until 1930.

Freehold
Opened around 1840, there were two 7½ feet diameter shafts initially of 147 yards depth, that eventually reached 245 yards. In 1896 there were 29 underground and 11 surface workers. However, by 1905 this had increased to a total of 205 men, which by 1927 had further increased to 314 at which it remained steady until closure in 1928.

Meadow
Opened prior to 1840, the horse tramway system connected this pit to the Lodge Furnaces and to the Donnington Wood Canal. It was closed in 1894.

The Cockshutts
Opened by 1840, this pit does not seem to have been connected to the rail system. Instead, there was a horse worked tramway linking it to the Lodge Furnaces. Closed by 1940.

Muxton Bridge
The exact date of opening is not known, but it was in operation by 1837 and closed in 1912. In 1896, there were 68 underground and 30 surface workers. The remains of the former engine house (built in 1844), which once contained a horizontal steam winding engine, are extant in the Granville Country Park which now covers this site.

Granville
Sinking started in 1860 to a depth of 409 yards, which by the 1950's had reached 444 yards. As mentioned below, it was linked underground to Grange colliery in April, 1952. Finally closed in May 1979, although the last train actually ran on 2 October 1979. The most prolific of the collieries, it supplied the LNWR, GWR and Cambrian Railways with locomotive coal, and latterly also to Ironbridge 'B' Power Station. In 1896, there were 177 underground and 67 surface workers. Later the pit had a fairly consistent workforce of around 300 men, but after the closure of the nearby Kemberton colliery in 1967, this grew to 900 men, but shrank again to around 600 in the early 1970s. Meanwhile, the annual output had grown from around 300-350,000 tons to 600,000 tons in the late 1960's.

Grange
Opened in 1864 with two 8 feet diameter shafts. In 1896, there were 239 underground and 60 surface workers, although this had fallen slightly to a total of 244 men in 1905. Connected underground to Granville in April 1952, and thus effectively closed as a separate colliery, although pumping continued until the closure of

16

Granville. Twin headshafts were installed in 1951, and subsequently used for upshaft ventilation from the Granville pit. These headshafts remain in situ as a local landmark, even though most people mistakenly believe them to be on the site of Granville pit.

Stafford
Sinking started on 24 November 1862, but the mine only reached the required reserves at 255 yards and opened on 8 December 1866. At this time the rail connection to Priorslee was put in. Utilising four shafts, in 1896 there were 231 underground and 48 surface workers, although this grew to around 400 men only five years later. Ironstone was also mined here, but this had ceased by 1924, so that the workforce at this time had fallen to 270 men. Coal winding ceased in 1926, and the mine was finally closed in 1928, although it remained open for drainage purposes until 1939.

Woodhouse
No precise opening date is available, but it was in use before 1864. In 1896, there were 202 underground and 55 surface workers. Ironstone was mined here to a depth of 311 yards. No.1 pit closed in 1931, after which it is noted that the workforce in 1932 was set at 740 men. No.2 pit subsequently closed in 1940, although pumping continued until the 1960s. Several of the colliery surface buildings survived into the mid-1970s before being demolished.

Hope
This was located near to Cefn-y-bedd, Flintshire (about four miles north west of Wrexham). The colliery was leased under an agreement dated 12 September 1872 with Sir G. H. Lockwood, and comprised two pits, of 651 feet (No.1) and 634½ feet (No.2). A third old shaft was stated to be about 390 feet deep. Rail access was from a line linking the nearby Hope Paper Mills to the Wrexham, Mold and Connah's Quay Railway (WMCQR). One siding led from this line into the Hope Colliery.

An agreement of 6 September 1875 with the Llay Hall Coal, Iron & Firebrick Co. Ltd. empowered this company to build a railway across the land of the Hope Colliery from the WMCQR at Caergwrle to their colliery, so long as they agreed to take traffic to and from the Hope Colliery. This railway was 1¼ miles long and opened in September 1877.

The 1876 Valuation lists the railway at Hope Colliery as comprising 395 yards of railway, plus a 20 ton weighbridge in a brick and slate house. There is no record of any locomotives having been used by the Company at this colliery, and with the small amount of track given above, it would not seem to be necessary. Locomotives of the WMCQR are presumed to have dealt with traffic up to September, 1877 and the Llay Hall Company's locomotives after that date.

The lease was terminated on 18 June, 1880 as the colliery had become uneconomic to work, and was subsequently abandoned by its owners.

Hadley
Company land at Hadley was used to sink coal pits nos. 1 to 7, which were in production, and recorded in the 1876 Valuation. These pits were leased to Nettlefold & Chamberlain by 1880 when they established their nearby Castle Ironworks at Hadley, and were operated by them until the surrender of the lease around 1890.

There was never any indication that these pits were provided with any form of rail access, and are presumed to have been small adits or gin pit type mines. These pits were included in the sale of land (known as 'The Hadley Estate') to Benjamin P. Blockley for £5,000 under an agreement dated 25 March 1895. Presumably the pits were worked out by this time, as the area was subsequently quarried by Blockley for clay for his brickworks, which were also established on this site.

In addition, there were many other smaller mines, which are listed separately in Appendix 1, along with those operated by chartermasters. The operating dates of these pits, which in some cases also mined ironstone, are not known. None of these were connected to the Lilleshall rail system, although most had some form of

Snedshill Brickworks, looking east, around 1900. [Shropshire Archives]

Granville Colliery, showing the pithead winding frames and engine houses in 1944. [Ironbridge Gorge Museum Trust]

tramway connection, either to nearby iron furnaces or to canal wharves, or both.

Maps showing the rail connections to the various works and mines are located at the end of this chapter.

Providing Local Facilities

It is not intended to detail all of the Company structures, but it may assist readers to appreciate the extent of its influence in the area to briefly mention some of those that were unconnected with the railways or the manufacturing processes.

Priorslee Hall was first leased along with other lands from the Jerningham family in 1788, who themselves had purchased the lands from Henry VIII, in the 16th century as a result of the Dissolution of the Monasteries. The hall was eventually allocated to the Company Manager, who during the first half of the 19th century was John Horton. In 1855, the hall was purchased for £24,000 along with the rest of the Priorslee estate from John Aglionby Slaney, and continued to become the residence of the successive Company Managers. The surrounding land continued to be farmed by the Company. Although the main offices were located at the New Yard Works during the 20th century, the hall became the administrative headquarters of the Company until its removal to the south of England. The hall stands today, forming the centrepiece of the Telford Campus of Wolverhampton University.

The Company provided a number of benefits for its employees from quite an early date. Houses were provided at Waxhill Barracks, Donnington Barracks and Lambs Lane, Wrockwardine Wood from around 1830, and although these were rather basic single storey wooden or brick affairs, as their names suggest, their provision was an advanced form of employee benefit at the time. The company went on to provide further, and more modern accommodation in the form of brick built terraced houses in the Oakengates and St. Georges areas, principally at Old Yard, Ivy Row and Mechanics Row for which the initial rent was between 7 shillings and 14 shillings per month in the first half of the 19th century. These were eventually furnished with running water from a reservoir at the summit of Red Hill, south of Granville Colliery, which is still in use by the Severn Trent Water Company. Gas was also piped to these houses.

The Lilleshall Cottage Hospital was opened by the Company in Albion Street, St. Georges in 1903, and lasted until 1928. It is now a residential property. Employees also enjoyed annual outings, although the extent to which the Company financed these is not known. However, the following extract from the Wellington Journal and Shrewsbury News of 29 June, 1895 illustrates the extent to which employees (actually from all departments, not just the collieries, as reported) enjoyed these facilities:
MINERS' EXCURSION – On Monday, (24 June, 1895) the annual excursion of the miners employed in the Lilleshall Company's Collieries was held, and Blackpool was the place selected. Between 800 and 900 availed themselves of the excellent train service of the L. and N. W. Railway, and started from Oakengates about 4.30 a.m., and returned to Oakengates about 1.30 a.m. on Tuesday morning, after having spent a very enjoyable day amid the many attractions of this favourite resort. Much praise is due to the committee for their excellent arrangements and exertions for the comfort of the party.

The employees' spiritual needs were not overlooked, and the Company donated land for building of churches and chapels at The Nabb, Priorslee, Donnington Wood (two), and Pains Lane (two).

It would perhaps, be pertinent at this stage to mention that the spelling of Priorslee as one word has been used throughout this book, except where quoting from original sources which may have used the alternative spelling of Priors Lee. Similarly, other place names spelt alternatively as one or two words are also quoted as used in the sources, for example, Muxton Bridge (Muxtonbridge) and Malins Lee (Malinslee).

Inside the machine shop at the New Yard Engineering Works, probably around 1920. The narrow gauge plateway, which was manually operated, was used for transferring heavy materials between machines. [Ironbridge Gorge Museum Trust]

BARN AND BARNYARD COLLIERIES (1883)

X Tramways to Old Lodge Furnaces

0 200 400 yards

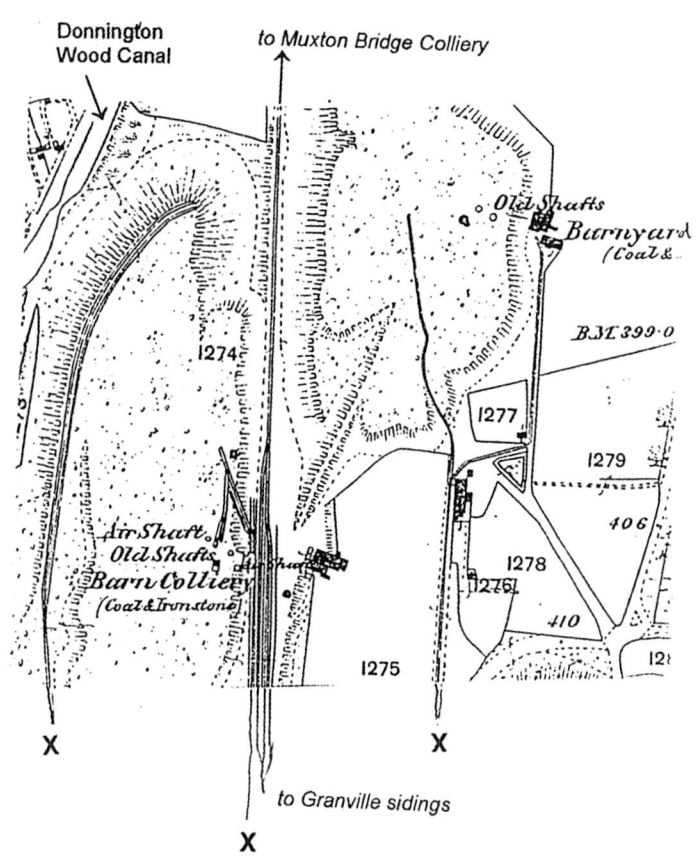

DARK LANE COLLIERY (1902)

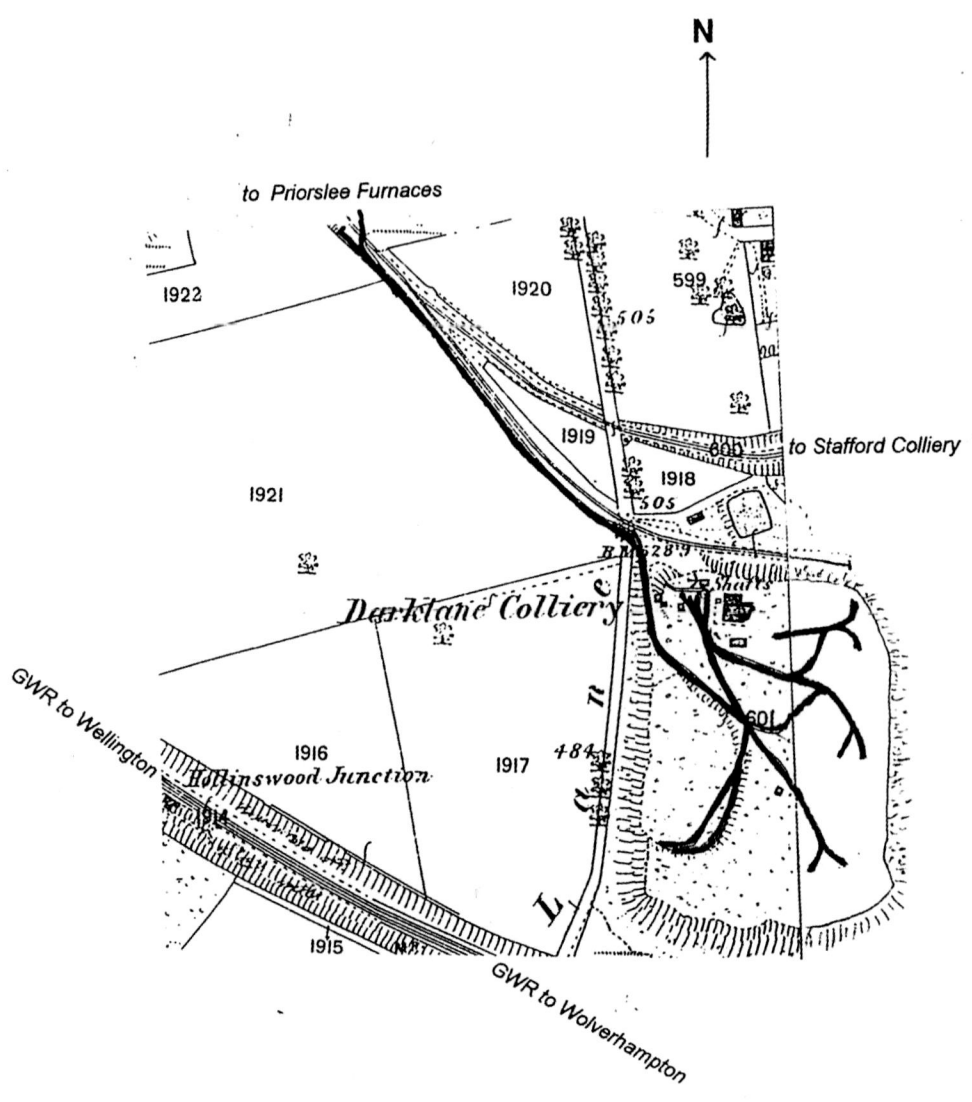

Tramway routes shown in heavy lines

DONNINGTON WOOD BRICK AND TILE WORKS (1927)

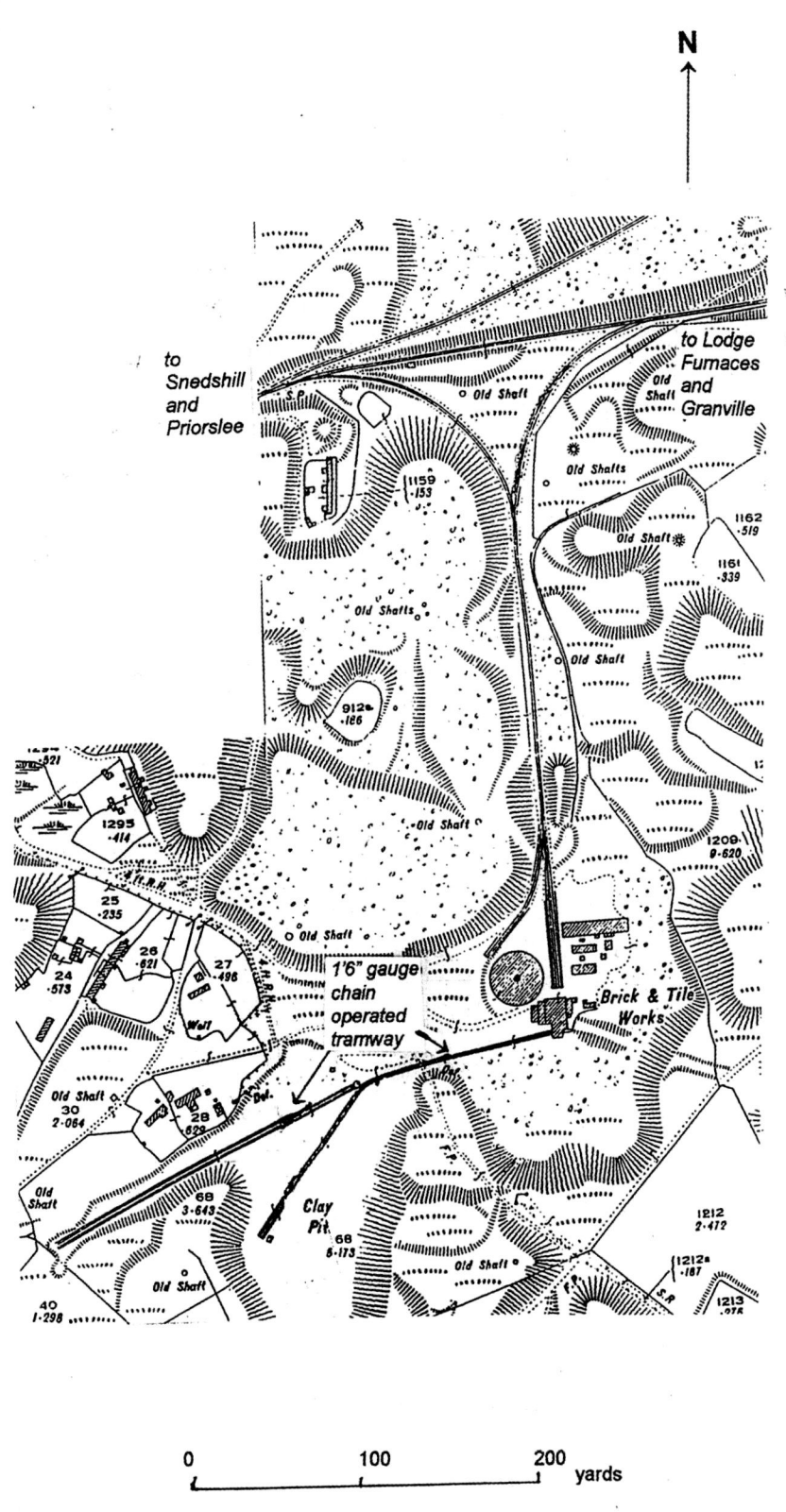

FREEHOLD COLLIERY (1927)

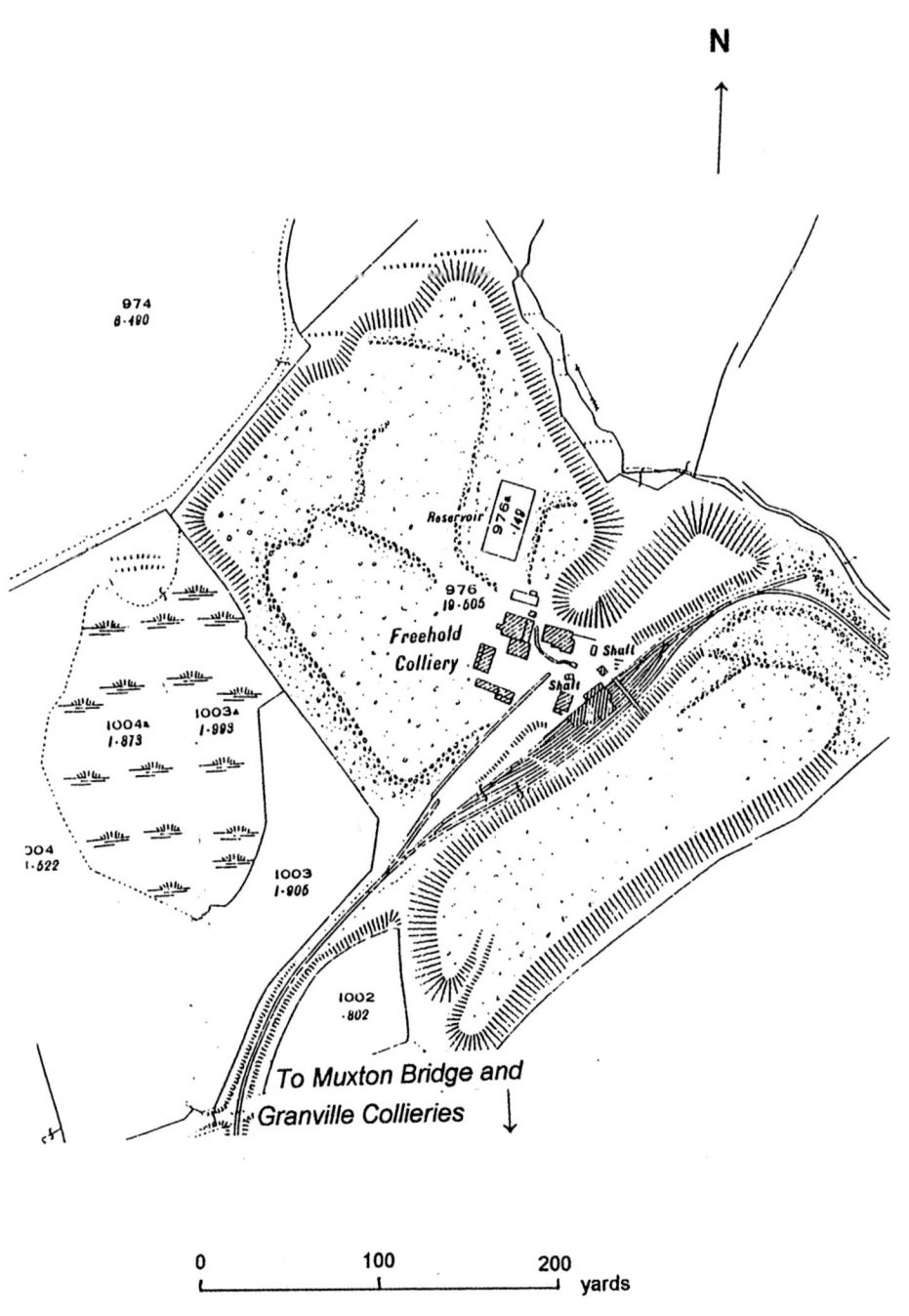

GRANGE COLLIERY (1902)

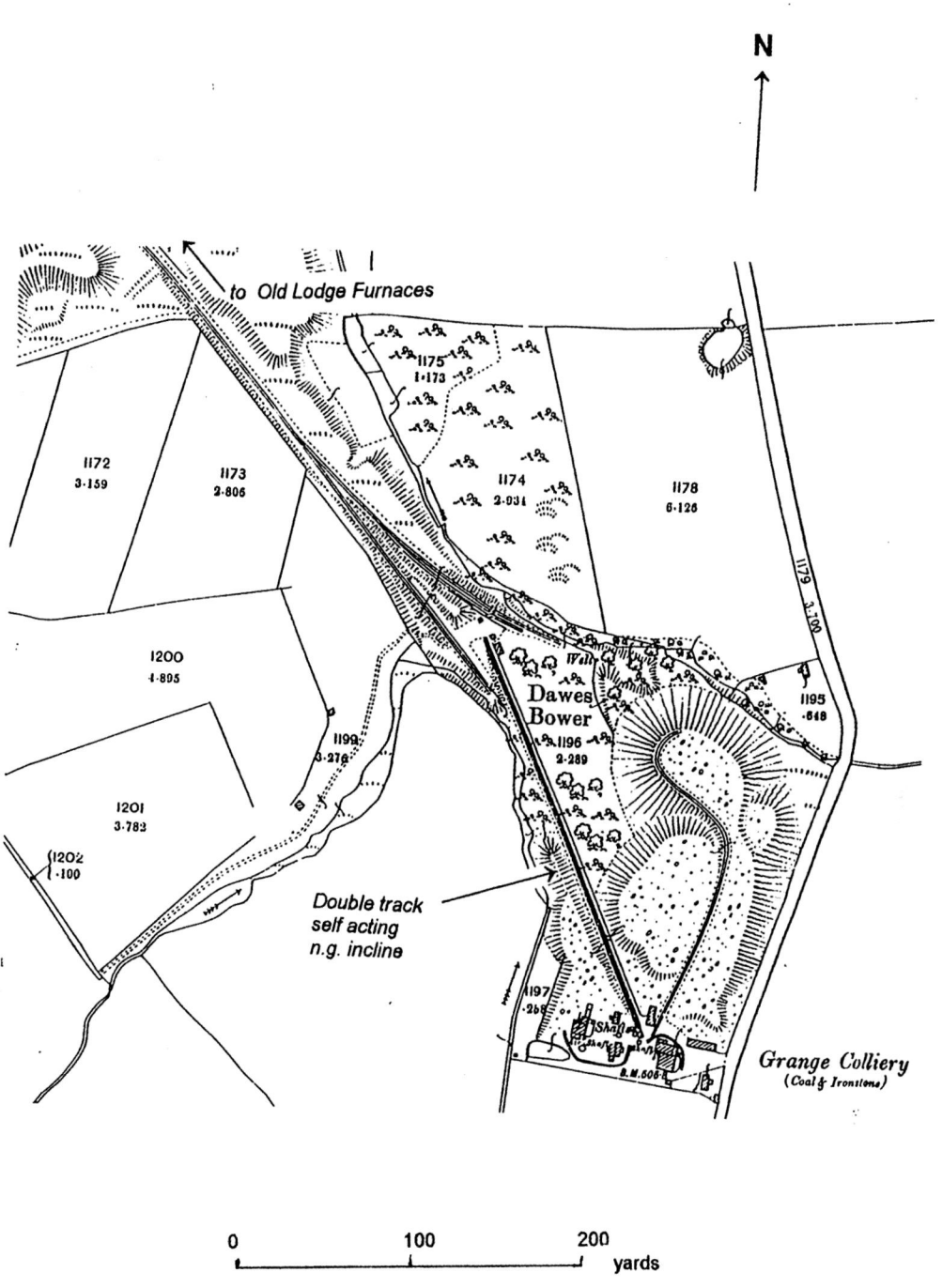

GRANVILLE COLLIERY (1927)

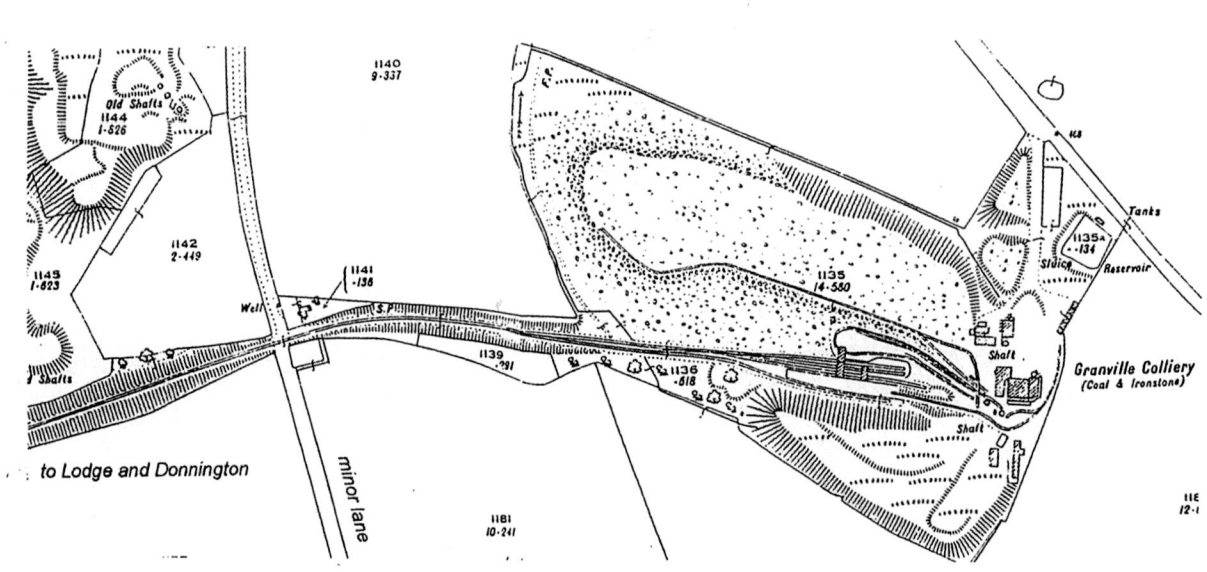

LAWN COLLIERY (1902)

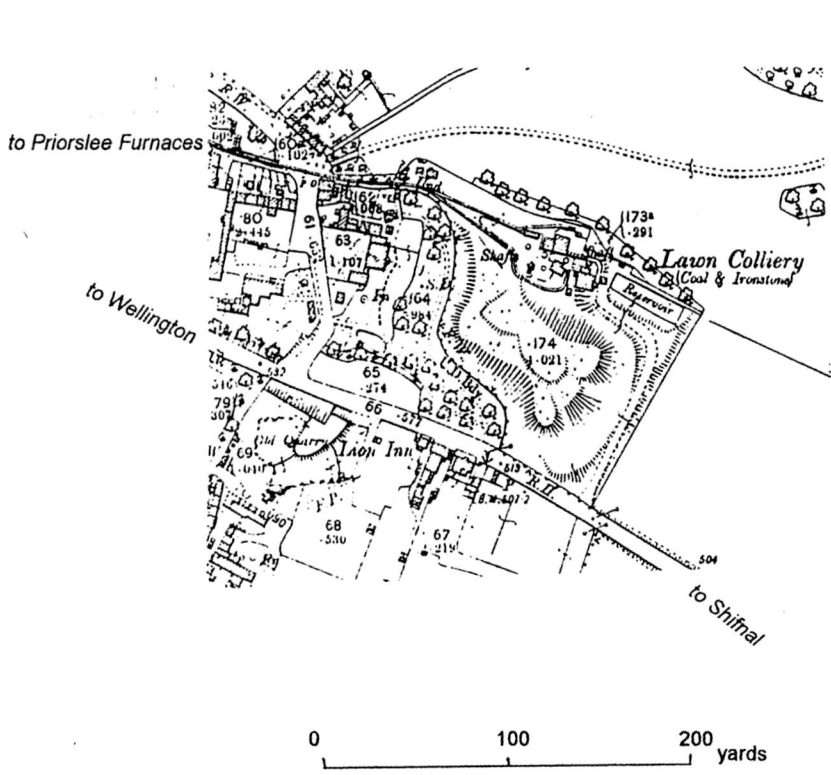

MUXTON BRIDGE COLLIERY (1902)

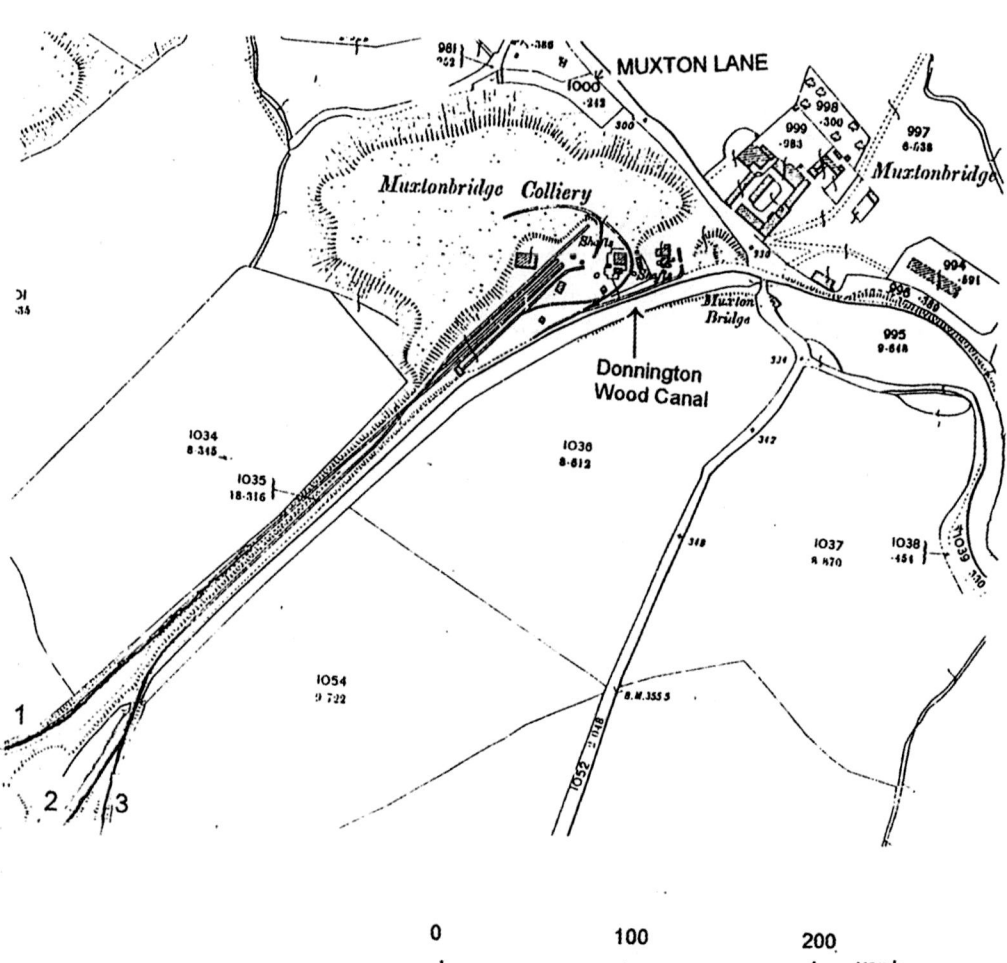

1. to Donnington exchange sidings
2. to Waxhill Barracks Colliery
3. to Granville sidings

OLD LODGE FURNACES (1881)

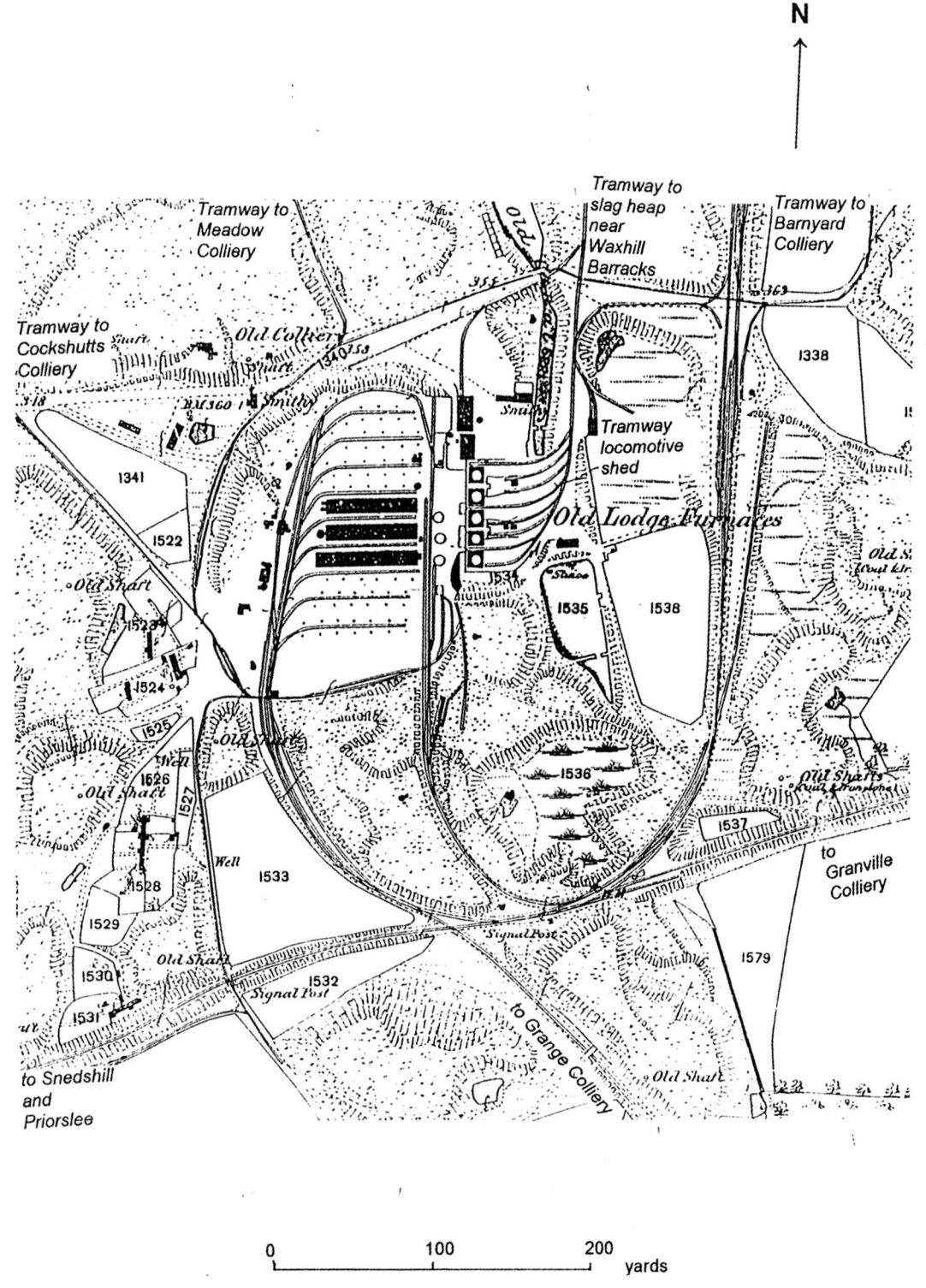

PRIORSLEE FURNACES (1927)

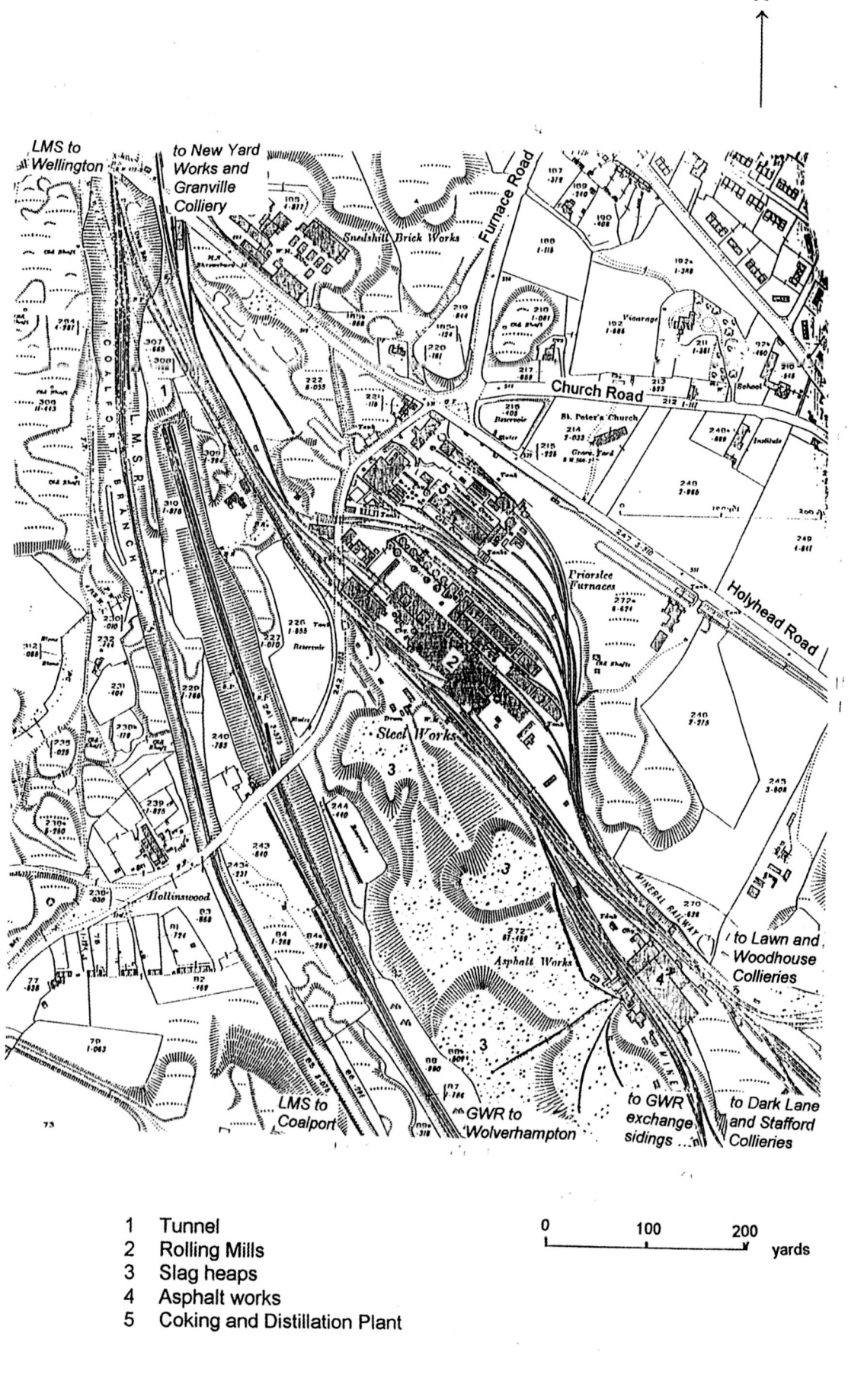

1 Tunnel
2 Rolling Mills
3 Slag heaps
4 Asphalt works
5 Coking and Distillation Plant

NEW YARD ENGINEERING WORKS (1927)

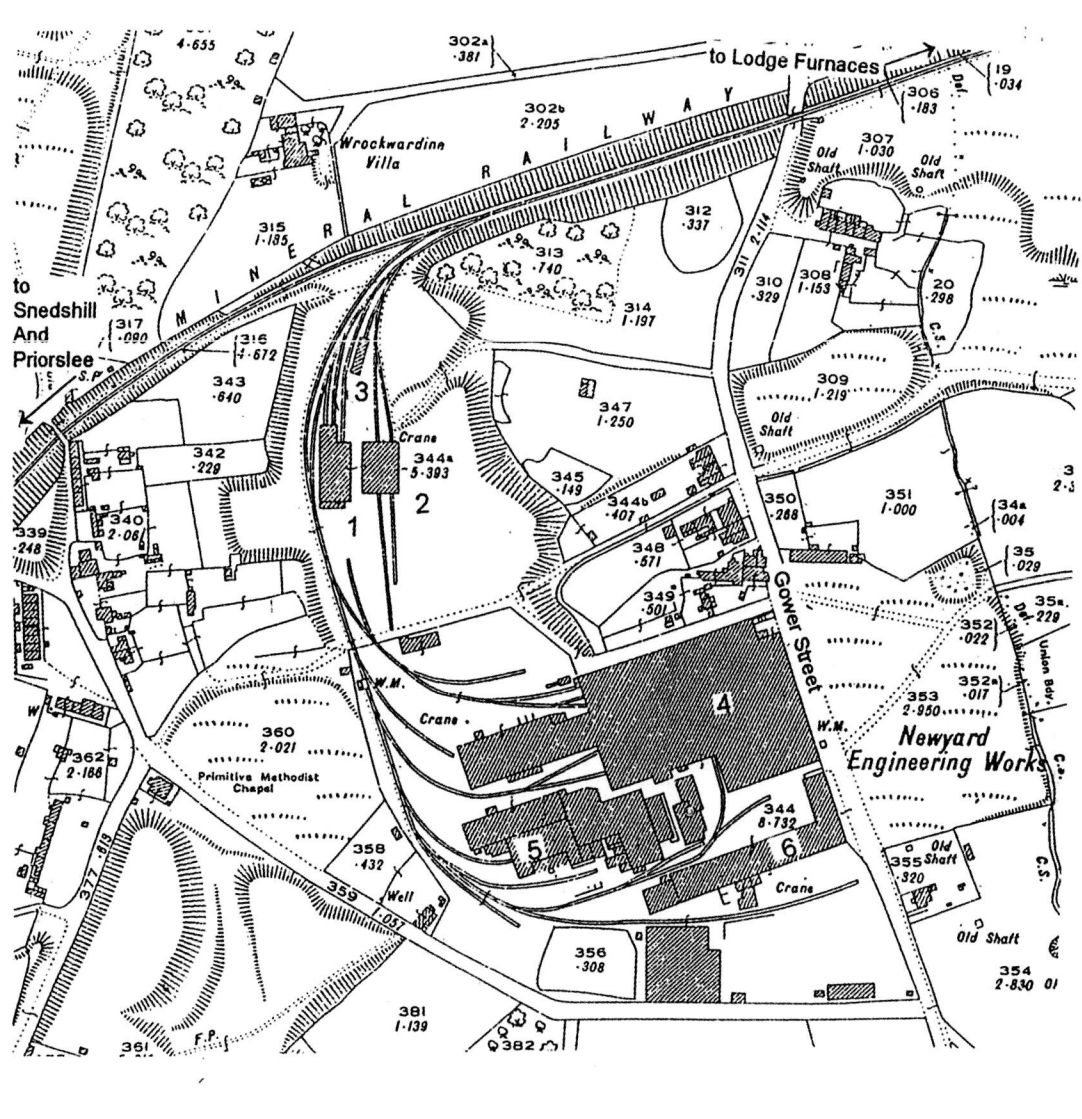

1 Locomotive running shed
2 Locomotive repair shed
3 Permanent way shed
4 Main erecting shop
5 Wagon repair shop
6 Sawmills

SHEPHERD SLAG CRUSHING PLANT (1927)

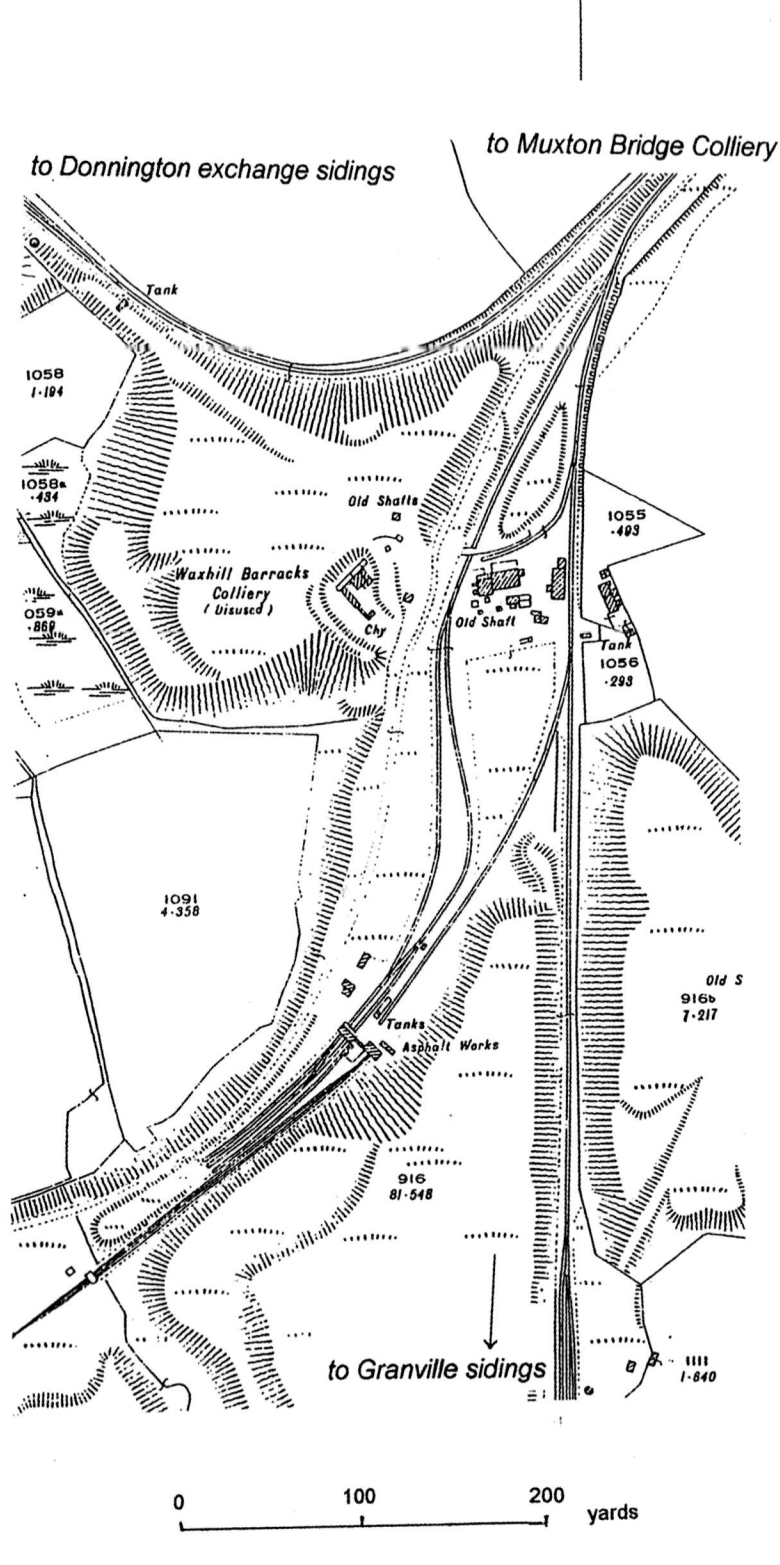

SNEDSHILL WORKS (1927)

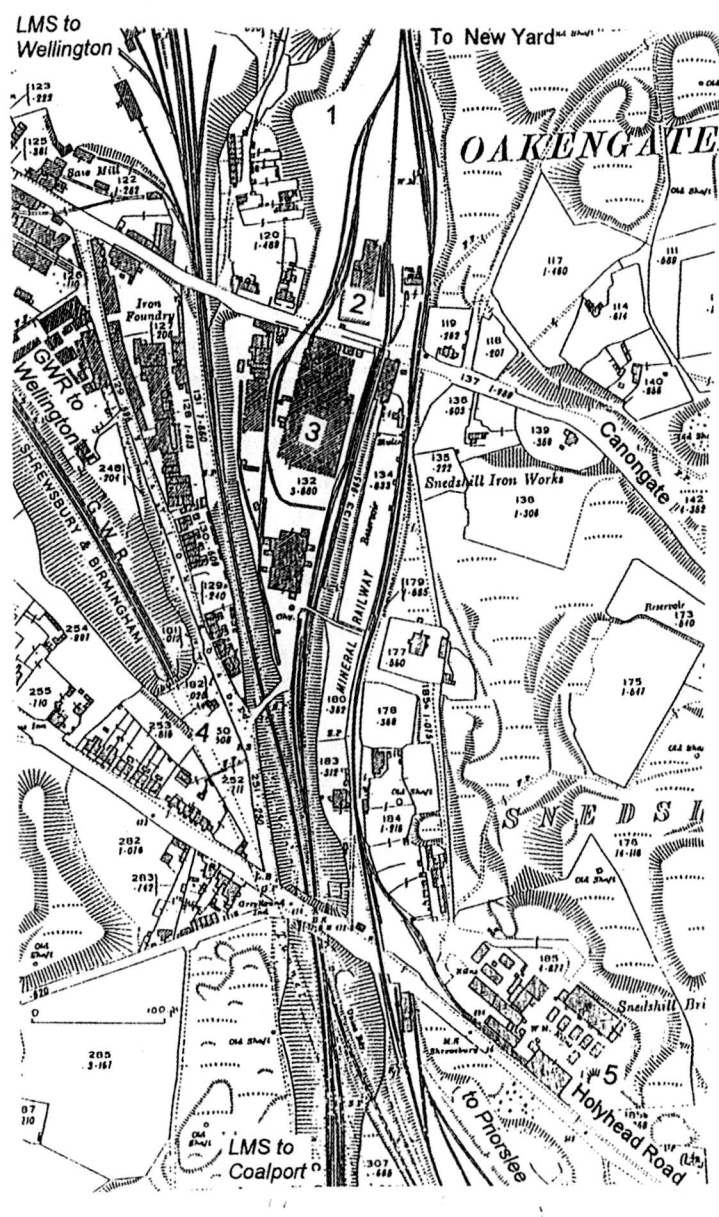

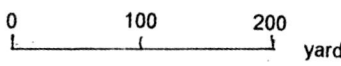

1   Landsale yard
2   Concrete works
3   Former Snedshill Forge
4   Tunnel
5   Snedshill Brick and Tile Works

STAFFORD COLLIERY (1902)

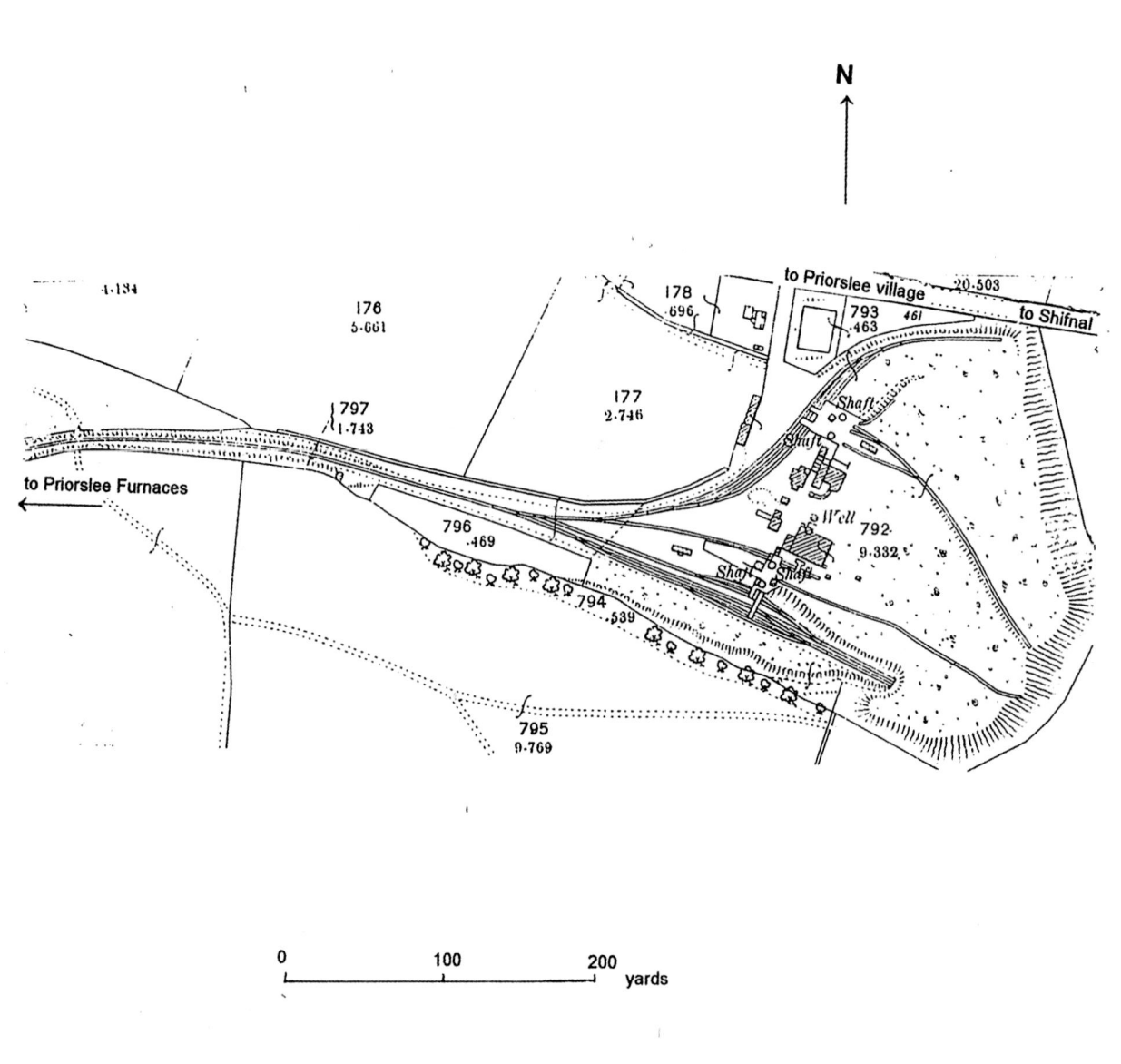

WAXHILL BARRACKS COLLIERY (1902)

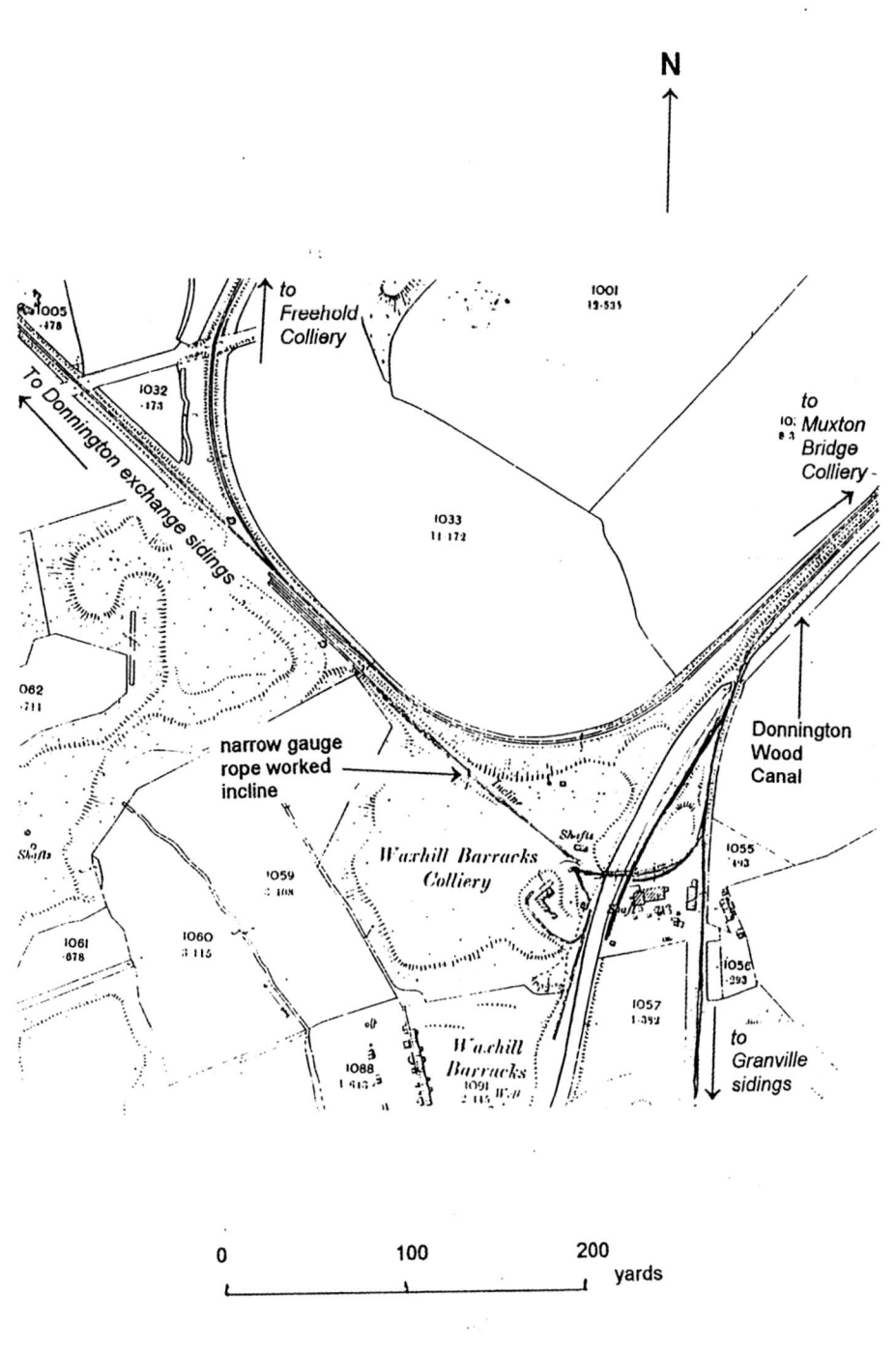

WOODHOUSE COLLIERY (1902)

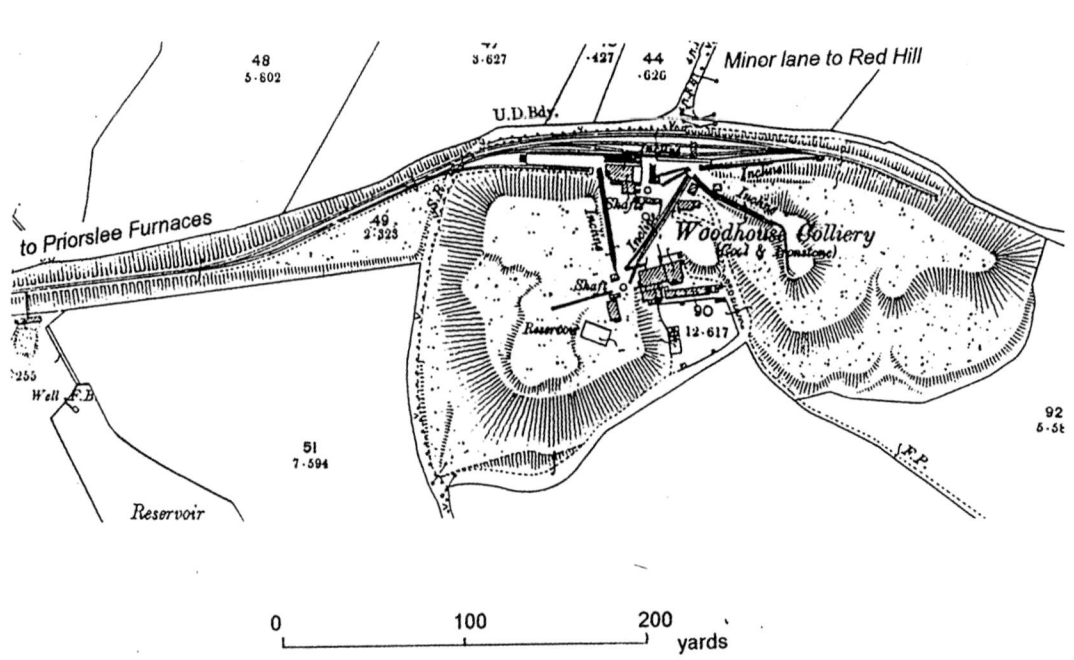

CHAPTER THREE
DEVELOPMENT OF THE TRANSPORT NEEDS

As with so many public railways, the history of this industrial railway actually begins with the early canals in the area. The first canal to serve the Company's needs was the Donnington Wood Canal, privately constructed by the 2nd Earl Gower, and opening in 1767. This ran north-east from coal pits at Donnington Wood to a roadside wharf at Pave Lane, about 1¼ miles south-east of Newport. One branch served the limestone quarries near to the village of Lilleshall, and another ran northwards to another coal wharf at Pitchcroft, just south-west of Newport, where there was also a limeworks and another limestone quarry. Most of the coal pits in this area were also producing ironstone, and a number of the pits solely mined ironstone.

The next canal to serve the Company's sites was the Shropshire Canal, for which Royal Assent was granted on 11 June 1788. The Company's interests were represented by the Marquis of Stafford, who subscribed £2,000 to the £50,000 nominal share capital of the canal company. This canal was authorised to connect with the Donnington Wood Canal in the north and with the River Severn near to Coalport in the south. The canal was to split into two branches at a place named as Southill Bank, which was near to the site of Snedshill Ironworks. The 'Western Branch' proceeded via Horsehay and Coalbrookdale to the River Severn near Ironbridge. The 'Eastern Branch' headed via Blists Hill and the Hay Inclined Plane where it met the River Severn near to Coalport.

The next element in the canal network was the opening of the two mile long Wombridge Canal in 1788. This joined the Donnington Wood and Shropshire Canals at their junction, at the foot of the Donnington Wood inclined plane, and served newly discovered reserves of coal and ironstone in the Wombridge area.

Subsequently a new canal, the Shrewsbury Canal, was promoted by the local ironmasters and the Marquess of Stafford to link the northern end of the Wombridge Canal via a 17 mile route to Shrewsbury. This canal opened in stages from 1794 to 1797, and the concern eventually purchased the Wombridge Canal so as to complete its route. Finally, the Birmingham and Liverpool Junction Canal (later to become the Shropshire Union Canal) opened a branch from Norbury on its Wolverhampton to Ellesmere Port main line to join the Shrewsbury Canal at Wappenshall (three miles north-west of Oakengates) in 1832.

Thus the Shropshire Canal served the Lilleshall Company's sites around Snedshill and Priorslee, completing the internal transfer of coal, iron and limestone to the Company's ironworks, and their subsequent shipment to customers via the connecting canal network.

However, in order to reach the workings of the pits, quarries and works that these canals served, a system of tramways was soon developed. These were almost certainly constructed using wrought iron rails from the start, and were definitely of plateway construction. A more conjectural subject is the actual gauge of these plateways. Various sources have quoted the numerous lines that sprang up all over the East Shropshire coalfield as being of 2ft 1½in, 2ft 2in or 2ft 3in gauge. Perhaps there were small differences between the different systems, or it may be that in the nature of such undertakings the gauge was only fairly 'nominal' anyway.

These short lines linking the workings to the canals, gradually lengthened as their usefulness became apparent. So it was that in October, 1797 the ironmaster Thomas Botfield agreed with his landlord, Isaac Browne to carry 1,200 tons of coal each month from Malins Lee (about two miles south of Oakengates): *to some convenient wharf or quay adjoining the River Severn, and to the railway intended to be made by John Bishton & Co. and the said Thomas Botfield, or to some intermediate wharf or bank between the said works and the River Severn upon the line of the intended railway.* This railway was working by 1799, running from Sutton Wharf, near Coalport, to Hollinswood, where it connected with several ironworks and mines to the north in the area of Priorslee. The total length of this line was about eight miles, and it is presumed to have been horse worked. Bishton and Onions, whose ironworks was situated at Snedshill, were certainly involved in the original line, and by 1812 it had become the property of the Company. This line is recorded on Robert Baugh's map of 1808, and again on the Ordnance Survey maps of 1814 and 1817, although in the latter two cases it is not shown in its entirety. It is recorded that the Company were sending down around 50,000 tons of coal annually and much iron. However, the Shropshire Canal was not enjoying the most robust of business climates, and attempted in June, 1812 to negotiate for the Company's business, although this seems to have been unsuccessful. However, in April, 1815 William Horton on behalf of the Company agreed that the tramway would be removed, and that its business would be transferred to the canal. In turn, the Company received compensation of some £500, as well as favourable tonnage rates.

Whilst this signalled the end of the Company's 'main line' tramway, those serving its pits and works continued to flourish. In 1833, the main tramways are described as running along Freestone Avenue to Lawn Pit, near to Priorslee Hall, and to Woodhouse Colliery. There were branches east of Stafford Street, Oakengates and north of Freestone Avenue. The main line then continued northwards crossing Station Hill, Oakengates to the east of the Shropshire Canal, and on to meet the Wrockwardine inclined plane near to Donnington Wood. By 1856, further tramways had been laid around the area of Snedshill Ironworks linking to the canalside warehouses, and branches reaching out to the waste heaps south and west of the ironworks. These spoil heap lines continued to expand in subsequent years around the Priorslee Ironworks, and south therefrom.

Meanwhile, and at least by 1837, several of the coal pits in the Donnington Wood area had been linked directly to the Old Lodge Furnaces, thereby eliminating the transhipment of coal via the canal network.

'Motive power' on all of these tramways is believed to have been provided by horses for the longer or steeper journeys, and by man-power for those of a short and level nature. It is nonetheless interesting to consider that wayleaves were granted in 1692 at Madeley and in 1749 at Coalbrookdale to permit the use of oxen. Admittedly this was over the roads of the area, but a good case can be made for their employment as motive power on the tramways, as surely local customs would be a powerful influence.

TRAMWAYS IN THE PRIORSLEE AREA (1883)

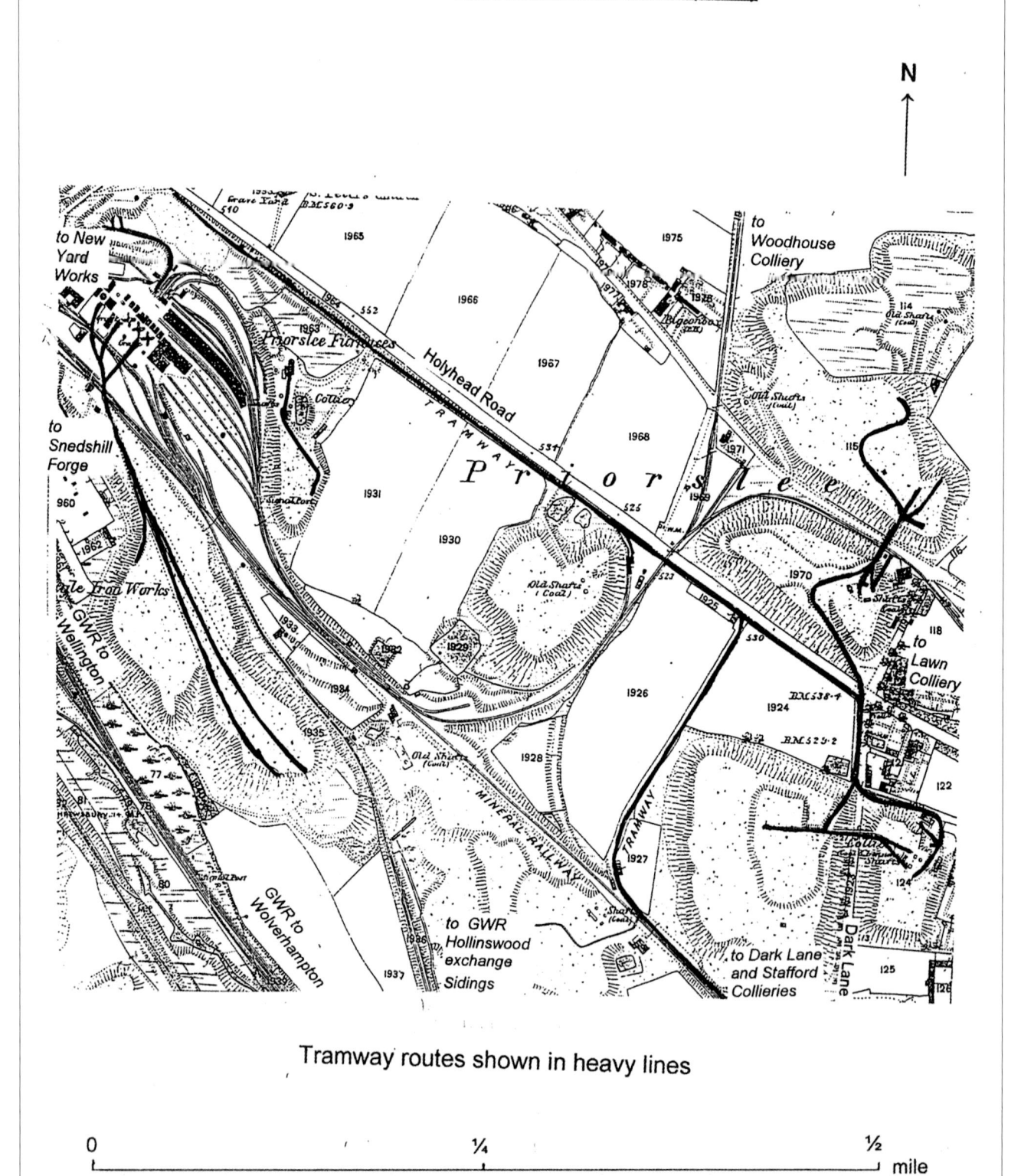

Tramway routes shown in heavy lines

CHAPTER FOUR
THE LILLESHALL COMPANY RAILWAY

The dawn of the 'Railway Mania' of the 1840s did not escape this corner of Shropshire. Whilst the canals still provided important transport facilities, they were becoming inexorably linked with the new-fangled railways. The Shropshire Union Railways and Canal Company (SURCC) had been formed on 3 August 1846, principally comprising the Birmingham and Liverpool Junction Canal, the Ellesmere and Chester Canal and the Shrewsbury Canal. Its enabling act permitted the SURCC to build railways, so the LNWR lost no time in controlling this potential competitor by leasing this company 'in perpetuity', obtaining the necessary enabling Act on 2 July, 1847.

In June 1849, the SURCC opened its line from Stafford to Wellington, which linked with the Shrewsbury and Birmingham Railway from Wolverhampton at Wellington (opened in November of that year) to continue as a joint line onwards to Shrewsbury. These two railways formed the northern and southern boundaries of the Company's operations at Donnington and Hollinswood respectively, and naturally enough became major interchanges for the Company's traffic, as we shall see.

Returning to the canals, the Shropshire Canal was leased by the SURCC in 1849 for a period of 21 years. This effectively put it under the control of the LNWR, who whilst perfectly happy to let the major part of the SURCC continue in its canal business until the grouping of 1923, nevertheless were not blind to the potential alternative uses that assets could be switched, especially when faced with changing circumstances. So it was that after the opening of the Company's railway, much of the former traffic that was routed via the Shrewsbury, Wombridge and Shropshire Canals instead went via the SURCC Newport Branch, then the Humber Arm to Lubstree Wharf and over the Company's railway. This also had an effect on the former Wombridge Canal, whose Trench Incline was very expensive to maintain, and which was also suffering from further mining subsidence and water leakage. The still independent Donnington Wood Canal also suffered from this withdrawal of traffic, even though a short branch had been built in the 1840s to serve the Lodge Furnaces. By 1873, the Lilleshall Branch of this canal was abandoned and the remaining sections became increasingly disused. Only about a one mile section, at the western end of the canal remained in use until the early years of the 20th century.

Realising that the opening of the main line railways would present much better transport opportunities, the Company decided to invest in their own modern system. After all, the Company at that time was at the forefront of what was the most modern technology of the day. No parliamentary powers were obtained for the building of the railway, despite the fact that it crossed (eventually) several major roads. Although unusual, the lack of an enabling Act was not unique, particularly as all of the land on which it ran was either owned or leased by the Company. It is unfortunate that the Board Minutes from this most important period have not survived. Therefore, the sequence of the construction of the railway, the contractors involved, the amounts involved and the necessary negotiations with the main line railway companies are simply not available. What we do know is that this was a period of massive capital investment, with the opening of Donnington Brickworks (1850), Priorslee Ironworks (1851) and later, the New Yard Engineering Works (1861).

The railway appears to have been firstly opened from the northern or Donnington end by conversion of existing tramways from Donnington LNWR exchange sidings to Freehold and Muxtonbridge mines, then after reversal, from there to the Lodge Furnaces serving the mines at Waxhill Barracks and Barnyard on the way. This can be traced on an 1853 map of the Company's property. At that time the southern section was still only served by tramways. However, it was not long before these were also utilised for much of the railway trackbed from Snedshill and Priorslee to The Nabb, where the new railway took a more direct line to the Lodge Furnaces, leaving the tramway formation near to the entrance to the New Yard Works. An 1854 plan of this anticipated route exists, but confirmation of its construction is only available on an 1857 map. As the second two locomotives (Neilson & Mitchell 63 and 64) were built in 1854, this does seem to confirm that the line was being built at that time, but was probably not completed until 1854 or even later. There is no indication of where locomotives may have been stabled at that time.

By 1862 the New Yard Works were open and a map of this time reveals that a line to the new Donnington Brickworks was also open, but that the locomotive shed and wagon workshop at the New Yard Works were not yet built. Once again there is no clue as to where the locomotives were stabled at this time. Certainly these facilities were

A wintry scene as a '94XX' pannier tank hustles two coal wagons and a brake van up the grade out of Oakengates, on its way to Stirchley during 1962/63. The exchange sidings are on the right, and the permanent way staff have evidently been busy defrosting the points. [A. J. B. Dodd]

LILLESHALL COMPANY RAILWAY SYSTEM

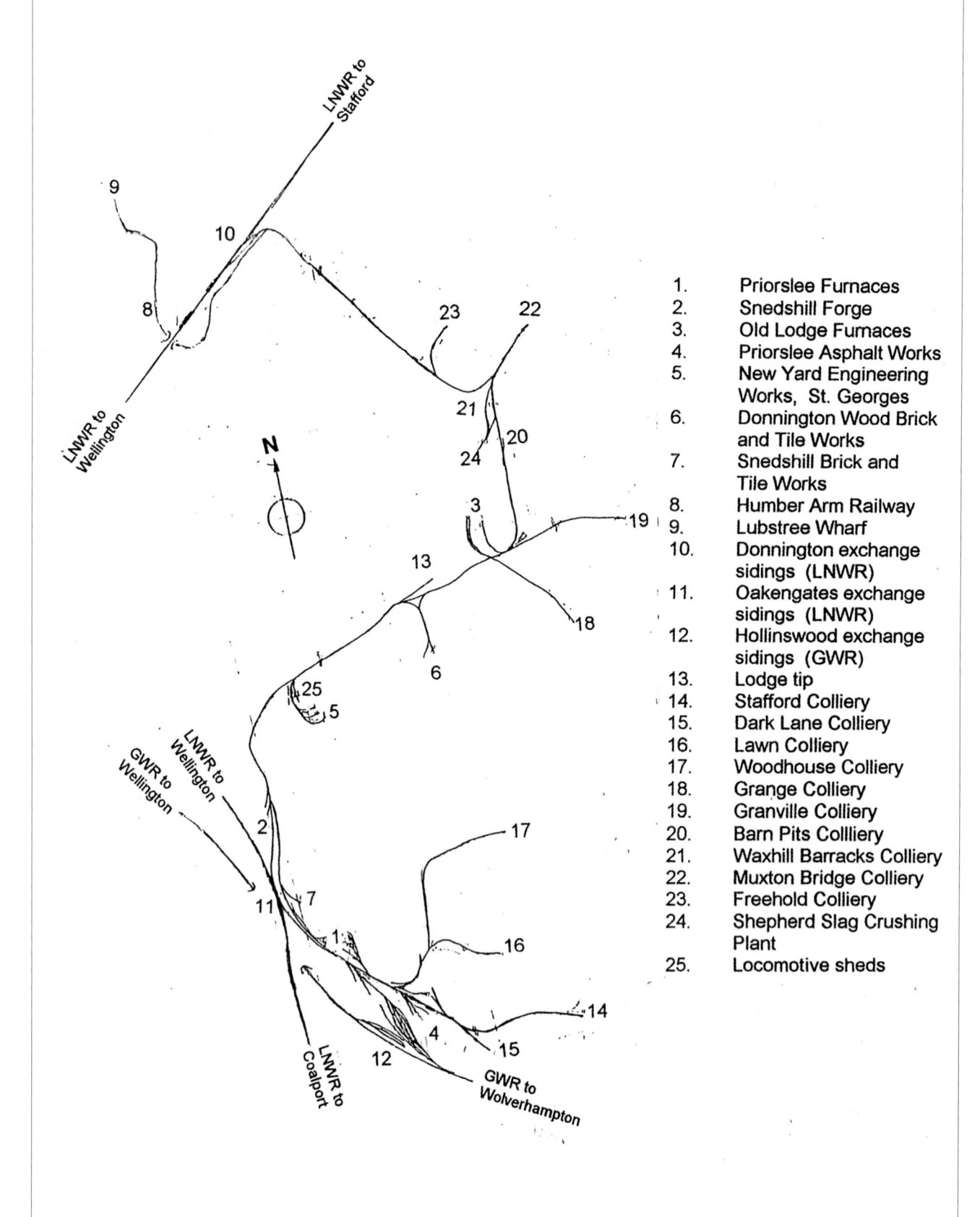

1. Priorslee Furnaces
2. Snedshill Forge
3. Old Lodge Furnaces
4. Priorslee Asphalt Works
5. New Yard Engineering Works, St. Georges
6. Donnington Wood Brick and Tile Works
7. Snedshill Brick and Tile Works
8. Humber Arm Railway
9. Lubstree Wharf
10. Donnington exchange sidings (LNWR)
11. Oakengates exchange sidings (LNWR)
12. Hollinswood exchange sidings (GWR)
13. Lodge tip
14. Stafford Colliery
15. Dark Lane Colliery
16. Lawn Colliery
17. Woodhouse Colliery
18. Grange Colliery
19. Granville Colliery
20. Barn Pits Collliery
21. Waxhill Barracks Colliery
22. Muxton Bridge Colliery
23. Freehold Colliery
24. Shepherd Slag Crushing Plant
25. Locomotive sheds

Looking north around 1956, with the Coalport branch line on the left, and the line from Priorslee Sidings on the right, which is diverging to run down to near the asphalt works. The Snedshill Sidings lie beyond the bridge. The substantial bridge carries the Holyhead Road. [A. J. B. Dodd]

A view of the Snedshill Sidings around 1950. The bridge over the Coalport branch carried an access road to the works in the centre right of the picture. These were originally the Snedshill Ironworks, but by this date had passed to John Maddock & Son Ltd. [Shropshire Archives]

in use by 1876. Southwards from Snedshill, the line crossed the Shropshire Canal (then still open), and again used parts of the tramway trackbed to reach the newly opened Priorslee Ironworks, then Lawn, Woodhouse and later, Stafford mines. A branch continued south-easterly to meet the Shrewsbury and Birmingham Railway (absorbed by the GWR as from 1 September, 1854) at Hollinswood, where further exchange sidings were provided.

The building of this line required an expertise that the Company, probably, would not have been possessed. Conversely, it would not have been short of any connections to the engineers and constructors necessary for the task. One suggestion is that Thomas Brassey constructed the line and, although there is no firm evidence for this, the surviving Impersonal Ledger for 1854 shows a balance of £405.13.8 owing *from* him, and brought forward on 1 January 1854. This was almost entirely cleared by a payment received on 24 March 1854 for £400. So although there were transactions between the Company and Brassey, it would have been expected that money would be *due to* him if he was installing a railway.

Further extensions to the line were made in the late 1860s and it has been suggested these were engineered by Joseph Fogerty, who by this time was living in the area. He had been working for the engineer John Fowler on the construction of the Severn Valley Railway in 1861. Later that same year he was engaged as Assistant Engineer for the construction of the Wenlock Railway from Much Wenlock to Craven Arms. Such further extensions of the Company railway are likely to have been related to the opening of several new collieries (Granville – 1861, Grange – 1864, Stafford – 1866) and possibly the Humber Arm Railway in 1870.

The enabling Act for the construction of the LNWR branch from Hadley Junction to Coalport was passed on 27 July 1857 and included a provision for the outright purchase of the Shropshire Canal, as this was required in part to form the trackbed of the proposed railway. The purchase was concluded on 5 February 1858 for the sum of £62,500. To enable the construction of the railway, the canal closed in June 1858 except for the portion from Tweedale Basin (near the foot of Windmill Farm inclined plane) to Coalport. This southern section remained intact, linking some of the smaller, local collieries to the Blists Hill ironworks. Eventually only a short section near to the top of the Hay inclined plane remained in use and even this became abandoned in the 1890s, although it was not officially closed until 1907.

The Coalport branch opened for freight traffic around September 1860 and passenger traffic commenced on 10 June 1861. As the line continued southwards from Oakengates, it passed close to Snedshill Ironworks, so the Company railway was extended in this direction to exchange sidings with the branch line. A further line was extended southwards from the exchange sidings to facilitate the transfer of traffic directly with the Priorslee Ironworks. In later years this became the most heavily used of the Company's exchange sidings.

By 1870, the Company's railway had taken over further parts of the disused section of the Shropshire Canal that passed by Snedshill and Priorslee, with the exception of the section opposite Snedshill Ironworks. Nearby was the main reservoir for the two works. Certainly the canal section was still extant in 1880, and seems to have been used as an additional reservoir for some time after. But by the turn of the century, it had gone out of use, and had been converted into further railway by the Company.

The opening of the New Yard Works in 1861 entailed the further provision of railway access to this large works, and this was joined to the existing railway at The Nabb by way of a south facing junction. The lines here eventually entered all of the workshops at this site, which were further extended in 1900 (with a new machine shop) and in 1902 when the Wagon Repair shops were built. The locomotive shed and repair shed were sited just off the access line, between the main line and the works. These were the sole locomotive facilities until the erection of a further running shed at Priorslee before the Second World War, and are discussed later.

A view from the 2.35pm passenger train from Coalport as it passes the Priorslee exchange sidings, on the last day of passenger services on the Coalport branch, 31 May 1952. The train engine is 2-6-2T No.40058. [T. G. Wassell]

CHAPTER FIVE
THE HUMBER ARM RAILWAY

The ¾ mile Humber Arm Branch was authorised as part of the Birmingham & Liverpool Junction Canal by an Act of 1827 and built by its successor, the Shropshire Union Canal Company. It ran for just over a mile from Kynnersley on the Shropshire Union's Newport Branch to the wharf at Lubstree, where the first cargoes were handled on 9 May 1844. Initially a tramway was constructed from Lubstree Wharf to Lodge Furnaces, a distance of some three miles. Curiously, both the wharf and the tramway were actually built by the Duke of Sutherland, on whose land both were situated.

During the first month, 320 tons of coal were shipped out (all from the Company) and 160 tons of fluxing limestone was delivered. The section from Lubstree to just south of where it passed beneath the LNWR line was converted in 1870 into a railway. It connected with the Company railway just beyond the Donnington exchange sidings, immediately prior to the Wellington Road crossing. The line became known as the Humber Arm Railway, running for a distance of just under 1½ miles, occupying a little over four acres in its entire length. The remainder of the tramway to Lodge Furnaces was removed at this time and the route given over wholly to road traffic. Immediately upon completion, the railway was leased by the Duke of Sutherland to the Company.

The line from Donnington to Lubstree ran at the southern side of the Company exchange sidings, and alongside the LNWR Stafford to Wellington line for about ¼ mile before turning south, then west and north through 270 degrees in a wide arc, whilst descending at 1 in 77 and passing beneath the LNWR line. From here the single line continued in a general north-westerly direction, descending firstly at 1 in 100 for about ¼ mile, then finally at 1 in 264 for about a further ½ mile until it reached the wharf. Just before the entrance to the wharf the line crossed over a minor road known as Humber Lane on the level. The formation then divided into two runround loops and three sidings, the easternmost of which ran alongside the wharf for transhipment with the canal barges and also ran through a canalside goods shed. At the far end of the yard, the canalside track continued into a single road locomotive shed. No major engineering works were required on the line, other than the short tunnel under the LNWR line, and a small bridge after about one mile, where the line crossed the Humber Brook. The line was carefully sited to avoid some marshy ground on its north-eastern side.

This branch line became particularly important for the shipment of limestone from Llangollen for use at the Company's ironworks, after the local supplies had been worked out. In the reverse direction, coal and pig iron was shipped out from this wharf to customers via the Shropshire Union system. As a measure of the importance of the traffic passing through the

The warehouse at Lubstree Wharf was once rail served, and the alignment of the photograph indicates the approximate route of one of the tracks. This building only lost its roof in recent years, but its survival must be questionable now. [Author]

Humber Arm, it is recorded that upon opening, the SURCC transferred 30 of its boats from its main fleet, exclusively for this traffic. The Company was paying the SURCC ½ d. per ton for all goods shipped through the wharf.

The Company records reveal that by 1897 signals had been erected on the railway although the method of operation is not known. A locomotive was outstationed at the wharf for the working of wagons to the exchange sidings at Donnington and for the shunting necessary to position wagons adjacent to barges at the wharf for loading and unloading. It is presumed that the locomotive returned to the later main shed at the New Yard Works for boiler washouts and routine maintenance. Although the wharf duties would only have required the attentions of one of the smaller Company locomotives, no information has surfaced to suggest any preferred locomotives.

At a Board meeting on 31 March 1913 permission was given for the lease to be renewed. This was done, and the annual rental of the line was fixed at £7.15s. 10d. being for a period of seven years, retrospectively from 25 December 1912. This new agreement evidently expired without legal renewal, and two years had elapsed before the matter was brought to the attention of the Board once more. However, the first suggestions that the line was no longer required emerged at a Board meeting on 1 September 1921 when consideration was given to closing of the railway. However, at the next meeting, on 7 October 1921, it was decided to continue with the tenancy of the railway. Matters evidently did not rest there, for less than a year later, on 26 May 1922 the Board Minutes record the following: *The Duke of Sutherland having decided to sell the site of this railway, correspondence with his agent was submitted* [to the meeting]. *The Board resolved that the offer of his Grace to free the Company from the obligation to restore the site, as per Clause 15 of the agreement dated 24 April 1913 for the sum of £500 be accepted, the Company to have the power to remove all rails and sleepers and any other plant thereon.* But at the Board meeting two months later, on 28 July, it was recorded that: *The purchase of the site of this railway from the Duke of Sutherland for the sum of £100 was approved, and authority was given to seal the conveyance in respect of this purchase.*

Two years later, the usefulness of the railway had finally come to an end, as the Board Minutes dated 29 July 1924 record: 'It was agreed to sell a portion of this railway land for the best price available.' The railway from the Donnington exchange sidings was truncated about 44 yards north of where it had passed beneath the LNWR line, and the track northwards to Lubstree Wharf was removed. Two months later, the Board meeting of 4 April recorded that: 'Instructions were given to accept Messrs. Ward's offer of £30 for the portion of the site of this railway as indicated.' This land was sold to Messrs. R.P.Ward and J.C Ward, and remains in the possession of their descendants to this day. The truncated spur now became a headshunt, and a new siding of about 125 yards was laid in, continuing directly southwards to Wellington Road. This was used as a sand siding for several years until these truncated remains were finally removed in the early 1930s, and the land was subsequently sold, although not recorded in Board Minutes. Some time after 1914, the western end of the line adjacent to the exchange sidings was connected to them, providing additional siding space there, and improving the operational aspects for traffic.

Strangely, although the Humber Arm Branch Canal was filled in many years ago, the wharf basin remains intact, fed by the nearby Humber Brook, and used by a local farmer as a source for irrigating nearby fields, notably during periods of drought. The original buildings at the wharf are still extant (at the time of writing), with the manager's house now restored and in private residence, the weighbridge hut in use as an office, and the locomotive shed and goods sheds becoming increasingly derelict. The latter had contained the pumping equipment necessary for raising the water from the basin to the fields.

A pastoral scene across the now isolated waters of the Lubstree Wharf in 2002. The warehouse is on the left; the restored house on the right was once the residence of the wharf manager. The scene remains unchanged in 2008.[Author]

LUBSTREE WHARF (1882)

1. Shropshire Union Canal (Humber Arm Branch), to Kynnersley
2. Humber Lane
3. Locomotive shed
4. Manager's house
5. Weighbridge office
6. Wharfside goods shed

The engine shed at the end of the Humber Arm Railway was located alongside the canal at Lubstree Wharf. This photograph from 2002 shows it to be in a fragile state, in which condition it remains in 2008. [Author]

CHAPTER SIX
THE NARROW GAUGE RAILWAYS

With the closing of the Lodge Furnaces in 1888, the tramways linking the nearby mines to these works and to the remains of the Donnington Wood Canal soon went out of use. This included the tramway that connected Barnyard Colliery to the Lodge Furnaces and crossed the standard gauge Granville to Donnington line. Similarly, the group of tramways in the Priorslee area were all removed by the turn of the century, as the extended standard gauge lines now linked all the remaining mines to the system. The only remaining tramway lines were those from the Priorslee Furnaces to the slag heaps, and from the older slag heaps (some of which owed their origin to the nearby earlier Eagle Ironworks) to the Asphalt Works. These are all believed to have been rope worked on their upper, steeper slopes, as at the Board Meeting on 29 March 1895 the minutes record: 'To consider rope haulage at Priors Lee furnaces. Proposed scheme sanctioned.' These were horse powered on the lower levels, and a map of 1922 indicates that at least one new such tramway was being installed at that time. However, the gauge of these tramways is not certain; in a report from the Company to Earl Granville dated 29 March 1899 it is given as 2ft 8in but in the 1915 valuation the 'cinder bank' tramway is given as 2ft 9in and confirmed as being rope or cable worked 'by a steam winch'.

The 3 foot gauge line at the Lodge Furnaces had been installed in 1869 for the opening of the calcining kilns in 1870, and by 1876 is recorded in the Company Valuation as comprising 2,261 yards (just over 1¼ miles) of tram railway and pig sidings, made of rails weighing 45lb per yard. Together with the sleepers, points and crossings, and 'cinder boxes, and tip and blast engine boilers', these were valued at £960.18s.6d. This line was worked by the three Company built 0-4-0 sidetanks built in 1869, and referred to in more detail in Chapter 7. The extent of the lines is indicated on the 1881 map of Old Lodge Furnaces.

The three locomotives were housed in an 'engine house' measuring 37 feet by 23 feet, and topped with a tiled roof, which was valued at £50. The 'Colliery Guardian' of 1 April 1870 records that 'three calcining kilns have lately been erected at the back of the furnaces ... a small engine raises the stone (*limestone*) to the top of them by a small incline.' In his 'Guide to the Iron and Steel Industry' in 1873, Samuel Griffiths wrote of the Lodge Furnaces: 'The saving of manual labour in this department is marvellous – locomotive engines are employed in all departments, removing the slag right away from the furnaces and take the pigs straight to the railway. Limestone, ironstone and fuel is supplied to the kilns and furnaces by the same motive power.' Again, the 1881 map of Lodge Furnaces illustrates the extent of this railway, and the location of the locomotive shed may be seen.

At Donnington Wood Brickworks, a smaller line was installed to connect the clay quarry to the brickworks. It is not clear when this was established, but it seems likely that it dates from some time after the First World War, as there is no mention of the system in the 1915 Company Valuation. Earlier Ordnance Survey Maps do show a tramway of some description, but this was initially possibly a conventional horse drawn or manual system. This line was latterly of 1ft 6in gauge and operated by an endless three eighths of an inch diameter chain system that was suspended over the tubs, which measured 30" x 20" x 12". A plate with a shaped slot was riveted to one end of

An interesting view along the 1ft 6in gauge chain operated plateway at Donnington Brickworks, looking towards the clay preparation shed, with the chain wheel and two tubs in the foreground. [Ironbridge Gorge Museum Trust]

A narrow gauge tub similar to those formerly used on the plateway at Donnington Brickworks, and now preserved at the Telford Steam Railway. [Author]

45

each tub, the chain engaging in this slot to pull the tubs along. The chains passed round 4 foot diameter guiding wheels from which the direction of the chain reversed. The drive for the chain was provided by a 50hp electric motor from the time that the Company was connected to the National Grid in 1931, but may have been steam driven in earlier times. However, such a system had one drawback in that it could not reliably go round curves. Therefore, where such changes of direction occurred, as at the one right-angled turn, and at the end of the system adjacent to the Hoffmann Kiln, the chain was guided upwards leaving the U-shaped tubs to proceed under gravity, or by manual power to their intended destination. Consequently, the line effectively operated in two sections; the upper section from the clay pit to the point known as the 'First Head', and then from there to the tipping dock. The upper section comprised a chain length of 600 yards, and the lower section of 540 yards. The tramway lines per the 1941 Valuation totalled 1,189 yards, which were valued at £200, and there were 24 tubs (otherwise also known as 'trams') valued at £60. This system continued in operation up to the closing of the brickworks in 1971. The cessation of this system must have come as a considerable relief to anyone living within earshot of the constant rattling of the chains and tubs.

The lines within each of the coal, ironstone and fireclay mines surfaced at the pithead to run the tubs to the screens. In most cases, these lines were extended from the screens to the spoil heaps nearby. The usual mixture of manual, horse or rope powered these lines depending on the availability of nearby power sources, steepness of the grade, and the loads to be worked.

One exception was the line from the pithead to the screens and standard gauge line loading point at Grange Mine. Due to the local geography, the pithead was some 30-40 feet above this loading point, which was situated some distance away at Dawes Bower. To connect the two, a dead straight double track rope worked tramway of just over 200 yards length was constructed. This tramway was self acting, whereby the descending loaded tubs powered the ascending empty tubs. The pithead winding gear could be brought into use to power ascending tubs, in circumstances where there were no corresponding descending loads. Temporary tramways ran out to the top of the spoil heaps. The tramways at Grange were all of 2ft. gauge (per the 1937 Valuation), and altogether totalled 2,700 feet of rails.

Ernie Woods can recall that when there was no one around, as a young lad, he and others would take an empty tub and ride it down the gradient. It can therefore be surmised that the gradient was not too steep!

The tramways at Woodhouse pit were also recorded as being of 2ft gauge, and totalled some 1,540 yards of tram rails. However, the tramways at Granville were of 2ft 6in gauge and per the 1937 Valuation totalled some 2,200 feet of rails.

A final small system was installed in the early years of operation at the Snedshill Brick and Tile Works for transport of clay from the quarry at the rear of the works, to the moulding shops and kilns. The lines are believed to have been manually worked. However, this source lasted only a few years before being exhausted, well before the start of the twentieth century, after which the tramway was extended towards further sources near to St.Georges, then abandoned altogether before the First World War.

The 1ft 6in gauge plateway at Donnington Brickworks connected the clay pits to the kilns. One of the tubs is running towards the guiding wheel for the overhead chain haulage system. A group of nine fully laden tubs are standing off the tramway, on the lower left. [Ironbridge Gorge Museum Trust]

Looking down into the clay quarry at Donnington Brickworks, showing the 1ft 6in gauge chain operated plateway, with a wagon approaching the direction wheel, around 1970. [Ironbridge Gorge Museum Trust]

CHAPTER SEVEN
LOCOMOTIVES BUILT BY THE LILLESHALL COMPANY

Locomotive building appears to have started with the completion of the New Yard Engineering Works at St. Georges during 1861. We have already seen that George Granville William Sutherland Leveson-Gower, who coincidentally became the 3rd Duke of Sutherland in 1861, had been apprenticed under McConnell at the LNWR Wolverton Works during the time that Wolverton was still building and repairing steam locomotives. Thus it is a fairly safe assumption to make that he was the inspiration behind the introduction of railway locomotives into the Company's product portfolio. It is also fairly safe to assume that some of the distinctive LNWR features introduced on the early locomotives, such as flared chimneys, Allen straight link motion, and Ramsbottom safety valves were likely to have been as a result of his influence.

The first manager of the New Yard Works was a John Lloyd, who according to the former Works Accountant, Thomas Hoggins, came from the 'Phoenix Works' in Stoke-on-Trent. This location will reveal its mysterious head once again in the chapter concerning the Lilleshall locomotive fleet, but for the moment, we can assume that this may be true, and that this person had already acquired a certain amount of experience with at least stationery steam engines (for colliery winding, blast furnace blowing, etc.), if not in the actual manufacture of locomotives.

The works were laid out for the construction of locomotives, as according to Hoggins, rails were laid in each bay of the fitting and erecting shops, with pits installed between the rails from end to end of each shop. The first recorded locomotive was constructed at the New Yard Works in 1862. An interesting insight into the Company's activities at this time is given in a short report in the 'Wellington Journal' of 3 October 1863, as follows:
Lilleshall Company's Engineering Yard. On Monday evening week [presumably 22 September] *the management of this yard treated a number of fitters who have been engaged in building two new locomotive engines, to some good brown stout and a few bottles of champagne.* The locomotives were probably RAVENHEAD (no.26) and DITTON (no.35) in the following list, as these seem to have been identical, but could equally have been RAVENHEAD and the Jarrow Chemical Co. loco, as these had sequential order numbers.

Hoggins also claimed that 'more than one locomotive was supplied to the Earl of Dudley for use on the Pensnett Railway'. However likely this may appear, there is no evidence of such construction, other than the entry given in the 'Questionable Lilleshall Built Locomotives' section of this chapter.

An interesting glimpse of what might have been is recorded in the Company 'Drawings for proposed machinery', in which a drawing (estimated from 1867/68) is listed for 'a 16 inch goods locomotive, Llanelly Co.' This was evidently a further attempt to get into the market for main line locos with an 0-6-0 tender or tank engine for the Llanelly Railway & Dock Co. (not to be confused with the later and perhaps better known Llanelly & Mynydd Mawr Railway) This venture must have been coincidental with the unsuccessful 2-2-2, also of 1867, and nothing more is

Lilleshall 0-6-0ST 116 of 1867 became No.1 MARQUIS at Cannock Wood Colliery in Staffordshire. As can be seen from this mid-1950s view, it was usually maintained in sparkling condition. [Allan C. Baker Collection]

Lilleshall 0-6-0ST No.4 RAWNSLEY was originally built in 1867 as Lilleshall's prototype 2-2-2 'express locomotive'. Failing to find a market, it was rebuilt in 1872 into the form shown here, at the Rawnsley locomotive shed on 17 May 1943. Despite the wartime conditions, it was always immaculately turned out, and regularly worked the 'Paddy Train' conveying miners from Hednesford to Rawnsley in three ancient six-wheeled carriages. It spent its entire working life, from 1873 until 1963, at Rawnsley. [J.H.L. Adams Collection: late A.C. Jarvis; Midland Railway Trust]

known of any proposals to build such a locomotive. An insight into the early production of locomotives was given in the following report from the 'Colliery Guardian' of 1 April, 1870: *Several locomotives have been turned out with 16 inch cylinders, six wheels coupled; tanks to hold 900 gallons of water; these are furnished with cabs and will take heavy trains up a gradient of one in forty five and are used in branch lines. Locomotives on a smaller scale are made extensively; some with 9 inch cylinders; six wheels, four coupled; 2ft 4in in diameter, gauge 2ft 7in and upwards. These will take loads of up to 20 tons up gradients of one in thirty.*

In his 'Guide to the Iron and Steel Trade' of 1873, Samuel Griffiths describes the Engineering Department as follows: *There are now in progress six locomotives, nine blast engines of various types, heavy pumping and winding machinery, steam hammers, etc ... A large business is done here in locomotives for colliery purposes and for this class of engine, the Phoenix Foundry has for a long time rivalled the engine shops of Manchester and the Tyne.*

It is worthy of note that Samuel Thomas Price, born at St. Georges, Oakengates on 1 December 1861 was apprenticed as an engineer at the Company. After completing his apprenticeship, he joined the Midland Railway at Derby Locomotive Works, and later still moved to the Meaford Pumping Station as Engineer. Around 1885/86, he joined William Gordon Bagnall at his newly established locomotive works in Stafford, and in later years became the Works Manager. He collaborated with Ernest Edwin Baguley to design the Baguley-Price valve gear used on many Bagnall locomotives. Despite the fact that he is reputed to have retired in 1915 due to ill health, he survived until December 1954, expiring at the ripe old age of 93!

Construction of the last recorded locomotive was in 1901, after a gap of several years, as the previous known locomotive to be constructed was in 1888. Evidently, this was a special concession, as by that time the Company had felt that it could not compete against the established volume manufacturers of locomotives. Alternatively, this last engine may not have been new, but a rebuild of an earlier locomotive.

In compiling the list of locomotives built by the Company, care has been taken to avoid the introduction of unreliable information. However, the paucity of available material means that some questionable information is included, but is indicated as such. The notable sources of information started with the various Industrial Railway Society (IRS) Handbooks and earlier Pocket Books where appropriate for each of the geographic regions, the Company's 1876 Valuation of Assets, Register of Drawings and various tracings and drawings (in the archives of the Ironbridge Gorge Museum Trust, and referred to as 'L Co'). The former Works Accountant at New Yard Works, Thomas Hoggins, compiled various lists of locomotives built by the Company from a register of customer orders. Apparently, after closure of the New Yard Works in 1931 he had retained this register without the knowledge of his employers, and even many years after his retirement felt that this was still confidential information, and so refused to let anyone else see it. Unfortunately this register has since been lost despite attempts by several persons (including the author) to trace it. Hoggins' position at the New Yard has been verified by reference to the Company salary ledger, and to the 1901 census. In 1952 he supplied a list to the late Ralph Russell (referred hereafter as the 'RR'), and in 1942/43 and in 1956/57 supplied lists to the late Selwyn Pierce Higgins (hereafter referred to as 'TH'). Reference has also been made to 'British Steam Locomotive Builders' by J.W. Lowe.

Early locomotives incorporated several distinctive features, notably covers over the slide bars on outside cylinder engines, horizontal cylinders, and combined front splashers with sandboxes. Saddle tanks were rounded on earlier locos, but from around the mid 1870s changed to a more square shape. Unsurprisingly, early locos were not originally fitted with cabs, and when fitted, the later ones were notable for the semi-elliptical shape of the side opening.

The TH lists include the works order numbers under which the locomotives listed thereon (which is not exhaustive), were constructed. As the works plates (not fitted to all locomotives) did not contain these numbers, and as they share the same sequence with all other machinery constructed at the New Yard Works, they are not considered as works numbers in the same way that they are normally used to identify the locomotives from other manufacturers. The actual worksplates were oval in shape, containing the words 'Lilleshall Co. Ltd.' along the upper border, 'Shropshire' along the lower border, and the year in the centre. On some, the words 'Engineers' appeared in the centre. The letters and numerals on the plates were raised.

For each locomotive, a short identification is given comprising the gauge, the works order number (in brackets), year built, wheel arrangement, inside or outside cylinders, cylinder dimensions (bore and stroke), and the allocated running number and/or name. Following this, any further technical details and dimensions are given, and then the history, where known, of the owners and uses of the locomotives and their final disposition. The various lists mentioned above have resulted in some contradictions, especially as to the cylinder dimensions, and so this information (quoting the applicable source) is given in the details of each locomotive. However, it should be borne in mind that the cylinders sizes on any locomotive could have changed during their lifetime, and minor variations, such as ¼in or ½in would be accounted for by a rebore during overhaul.

A review of the Company records and comparison to known locomotives reveals a local terminology, in that the terms 'tram tank' or 'tram loco' are used to describe side tank locomotives. Correspondingly, the term 'tank loco' was used to indicate a saddle tank locomotive.

The following list is inevitably far from complete, and any comments relating to the details or history of these locomotives will be much appreciated.

The celebrated Lilleshall 0-4-0ST No.4 CONSTANCE of 1865 stands out of use near to the running shed at Priorslee Furnaces on 19 June 1954, in company with two slag ladles and 0-6-2T No.5. [F. W. Shuttleworth]

LOCOMOTIVES BUILT BY THE LILLESHALL COMPANY

Gauge	Order No.	Date Built	Wheels	Cylinders	No./ Name

4' 8 ½"   (15)   1862   0-4-0ST   OC   13" x 20" (IRS, TH, RR)   21

Delivered December, 1862. Driving wheels 3' 9" diameter. Exhibited at the London Exhibition in 1862, probably bearing the name "LILLESHALL" (although afterwards more likely simply known as "LILLESHALL"). Sold to T. Savin, contractor, "as new" in December, 1862. It is not known where it worked, although it may have carried the name ABERYSTWYTH at some time, and this may be a clue that it was used on the construction of the Aberystwyth & Welsh Coast Railway. Savin is well known for informally moving his various assets from one enterprise to another, and this loco was transferred to the Oswestry & Newtown Joint Committee (formed 3 December, 1863 to operate the Llanidloes & Newtown Railway, Oswestry & Newtown Railway, and to take over the Newtown & Machynlleth Railway). This became the Cambrian Railways on 25 July, 1864. The loco was used as a "ballast engine" and became their no. 21. Per an unconfirmed report, it was sold in January, 1868 to the Black Park Colliery, Chirk for £850. Subsequent disposal unknown.

A print of the locomotive, and the related technical description of this locomotive from "The Colliery Guardian" of 1 November, 1862 are attached as Appendix 2.

Gauge	Order No.	Date Built	Wheels	Cylinders	No./ Name

4' 8 ½"   (26)   1863   0-4-0ST   OC   10" x18" (TH,RR)   RAVENHEAD

Per the RR list, this was originally supplied in September, 1863 to the Ditton Brook Iron Company, near Widnes which is felt to be in error. The two TH lists each show this as being delivered to the order of a Mr. James Haddock, who is believed to have been one of the partners in the firm of Bromilow and Haddock, owners of the Ravenhead Colliery, near St. Helens. It is assumed that this engine worked from the colliery to the new canal wharf that opened around the time of its delivery. Further details on this system are included in "The Industrial Railways of St. Helens, Wigan and Warrington – Part One, St. Helens" by C.H.A. Townley and J.A.Peden (IRS, 1999). There is a possibility that after a rebuild (see next paragraph), it was transferred to the Ravenhead Plate Glass Works. It is believed to have been finally scrapped around 1920.

However, there are some further facts that tend to 'muddy' the story somewhat. Firstly, in Rosling Bennett's "The Chronicles of Boulton's Siding", it is suggested that RAVENHEAD was sold to Isaac Boulton. That RAVENHEAD was known to have worked at Ravenhead later, in fact suggests that its visit to Boulton's works was more likely for repairs, such as a new boiler than a transfer of ownership.

Secondly, Trevor Lodge commented in the "Industrial Railway Record no. 135" (December, 1993) that IRS records contain a note from the late R.H. Inness to the effect that RAVENHEAD had worked at the Ditton Brook Iron Company's colliery at Holland Moor, near Wigan. In the light of the discovery of **two** locomotives delivered to the Ditton Brook Iron Company (see below), it seems that Inness must have been mistaken as to the identity, especially as they were very similar.

Gauge	Order No.	Date Built	Wheels	Cylinders	No./ Name

3' 6"   (27)   1863   tram tank   6" x 12"   (TH)

Almost certainly an 0-4-0T with outside cylinders. Delivered in September, 1863 to Jarrow Chemical Company, near Tyne Dock, where it is believed to have worked on the extensive internal works tramway system. This works was closed shortly after the company was merged to form The United Alkali Co. Ltd. on 1st November, 1890. It is not known whether this locomotive survived to form part of the 1890 merger, and if it did, its subsequent disposal is similarly unknown.

Gauge	Order No.	Date Built	Wheels	Cylinders	No./ Name

4' 8 ½"   (35)   1863   tank loco   10" x 18" (TH)   DITTON

Delivered in December, 1863 to the Ditton Brook Iron Company, near Widnes. Almost certainly this was an 0-4-0ST with outside cylinders. Its eventual fate is not known.

Gauge	Order No.	Date Built	Wheels	Cylinders	No./ Name

4' 8 ½"   1864   0-4-0ST   OC   13" x 20" (RR)   19

Per the RR list, this was supplied new in June, 1864 to T. Savin & Co., Brecon, so it is believed to have been part of his contractor's fleet at this time. However, no further reports of this locomotive's movements have been traced, even though much of Savin's history has been reported in detail. There again, several of Savin's locomotives seem to have "disappeared" around the time of his bankruptcy! There is a possibility that this locomotive has been confused with LILLESHALL (15 of 1862, above) and its history is therefore unknown. The running number 19 most definitely is not that from the later Cambrian Railways sequence, as has been claimed by some sources.

In a view believed to date from the 1920s, 0-6-0ST No.6 (134 of 1869) is posed at the entrance to New Yard Works. [F. Jones Collection]

Lilleshall's 0-6-0ST No.7 (135 of 1870) was identical to No.6, except for minor details, such as differing rivet spacing on the saddle tank, and a smaller running plate toolbox. [F. Jones Collection]

LILLESHALL (15 of 1862, above) and its history is therefore unknown. The running number 19 most definitely is not that from the later Cambrian Railways sequence, as has been claimed by some sources.

Gauge	Order No.	Date Built	Wheels	Cylinders	No./ Name
4' 8 ½"	(43)	1864	0-4-0ST	OC 10" x 18" (TH,RR)	1 DEFENCE

Delivered new in July, 1864 to William Harrison Ltd., Brownhills Colliery, Staffs. Subsequent disposal unknown.

Gauge	Order No.	Date Built	Wheels	Cylinders	No./ Name
2' 7 ½"	(61)	1865	0-4-0T	OC 8" x 14" (IRS)	FREE MINER

Delivered new in February, 1865 to Cornelius Brain, Colliery, Cinderford, Gloucestershire. The TH list gives the cylinders as 10" x 12", and the RR list as 6" x 12". Possibly scrapped by c 1906. **Note 1.**

Gauge	Order No.	Date Built	Wheels	Cylinders	No./ Name
3' 2 ½"		1865	0-4-0T	11" x 18" (RR)	CORNGREAVES

Delivered new in April, 1865 to the New British Iron Co. Ltd., Corngreaves Brickworks, Collieries and Furnaces, Cradley Heath, Staffs. Business became W. Bassano & Co. c 1891, then R. Follows from 1901. Subsequent disposal unknown.

Gauge	Order No.	Date Built	Wheels	Cylinders	No./ Name
4' 8 ½"	(89)	1865	0-4-0ST	OC 13" x 21" (L Co)	No. 4 CONSTANCE

Delivered on 5 September, 1865. The TH and RR lists give the cylinder stroke as 20". Driving wheels 3' 6" diameter, boiler pressure 150 lbs per square inch, weight 23 tons. New to Lilleshall Company for own use. Fitted with a new boiler in 1896, and again in 1916 when the Salter spring balance safety valves were replaced by Ramsbottom type. New frames were probably fitted at this time. Scrapped circa February, 1957.

Gauge	Order No.	Date Built	Wheels	Cylinders	No./ Name
4' 8 ½"		1866	0-4-0ST	OC 13" x 20" (TH)	

Delivered in April, 1866 to Robert Heath, who had a number of enterprises in North Staffordshire. The only site that is appropriate is the system serving Norton and Victoria Collieries, Ford Green Iron Works, and the Norton and Biddulph Valley Iron Works. IRS "Industrial Locomotives of North Staffordshire" lists two locomotives, Robert Heath's No.1 and No.2 as being of unknown identity, which are suitable candidates for this locomotive. The second locomotive may also have been built by Lilleshall, as unconfirmed suggestions have been made that more than one was supplied to Robert Heath. However, there is no firm evidence of such a second locomotive. These two locomotives are recorded as being derelict around 1885 and scrapped soon after.

Gauge	Order No.	Date Built	Wheels	Cylinders	No./ Name
4' 8 ½"	(98)	1866	0-4-0ST	OC 13" x 21" (L Co)	No.5

Delivered new on 17 April, 1866 to Lilleshall Company for own use. Cylinder dimensions confirmed by the 1876 Valuation, although the TH list gives the cylinder stroke as 20". 1915 Valuation records that a new boiler was fitted in 1895, but that at this later date "a new boiler is to hand". Wheels were 3' 6" diameter. Sold in February, 1929 to Victoria Coal & Iron Co. Ltd., Wellington, who as dealers hired it to Netherseal Colliery Co. Ltd., Linton, Derbyshire. Scrapped on site, c 1934 possibly by the Victoria Coal & Iron Co. Ltd. who were also scrap dealers.

Gauge	Order No.	Date Built	Wheels	Cylinders	No./ Name
4' 8 ½"	(90)	1866	0-4-0ST	OC 13" x 20" (TH,RR)	No.6

Delivered new in November, 1866 to Dalmellington Iron Co. Ltd., Waterside, Ayrshire.. The outside cylinders have been alternatively quoted as being 14" x 21" by David Smith in his book "The Dalmellington Company – Its Engines and Men" (David & Charles, 1967), with wheels 3' 8" diameter, wheelbase of 7' 0" and an overall length over buffers of 20 feet. It featured a round topped saddle tank, centrally positioned dome, Allen straight link motion, shields over slide bars, Ramsbottom safety valves, a weatherboard and boiler with a working pressure of 120 psi. It was kept at the Burnfoothill shed, where it remained working on the remote, and elevated section of the line serving the company's ironstone pits for most of its life. The slide bar shields were removed at an early date, and later the safety valves were moved to the top of the dome. About 1896, a large cab replaced the weatherboard, which must have come as some relief to the engine men who had endured thirty years in primitive conditions.

By 1899 there was a 23" crack in the top and side of the firebox, and so it was laid up to await a new boiler. However, the needs of other locos were considered more pressing, so No.6 was simply "patched up" and ran for a further seven years until it was fitted with a new boiler, supplied by Andrew Barclay of Kilmarnock in 1906. However, its duties at Burnfoothill were taken over by Markham 0-4-0ST no.15 in 1909, so it returned to the main works on various duties, including haulage of molten slag to the Slag Hill. Around 1909, the overall cab was removed, and the chimney hinged at its base so as to fold sideways – presumably in order to clear some low structure in its new duties. Scrapped on site 1911, its 1906 boiler was evidently still in good order, as it was removed and sold intact.

Lilleshall's 0-4-0ST No.5 (98 of 1866) was virtually identical to No.4 CONSTANCE. Both locomotives had a single (upper) slide bar, which was a feature common to all outside cylinder Lilleshall-built locomotives. [F. Jones Collection]

0-4-0ST No.4 CONSTANCE (89 of 1865) was the company's longest serving locomotive, not being scrapped until 1957. This is another of the posed views of the Company locomotive fleet from the 1920s. [F. Jones Collection]

Gauge	Order No.	Built Date	Wheels	Cylinders	No./ Name
(3 ft ?)	(99)	1866	Tram Tank	6" x 12" (TH)	

Almost certainly an 0-4-0T, with outside cylinders. Delivered new to the Hodbarrow Iron Co. for use on their tramway running from the "Old Mine" to the pier at Crab Marsh for shipping the iron ore, which is believed to have been of 3 feet gauge. Hodbarrow board minutes authorised the purchase of this locomotive from Lilleshall on 29 December, 1865. In August, 1866 the sum of £420 was paid to Lilleshall, although it is not certain that this was the full purchase price. This system was discontinued around 1877, and the loco is believed to have been sold. It may be the one advertised in the "Machinery Market" for 2 September, 1878 as follows: "One side tank loco, 3 ft. gauge, 4 wheels, 6" x 12" cylinders, Wilson's patent feed pump. Recent overhaul, including a new copper firebox. Makers, the Lilleshall Co. Price offered £370 (in Northumberland)". Any further history is unknown.

Gauge	Order No.	Built Date	Wheels	Cylinders	No./ Name
4' 8 ½"	(101)	1867	2-2-2	IC 16" x 21" (RR, TH)	
		Rebuilt 1872	0-6-0ST	IC 17" x 21" (IRS)	4 RAWNSLEY

Exhibited as first built as an "express engine" at the 1867 Paris Exhibition where it gained a silver medal. However, it failed to attract any main line buyers, and after return to the Company was rebuilt as shown.

Further dimensions and details concerning the original locomotive are given in Appendix 4, "Lilleshall's Express Locomotive".

Supplied "as new" in its rebuilt form in July, 1873 to Cannock & Rugeley Collieries Ltd., Rawnsley, Staffs. Acquired by NCB on 1 January, 1947. Scrapped at Cannock Wood Colliery in March, 1962 by J. Cashmore.

Gauge	Order No.	Built Date	Wheels	Cylinders	No./ Name
4' 8 ½"	(109)	1867	0-4-0ST	11" x 18" (TH, RR)	

Delivered new in May, 1867 to John Hunter, who was General Manger of the Dalmellington Company from 1848 to 1886. There is no confirmation of this loco being delivered to Dalmellington, and IRS Handbook N does not give any suitable unidentified candidates. It may be that John Hunter had other business interests in the area that would have employed this locomotive, but none have come to light. However, see the 1868 engine for New Cumnock Collieries, below. The earlier TH list gives the cylinder dimensions as 11" x 12", although this looks unreasonable. No further details are known of this engine.

Gauge	Order No.	Built Date	Wheels	Cylinders	No./ Name
4' 8 ½"	(116)	1867	0-6-0ST	IC 17" x 22" (IRS)	1 MARQUIS

Delivered in September, 1867. Driving wheels 3'6" diameter. The weight in working order was 38 ½ tons and the overall length was 27 feet 8 inches. It featured a polished brass dome. The TH list gives cylinder bore as 16". New to Cannock & Rugeley Collieries Co. Ltd.,Rawnsley, Staffs. Acquired by NCB, 1 January, 1947. To Grove Colliery, Little Wyrley, Staffs.15/1/62; to Cannock Central Workshops, Staffs. March / April, 1963. Scrapped on site by L. Wallace of Cannock, May 1964.

Gauge	Order No.	Built Date	Wheels	Cylinders	No./ Name
4' 8 ½"	(112)	1867	0-6-0ST	IC 14" x 21" (RR)	WARRIOR

Delivered new in December, 1867 to William Harrison Ltd., Brownhills Colliery, Staffs. The TH list gives the cylinders as 14" x 18". Scrapped c 1934

Gauge	Order No.	Built Date	Wheels	Cylinders	No./ Name
4' 8 ½"		1868	0-4-0ST	OC 11" x 18" (IRS, RR)	2

Delivered new in February, 1868 to Thos. Kinnersley & Co. Ltd., Clough Hall Ironworks, Kidsgrove, Staffs. When the ironworks closed in 1890, it is believed to have passed to Lincoln Wagon & Engine Co., Lincoln. There are no further details of its disposal.

Gauge	Order No.	Built Date	Wheels	Cylinders	No./ Name
3' 2 ½"		1868	0-4-2T	OC 9" x 16" (RR)	LION

Delivered new in March, 1868 to New British Iron Co. Ltd., Corngreaves Brickworks, Collieries and Furnaces, Cradley Heath, Staffs. Business later became W. Bassano & Co. c 1891, then R. Follows from 1901. Scrapped or sold before 1901.

FREE MINER was works number 61 of 1865, built to the unusual gauge of 2ft 7 ½in for the Trafalgar Colliery Company of Cinderford, Gloucestershire where it was photographed around 1880. [Allan C. Baker Collection]

Amongst the Company's wide range of steel products was the supply of steel girders. This one was used to support the bridge carrying the Shrewsbury & Birmingham Railway over the jucntion of Bridge Street and Church Street in Oakengates. As can be seen, it was manufactured in 1848, and performs its original role to this day. [Author]

Gauge	Order No. Built	Date	Wheels	Cylinders	No./ Name
4' 8 ½"	(117)	1868	0-6-0ST IC	17" x 22" (IRS)	2 ANGLESEY

Delivered in March, 1868. Driving wheels 3'6". Very similar to MARQUIS (above), and also similarly, the cylinder bore is given on the TH list as 16", but the weight was 39 tons, and the overall length was 27 feet 10 inches. New to Cannock & Rugeley Collieries Co. Ltd., Rawnsley, Staffs. Acquired by NCB, 1 January, 1947. Transferred temporarily to West Cannock No.5 Colliery after August, 1957 and returned by July, 1958. Scrapped at Cannock Wood Colliery in March, 1962 by J. Cashmore.

Gauge	Order No. Built	Date	Wheels	Cylinders	No./ Name
4' 8 ½"	(91)	1868	0-4-0ST	OC 13" x 20" (RR)	UXBRIDGE

Delivered new in November, 1868 to Cannock & Rugeley Collieries Co. Ltd., Rawnsley, Staffs. Sold in July, 1892, but destination unknown.

Gauge	Order No. Built	Date	Wheels	Cylinders	No./ Name
4' 8 ½"		1868	0-4-0ST	OC	No.1

Delivered new in 1868 to New Cumnock Collieries, Ayrshire. This may be the same loco as 109 of 1867, above. Scrapped 1934.

Gauge	Order No. Built	Date	Wheels	Cylinders	No./ Name
2' 7 ½"	(140)	1869	0-4-2T	OC 8" x 14" (TH, RR)	TRAFALGAR

Delivered new in April, 1869 to Cornelius Brain, Colliery, Cinderford, Gloucestershire. An early photograph of this locomotive reveals that it was supplied without a cab, and that the trailing wheels were only about 6" diameter less than the driving wheels. The safety valves were mounted on a 'haystack' firebox. Scrapped c 1906. **Note 1.**

Gauge	Order No. Built	Date	Wheels	Cylinders	No./ Name
3' 0"	(141)	1869	0-4-0T	8" x 14" (TH)	COMET

Delivered new in April, 1869 to Evans & Bowen, whose location is not presently known. The earlier TH list gives the cylinder bore as 8", and both the Register of Drawings and the later TH list as 8 ½". Subsequent history unknown.

Gauge	Order No. Built	Date	Wheels	Cylinders	No./ Name
4' 8 ½"		1869	0-4-0ST	OC 12" x 18" (RR)	SHIFNAL

Delivered new in July, 1869 to Old Park Iron Co. Ltd., Wellington, Shropshire. From 1872, this became Wellington Iron & Coal Co. Ltd., Old Park Ironworks. Subsequent disposal unknown.

Gauge	Order No. Built	Date	Wheels	Cylinders	No./ Name
3' 0"	(137)	1869	0-4-0T	OC 7" x 12" (L Co)	
3' 0"	(138)	1869	0-4-0T	OC 7" x 12" (L Co)	
3' 0"	(139)	1869	0-4-0T	OC 7" x 12" (L Co)	

The first two were delivered in October, 1869 and November, 1870 respectively for Lilleshall's own use at Lodge furnaces, Oakengates which were closed by 1888. The third locomotive must have followed soon after. Per the TH and RR lists the cylinder bore of the first two was 6", but per the 1876 Valuation it was 7". Two of these were believed sold around 1881, but subsequent disposal unknown. The fate of the third loco is similarly unknown.

Gauge	Order No. Built	Date	Wheels	Cylinders	No./ Name
4' 8 ½"	(134)	1869	0-6-0ST	OC 13" x 21" (L Co)	No.6

Delivered on 7 December, 1869 to Lilleshall Company for own use. Cylinder dimensions confirmed by the 1876 Valuation, although per the TH and RR lists the cylinders were 13" x 20", and per the 1915 and 1937 Valuations they were 13 ¼" x 20". Wheels were 3' 8" diameter. Received a new boiler in 1899, and again in 1923. Sold to NCB, Granville Colliery, c6/1950. Scrapped on site between August, 1955 and May, 1956 by Bell of Doncaster.

Another of the Rawnsley locomotives built by Lilleshall was 0-6-0ST MARQUIS, completed in 1867. [F. Jones]

No.2 ANGLESEY of the Cannock & Rugeley Collieries was identical to MARQUIS, but built in the following year, 1868. [F. Jones]

Gauge	Order No. Built	Date	Wheels	Cylinders	No./ Name

4' 8 ½"   1869   0-6-0ST   IC   14" x 21" (IRS, RR)   No.3
Delivered new in December, 1869 to Thomas Kinnersley & Co., Clough Hall Collieries & Ironworks, Kidsgrove, Staffs. Believed to have passed to Lincoln Wagon & Engine Co., Lincoln in 1891 when the ironworks closed. Subsequent disposal unknown, but see the entry under "SONS" in the section headed "Unknown Identities" below.

Gauge	Order No. Built	Date	Wheels	Cylinders	No./ Name

2' 7 ½"   (158)   1870   ank loco   8" x 14"   (TH)   DYFFRYN
Delivered new in March, 1870 to Dyffryn Co. (per the TH list – actually the company name was Dynevor United Co.), Main Colliery, Skewen, near Neath. The Register of Drawings and the later TH list gives the cylinder bore as 8 ½". The narrow gauge line here was abandoned in 1899 and replaced by a standard gauge line. This was one of six narrow gauge locos subsequently put up for sale.

Gauge	Order No. Built	Date	Wheels	Cylinders	No./ Name

4' 8 ½"   (135)   1870   0-6-0ST   OC   13" x 21" (L Co)   No.7
Completed on 21 June, 1870 for the Lilleshall Company's own use. Cylinder dimensions confirmed by the 1876 Valuation, but the TH and RR lists give the cylinder stroke as 20". It was identical to No.6 delivered in the previous year, and received a new boiler in 1898, and again in 1917 when it was recorded as being "rebuilt" at the New Yard Works. It was disposed of during 1948, and is presumed to have been scrapped on that date, although there is no evidence of its actual disposal.

Gauge	Order No. Built	Date	Wheels	Cylinders	No./ Name

2' 7 ½"   (159)   1870   0-4-2T   OC   8" x 14"   (TH)   THE BROTHERS
Delivered new in August, 1870 to Cornelius Brain, Colliery, Cinderford, Gloucestershire. The Register of Drawings gives the cylinder bore as 8 ½". Possibly scrapped c 1906.

Gauge	Order No. Built	Date	Wheels	Cylinders	No./ Name

4' 8 ½"   (161)   1870   0-4-0 tank   OC   10" x 14" (TH)   DITTON No.2
Delivered new in November, 1870 to Ditton Brook Iron Company, near Widnes. A cylinder stroke of 18" is quoted by the later TH list, the RR list and the Register of Drawings. Subsequent disposal unknown.

Gauge	Order No. Built	Date	Wheels	Cylinders	No./ Name

4' 8 ½"   (160)   1870   0-6-0ST   IC   17" x 22" (IRS)   CANNOCK WOOD
Delivered on 6 December 1870. Driving wheels 3' 6" diameter. The TH lists give the cylinders as being alternatively 16" x 20" and 16" x 22", the latter also being given in the RR list. New to Cannock & Rugeley Collieries Co. Ltd., Rawnsley, Staffs. Sold to Walsall Wood Colliery Co. Ltd., Walsall Wood, Staffs. 1882. Subsequent disposal unknown.

Gauge	Order No. Built	Date	Wheels	Cylinders	No./ Name

(Narrow) (162)   1870   Tram loco   6" x 12" (TH)
These cylinder dimensions conflict with the Register of Drawings which give them as 10" x 18". Delivered new to Rosedale & Ferryhill Iron Co., Ferryhill, Co. Durham. Subsequent disposal unknown.

Gauge	Order No. Built	Date	Wheels	Cylinders	No./ Name

2' 6"   (171) 1870   6w tank tram   6" x 12"   (TH)   JOHN KING
Delivered new to the Cape Copper Co. Ltd., South Africa, where they had just established interests in Namaqualand. Locomotives were used on a relatively flat section of line between Port Nolloth and either Abbevlaack (22 miles), or to the 35 mile point. This loco was probably an 0-6-0 tank and tender loco, and similar to MINER (see below). Neither were a success in this arid land, being too light and suffering boiler problems as a result of the poor local water. Both were withdrawn from "main line" service by 1876. Nothing further is known of its fate.

This photograph from around 1900 shows a proud workforce at William Harrison Ltd., Brownhills Colliery, Staffordshire posing in front of WARRIOR (works No.112) of 1867. This engine had flat sides to the saddle tank. [F. Jones Collection]

There is some doubt as to the original identity of this locomotive, 0-6-0ST SONS, at the Old Coppice Colliery, Cannock, Staffordshire although there is no question that it was built by Lilleshall. It has the typical flat saddle tanks, cab and smoke box shapes characteristic of these locomotives. [F. Jones]

Gauge	Order No. Built	Date	Wheels	Cylinders	No./ Name
2' 6"	(190)	1871	6w tank tram	7" x 14" (TH, RR)	MINER

Delivered new in September, 1871 to the Cape Copper Co. Ltd., this was similar to JOHN KING, but with larger cylinders, and was also probably a tank and tender loco. As mentioned above, it was withdrawn from service by 1876. However, MINER was subsequently returned to service on ballast trains between 1880 and 1883, but was out of traffic again in 1884 and 1885, awaiting boiler repairs. These do not appear to have taken place, as in the annual reports it was subsequently listed as "dismantled" until 1889. After this date it was no longer referred to again.

Gauge	Order No. Built	Date	Wheels	Cylinders	No./ Name
3' 2 ½"		1872	0-4-2T	OC 9" x 16" (RR)	CORNGREAVES

Delivered new in January, 1872 to New British Iron Co. Ltd., Corngreaves Brickworks, Collieries and Furnaces, Cradley Heath, Staffs. Business later became W. Bassano & Co. c 1891; R. Follows, 1901. Loco scrapped at an unknown date.

Gauge	Order No. Built	Date	Wheels	Cylinders	No./ Name
2' 7"	(216)	1872	Tank	8 ½" x 14" (TH)	NEATH ABBEY

Delivered now to Dyffryn Main Colliery Co. (actually this was, correctly, Dynevor United Company), Main Collieries, Skewen, near Neath. The narrow gauge line was abandoned in 1899, and replaced by a standard gauge line. This loco was one of six then put up for sale in 1899. Subsequent history not known.

Gauge	Order No. Built	Date	Wheels	Cylinders	No./ Name
4' 8 ½"	(181)	1873	4w tank loco	10" x 18" (TH)	

Almost certainly this was an 0-4-0ST with outside cylinders. Delivered new to West Stockton Iron Co., Stockton-on-Tees, Co. Durham. No further history known.

Gauge	Order No. Built	Date	Wheels	Cylinders	No./ Name
4'8 ½"	(187)	1873	0-4-0ST	OC 10" x 18" (TH)	No.4

Per the TH list, this was delivered new to Thos. Kinnersley & Co. in July, 1873. After the closure of the ironworks in 1890, it was probably moved with the rest of the locos to the Lincoln Engine & Wagon Co. Ltd., Lincoln, who advertised an "0-4-0 10" x 18" cylinders by Lilleshall Iron Co." in "The Engineer" of 11 April and 1 August 1890, and in "The Colliery Guardian" of 13 April 1890. It was probably subsequently purchased sometime between 1890 and 1897 by Brooks, Shoobridge & Co., (later Hilton, Anderson, Brooks & Co. Ltd., and later still, Associated Portland Cement Manufacturers Ltd.) of Grays, Essex. Photographic evidence reveals that the "No.4" plate was removed at this location. There are no details as to the eventual disposal of this engine.

Gauge	Order No. Built	Date	Wheels	Cylinders	No./ Name
4' 8 ½"	(233)	1874	0-6-0 tank	`14 ½" x 18" (IRS, RR)	

Delivered new in February 1874 to Thomas Kinnersley & Co., Clough Hall Collieries & Ironworks, Kidsgrove, Staffs. Believed to have passed to Lincoln Wagon & Engine Co., Lincoln in 1890 when the ironworks closed. This is another candidate for the identity of "SONS", listed in the "Unknown Identities" section below. Subsequent disposal unknown.

Gauge	Order No. Built	Date	Wheels	Cylinders	No./ Name
3' 0"		1877	0-4-0 tank	7" x 12" (IRS, TH, RR)	APE
3' 0"	(302)	1877	0-4-0 tank	7" x 12" (IRS, TH, RR)	TIGER

Tank engines of unconfirmed type, but almost certainly side tanks. Built with 22" wheels. Delivered new in 1877 (TIGER during September) to Stanier & Co., Silverdale, Newcastle-under-Lyme, Staffs. Gone by February, 1903. Subsequent disposal unknown.

Gauge	Order No. Built	Date	Wheels	Cylinders	No./ Name
4' 8 ½"	(277)	1880	tank	11" x 18" (TH)	

Details per the TH lists give the customer as Lilleshall Company. However, all Lilleshall fleet locos are accounted for. Therefore, the alternatives are that this loco was built for stock, or that the order was diverted to an outside customer, or that the information was simply incorrect. Either way, nothing more has been traced of this locomotive, which was probably an 0-4-0ST with outside cylinders.

Brooks, Shoosmith & Co. of Grays, Essex acquired this 0-4-0ST (187 of 1873) some time between 1900 and 1908; this photograph was probably taken shortly afterwards. [F. Jones Collection]

Lilleshall's standard design of narrow gauge 0-4-0T (no.331 of 1881) was originally supplied as a 2ft 8in gauge locomotive to the Heyford Iron Co. of Northamptonshire. It is believed to have been subsequently regauged to 2ft. 4in and used at the British Quarrying Co. Ltd., Glyn Ceiriog. Here it is some time during the Second World War, and looking decidedly forlorn. It lingered on in this condition for many years, being mostly cut up in 1944, although some remains lingered on until 1956. [F. Jones Collection]

The Dalmellington Iron Co. Ltd. of Waterside, Ayrshire purchased this locomotive as their No.6, new in 1866 (works No.90). The first photograph shows it in its original condition, the second as rebuilt around 1896 with a large cab replacing the weatherboard. [F. Jones Collection]

Truly derelict. This 0-4-0ST was simply abandoned at the Devon Basalt & Granite Co. Ltd., near Christow, Devon after their Dixon's Quarry was closed in 1932, and finally disappeared around 1934. It was possibly the last Lilleshall locomotive, being built in 1901, though this may be the date of its refurbishment at the works. [F. Jones Collection]

Lilleshall 0-6-0ST No.2 (341 of 1886) outside the locomotive shed at New Yard around 1935. [Ironbridge Gorge Museum Trust]

Gauge	Order No.	Date Built	Wheels	Cylinders	No./ Name
2' 8"	(331)	1881	Tram tank	7" x 12" (TH)	LAURA

Almost certainly, this was another 0-4-0T with outside cylinders, as determined from its later history. Delivered new to Heyford Iron Co., Northamptonshire. It is not clear whether it went to this company's ironstone quarries at Gayton Wood or to the ironworks at Heyford. The quarries were not directly connected to the ironworks, and being some three miles away to the north-west, all ironstone was conveyed over the LNWR mainline from Blisworth. Eric Tonks' seminal work of the ironstone quarries, and subsequent research published in the IRS Handbook for this area, suggest that the quarry was worked by a 2' 10" system and standard gauge feeder line to the LNWR. The consequence is that this loco probably worked on a 2' 8" gauge line charging the furnaces, and on the slag line, similar to those at the Company's Lodge Furnaces. The ironworks closed in the depression of the early 1890's, and LAURA may have been sold to Charles D. Phillips, dealers of Emlyn Engineering Works, Newport, Monmouthshire. A rather anonymous advertisement for sale in the Philip's Plant & Machinery Register of May/ June 1900 as "26764. Lilleshall Iron Co., new copper firebox, 2' 8" gauge, perfect condition, £180" is believed to relate to this engine. It is believed to have then gone to Glyn Ceiriog Granite Co., Hendre, Denbighshire c 1900, where the gauge was 2' 4", so a regauging was necessary. This loco carried a plate "Lilleshall Company, Engineers, 1880, Shropshire" and featured a stovepipe chimney, a rather tall firebox and a fully sheeted cab, which appears to have been added at Hendre.

The operation was taken over by British Quarrying Co. Ltd. in 1929, who offered the loco for sale in 1942. There were no takers, and so the loco was cut up on site during 1944, although some parts remained there until 1956.

Gauge	Order No.	Date Built	Wheels	Cylinders	No./ Name
4' 8 ½"		1882	0-4-0ST	OC 12" x 18" (IRS, TH, RR)	ALTHORP (possibly later PHYLLIS or WASP)

Delivered new in January, 1882 to Shelton Bar Iron Co. Ltd., Etruria, Stoke-on-Trent, Staffs. Either this loco, or WALMER (below) is listed unnamed as having been delivered in 1883 under works order no. 371. Sold or scrapped after 1901, but before 1902.

Gauge	Order No.	Date Built	Wheels	Cylinders	No./ Name
4' 8 ½"		1882	0-4-0ST	OC 12" x 18" (IRS, TH, RR)	WALMER

Delivered new in November, 1883 to Shelton Bar Iron Co. Ltd., Etruria, Stoke-on-Trent, Staffs. May be works order no. 371 (see ALTHORP above). Sold or scrapped after 1901 and before 1910.

Gauge	Order No.	Date Built	Wheels	Cylinders	No./ Name
4' 8 ½"	(341)	1886	0-6-0ST	IC 15" x 22" (TH)	No.2

Delivered on 30 June, 1886 for company's own use. The 1915 and 1937 Valuations give the cylinders as 15 ½ " x 18", and J. W. Lowe gives them as 14" x 22". Wheels were 3' 5" diameter. Received a new boiler at Lilleshall in 1903, and again in 1925. Sold or scrapped around 1948.

Gauge	Order No.	Date Built	Wheels	Cylinders	No./ Name
4' 8 ½"	(419)	1888	0-4-0ST	OC 14" x 18" (IRS, TH, RR)	ALICE

Delivered new in March, 1888 to Shelton Iron & Steel Co. Ltd., Etruria, Stoke-on-Trent, Staffs. Sold or scrapped after 1901

Note 1.
This business later became T.B. & W.B .Brain from 1869, then J.B. & W.B. Brain from 1874, then Trafalgar Colliery Co. Ltd., Drybrook Road, Cinderford, from 22 December 1883.
Two six wheel 8" x 14" locos built by Lilleshall were advertised in the Colliery Guardian on 2 January 1891 and 29 January 1892 "in consequence of abandonment of pit cart railway". The abandoned railway was the 1 ½ mile section from Laymoor to the GWR sidings at Bilson Junction. The two locos advertised for sale were TRAFALGAR and THE BROTHERS. However, neither were sold and TRAFALGAR continued in use on the northern extension of the tramway from Bilson to the Golden Valley Iron Mine at Drybrook until around 1906, when it was eventually scrapped. The other two locos are believed to have been cannibalised to keep TRAFALGAR in running order, and these were therefore presumably scrapped at some time prior to 1906.

UNKNOWN IDENTITIES

Gauge	Order No.	Date Built	Wheels	Cylinders	No./ Name
4' 8 ½"		1901	0-4-0ST	OC	3 ALDERMAN

The 1901 build date is given in a typewritten list retained at the Shropshire Records & Research Centre, Shrewsbury. This list seems to have been used by Gale and Nicholls in their book on the history of the Company, and contains many errors. This entry follows those for a Lilleshall no.3 (presumably PHOENIX), and for a loco belonging to the Earl of Dudley's Pensnett Railway, also in 1901. Both of these were rebuilds or overhauls, and certainly not 'new construction'. Therefore, it is the author's view that new construction had almost certainly ceased by this date, and that this loco too was a 'rebuild'. Photographic evidence shows that it was definitely a Lilleshall product, being very similar to the 1873 loco (Job no.187) that eventually found its way to Brooks, Shoobridge & Co. Arrived at Devon Basalt & Granite Co. Ltd., Dixon's Quarry, near Christow, Devon on an unknown date. It became increasingly derelict after the quarry closed in 1932, and was sold or scrapped around 1934.

Gauge	Order No.	Date Built	Wheels	Cylinders	No./ Name
4' 8 ½"		?	0-6-0ST	IC	EMLYN later SONS

Almost certainly a Lilleshall product, however its identity and early history are unknown, although it has been suggested that this was one of the two 0-6-0ST supplied to Thos. Kinnersley & Co. Ltd. in 1869 and 1874 (No.3 and untitled) respectively. As EMLYN it was sold by Charles D. Phillips Engineering Ltd., Emlyn Engineering Works, Newport, Monmouthshire in 1914 to T.A. Hawkins & Sons Ltd., Old Coppice Colliery, Cannock, Staffs., where it was renamed SONS. Scrapped on site around 1936.

QUESTIONABLE LILLESHALL BUILT LOCOS

Gauge	Order No.	Date Built	Wheels	Cylinders	No./ Name
4' 8 ½"		1862?	2-2-2	IC	

A photograph in the possession of the Ironbridge Gorge Museum Trust is labelled as being of such a locomotive, and that it was displayed at the London Exhibition of 1862. However, no such exhibit has been traced at this exhibition. Furthermore, the engine in the photograph, which is a 'rear three-quarter' view, appears identical to the 2-2-2 built in 1867. In an article on page 536 of the December, 1979 issue of "The Railway Magazine", C. Hamilton Ellis makes reference to this engine, but gives no further details. No reference to this engine has been found elsewhere, and so no further details are known. The existence of this engine is seriously in doubt, and your author believes that this engine has been mistaken for the 1867 engine, but as it was mentioned by so eminent a railway historian, it is recorded here.

Gauge	Order No.	Date Built	Wheels	Cylinders	No./ Name
2' 6"		?	0-6-0WT	IC	DOCTOR JIM

Received by the Earl of Dudley's Pensnett Railway (date unknown) in part payment of a debt from Nora Hingley, Netherton, near Dudley. This may have been the loco engaged at the Earl of Dudley's Baggeridge Colliery during trial borings and construction work from 1896. The narrow gauge railway here ran from Himley No.5 pit to convey construction materials, and was possibly not used by 1905. This loco was sold or scrapped by 1933. If this was a Lilleshall built loco, it is the only known example built as a well tank, thus casting doubt on it being built by Lilleshall.

Gauge	Order No.	Date Built	Wheels	Cylinders	No./ Name
4' 8 ½"		?	0-4-2ST	IC	HARDMAN

At Josiah Hardman (Ltd., from 1901), Chemical Manufacturers, Milton, Stoke-on-Trent, Staffs. From early 1890's. *per Industrial Locomotives of North Staffordshire, p.98* - "Photographic evidence suggests a Neilson, RS or Lilleshall built loco. (Could be one of the Lilleshalls, ex Shelton or Birchenwood.)". However, despite the fact that the two photographs available do not show a great deal of detail, in the opinion of the author, this locomotive does not possess the features of a Lilleshall locomotive

REGISTER OF DRAWINGS

Order No.	Locomotive Description	Build Date	Identity
90	Ramsbottom safety valves (with 91)	1866	Dalmellington No.6
91	Ramsbottom safety valves (with 90)	1868	UXBRIDGE
101	Express passenger locomotive	1867	4 RAWNSLEY and tender
109	Locomotive tank engine	1867	John Hunter loco
112	Slide valves	1867	WARRIOR
116	Slide valves (with 116)	1867-8	1 MARQUIS
117	Slide valves (with 117)	1867-8	2 ANGLESEY
134	13" locomotive (with 135)	1868-9	No.6, Lilleshall
135	13" locomotive (with 134)	1868-9	No.7, Lilleshall
137	Tram locomotive (with 138/9)	1868-9	Lodge furnaces
138	Tram locomotive (with 137/9)	1868-9	Lodge furnaces
139	Tram locomotive (with 137/8)	1868-9	Lodge furnaces
140	Engine 8" x14" 2' 7 ½" gauge	1868-9	TRAFALGAR
141	Engine 8 ½" x 14" 3' 0" gauge	1868-9	COMET
158	8 ½" tank locomotive (with 159)	1870	DYFFRYN
159	8 ½" tank locomotive (with 158)	1870	THE BROTHERS
160	Slide valve, (as order nos. 116 and 117)	1870-1	CANNOCK WOOD
161	10" x 18" tank locomotive (with 162)	1870-1	DITTON No.2
162	10" x 18" tank locomotive (with 161)	1870-1	Ferryhill Ironworks loco

This list is reproduced from a small notebook evidently compiled by someone in the design department, which records many (but not all) of the machines constructed by the Company. Only the locomotives are listed here, and although their identities were not all given in the original register, it has been possible to confirm these by reference to other records. The detail in the register associated with each locomotive is such as to assume that drawings were only prepared for a limited number of components in each case. Alternatively, these may be only those drawings that the compiler actually worked on.

Lilleshall-built 0-4-0ST No.4 CONSTANCE in steam on 29 September 1938, probably at Priorslee. Note the typical Lilleshall practice of providing only one slide bar. [Author's collection]

CHAPTER EIGHT
LOCOMOTIVES OF THE LILLESHALL SYSTEM

As we have seen, the Lilleshall system was extensive and therefore required a considerable number of locomotives to operate it. In addition, much of the traffic was heavy, so it comes as no surprise to find that the company turned to acquiring former main line company locomotives for some of the more arduous duties. The total number of locomotives available for service rose from four during the mid-1850s to eight by 1870, down to five by 1875, then six by 1886, increasing to nine in 1900 until 1920 when there were eleven.

By the early 1930s the number was back down to nine, which was maintained throughout the war years. After the war, five sufficed, although during the last two years of operation five locos were scrapped and two more acquired. At the close of the system in 1959 there were only three still extant, all in working order.

An illuminating comment was made in the detailed, 62 page report dated 29 March 1899 from the Company to Earl Granville concerning the state of the locomotive fleet: *The condition of the locomotives is discreditable and obvious to the most superficial examination. Without going into detail we quote the fact that during the 10 months of 1898 some 100 safety plugs were used, owing perhaps in a measure to the use of bad water but mainly to the carelessness of the drivers, who, it would appear are not subject to proper discipline and control.* The writer (anonymous) seems to have reported the situation with some degree of success, as there were several new locomotives obtained during the next two years. Unfortunately, it has not been possible to discover whether the enginemen were advised to realise the errors of their ways.

The Company advertised the commencement of locomotive building in the specialist press (see Appendix 2: Advertisement reproduced from the 'Colliery Guardian' of 6 December 1862) in which it mentioned 'after twelve years experience in the working of five locomotives, of various makes, in the Lilleshall Works'. This confirms, firstly, that the earliest locomotive was in use in 1850, and secondly, that the five locomotives were therefore the four from Neilson & Mitchell, as listed below, plus PHOENIX.

The Lilleshall-built locomotives did not carry worksplates, as such. Instead, the oval plates affixed to the cabsides were similar to worksplates, but contained 'Lilleshall Co. Ltd.' along the upper border, 'Shropshire' along the lower border, and the running number, as 'No. x' in the centre. However, No.9 (Robert Stephenson 1800 of 1866) also carried this plate, which differed in that 'Oakengates' replaced 'Shropshire' on the lower border.

Andrew Barclay 0-6-0T No.11 (1486/1916) on a warm 19 June 1954, outside the locomotive shed at New Yard Works preparing for another turn of duty. [F. W. Shuttleworth]

Also out of use on 19 June 1954 was former GWR 0-6-2T No. 251, Lilleshall's No.5, alongside the 'balloon' water tank at Priorslee Furnaces. The water hoses can be seen beneath the tank. [F. W. Shuttleworth]

The following list of locomotives is largely abstracted from the IRS Industrial Locomotive Handbook G covering Shropshire. Additional details have been added from the Company Valuations of 1876, 1915 and 1937, and certain information supplied by the Lilleshall loco foremen, Mr. Ware in 1944 and Mr. E. Owen in 1953. However, the various sources of information have resulted in a number of discrepancies concerning the cylinder dimensions, and driving wheel diameters. Consequently, these dimensions are not generally listed in the following text. Instead, they are shown in tabular form in Appendix 8. In compiling this data, I have formed my own opinions as to which are the most reliable sources, only to find obvious errors in those considered safe. Therefore, I leave the reader to determine that which is thought to be the most appropriate. Two aspects of cylinder dimensions should be borne in mind. Firstly, the bores may well have been increased (as I've already stressed) by ¼in or even ½in during the life of the locomotive, from reboring during overhaul. Secondly, some of the locomotives were extensively rebuilt during their lifetimes, and may well have been fitted with new cylinders, which themselves may have been of differing dimensions. So some of the information may not be as incorrect as it first appears, but the lack of locomotive record cards (as with main line companies) means that we are not able to confirm such alterations.

It is unfortunate that none of the Lilleshall fleet survived long enough to have reached the 'preservation era'. The last remnants were, as will be seen below, scrapped during the 1950s, by Bell of Doncaster, who acted as dealers in second-hand plant and equipment (including the last two locos for the Company) as well as being scrap dealers. Local scrap dealer Jim Rollason was able to confirm this information.

Robert Stephenson 0-6-0ST 1800 of 1866 was Lilleshall's No.9, acquired by the company some time between 1900 and 1904; it lasted until 1929, until sold for scrap. This view at the entrance to the New Yard Works dates from the 1920s. [F. Jones Collection]

68

Running No. / Name	Wheels	Cylinders	Builder	Works No.	Date Built
			Neilson & Mitchell	46	1850

The Neilson works list records this locomotive as having 10' x 18' cylinders, and its destination as being 'Lilleshall & Co (Shipment)'. Quite what the reference to 'shipment' is supposed to denote is open to speculation. Although there is no indication of the wheel arrangement, the cylinder size is the same as the following loco in the Neilson list (which was Dalmellington Co's no.1) and which was an 0-4-0ST with outside cylinders. Therefore, it is presumed to have been of the same configuration. It is presumed to have initially worked on the Donnington to Muxton Bridge line, which was the only section of standard gauge line open in 1850. Nothing more is known of its destination, nor its subsequent fate.

Running No. / Name	Wheels	Cylinders	Builder	Works No.	Date Built
No.1 GRANVILLE	0-4-0T	OC	Neilson & Mitchell	63	1854

Supplied new, presumably upon the expansion of the system. There is some question as to whether this locomotive was supplied with a side or a saddle tank. The confusion probably arises from the square shaped saddle tanks fitted by Neilson at this time, now referred to as 'box tanks'. According to the 1915 Valuation, No.1 is stated to have been bought second-hand, but this may more likely relate to the boiler which it had received in 1900. In an internal report dated 6 May 1915, the loco foreman at the time, states that GRANVILLE 'is too light for any work outside the yard'. This is taken as restricting its use to shunting activities, and precluding its use on trip duties to/ from the collieries and exchange sidings. An unconfirmed note from the loco foreman in 1953 (Mr. E. Owen) states that this loco was scrapped in 1919. The 1937 Valuation simply comments that this loco had been 'broken up', without giving any date.

Running No. / Name	Wheels	Cylinders	Builder	Works No.	Date Built
No.2	0-4-0ST	OC	Neilson & Mitchell	64	1854

This was also supplied new upon the opening of the system. The subsequent disposal is unknown, although a later pencil note in the 1876 Valuation simply records 'scrap', reducing the value from £250 to a mere £30, so it is fairly safe to assume that it was scrapped shortly afterwards. Certainly it must have gone by 1886, when a replacement no.2 was introduced.

Running No. / Name	Wheels	Cylinders	Builder	Works No.	Date Built
No.3	0-4-0ST	OC	Neilson & Mitchell	50	1851

Because the Neilson Works List does not ascribe the wheel arrangement and configuration of the tank, this has been taken by some persons to assume that it was an 0-4-0 tender engine as for the preceding engine in the list. However, examination of the Neilson Works List reveals that all positively identified tender engines had bores of at least 14', and the 10' x 18' dimensions of this engine were standard dimensions for saddletanks.

There must either have been some problem in the delivery of this engine, so that it arrived after the previous two (hence being numbered '3'), or it was not new when delivered, or it was simply numbered out of sequence. However, other scenarios could equally be propounded. The subsequent disposal is unknown, although it is presumed to have gone by 1859, but see the next entry.

Running No. / Name	Wheels	Cylinders	Builder	Works No.	Date Built
No..3 PHOENIX	0-6-0T	IC	Phoenix Foundry		c1859

The origins of this locomotive have proved particularly elusive, and the available evidence is mainly conjectural and inclined to be lengthy. So the various pieces of evidence are discussed separately in Appendix 3. The conclusion is that this locomotive was rebuilt from an earlier, unknown, locomotive by the Company, possibly in the Old Yard Works, and being completed in the New Yard Works, which was also known as the Phoenix Foundry.

IRS Handbook G records that it was disposed some time after 1914. However, it was recorded in the 1915 Valuation, so it must have been disposed of after 1915. Additionally, the record states that this loco was 'bought second-hand' (but no date is given), although this may relate to the boiler, as it had received a new boiler in 1897.

Running No. / Name	Wheels	Cylinders	Builder	Works No.	Date Built
No.4 CONSTANCE	0-4-0ST	OC	Lilleshall	89	1865

Completed on 5 September, 1865, this became the longest serving engine on the system. It was named after Lady Constance Gertrude Leveson – Gower, daughter of the 2nd. Duke of Sutherland, who in 1852 married Hugh, Lord Grosvenor, later to become the Duke of Westminster. As a result it was colloquially also known as 'The Countess'. This loco had received a new boiler in 1896 and was further rebuilt at New Yard in 1916, including another new boiler. The boiler pressure was 150 lbs per square inch (140 lbs in 1915), and the total weight was 23 tons.

The 1916 rebuild was probably the occasion when new frames were fitted. Mr. Ware (loco foreman in 1944) told Seymour Pierce Higgins that there was practically nothing left of the original locomotive.

It survived until around February 1957, when it was scrapped on site by Bell of Doncaster.

Running No. / Name	Wheels	Cylinders	Builder	Works No.	Date Built
No.5	0-4-0ST	OC	Lilleshall	98	1866

Identical to No.4, and completed on 17 April 1866. According to the 1915 Valuation, it had received a new boiler in 1895 and another new boiler was 'on hand' at this time. Per an entry in the company's Impersonal Ledger, this engine was finally sold out of service on 28 February, 1929 for £190 to the Victoria Coal & Iron Co. Ltd., who were dealers of nearby Wellington. This company hired the loco to Netherseal Colliery Co. Ltd., Netherseal Colliery, Linton, Derbyshire. It evidently had a short career there, as it was scrapped on site there in 1934, probably by the Victoria Coal & Iron Co. Ltd. who also operated as scrap merchants.

This Hudswell Clarke 0-4-4T (612 of 1902) was No.12 in the company fleet, and despite the unusual wheel arrangement for an industrial locomotive, was apparently quite successful, being used from around 1919 until 1932. [F. Jones Collection]

Former Taff Vale Railway 'U' class 0-6-2T No.72 passed to the Great Western to become GW No.589, before being acquired by the Company in May 1932. On vesting day, 1 January 1948, it passed to the NCB for use at Granville Colliery, but does not seem to have been used much. Here it is dumped, partially off the rails in the colliery sidings around 1951, approximately two years before it was finally cut up. [F. Jones]

Running No. / Name	Wheels	Cylinders	Builder	Works No.	Date Built
No.6	0-6-0ST	OC	Lilleshall	90	1869

Completed on 7 December, 1869 this was a larger engine. It received a new boiler in 1899, and was further rebuilt at New Yard in 1923 including another new boiler. The working boiler pressure was 150 lbs per square inch (130lbs in 1915), and the approximate weight was 28 tons per Mr. E. Owen. It was sold to the NCB for use at Granville Colliery arriving there between April and September, 1950. It was finally scrapped on site between August 1955 and May 1956 by Bell of Doncaster.

Running No. / Name	Wheels	Cylinders	Builder	Works No.	Date Built
No.7	0-6-0ST	OC	Lilleshall	135	1870

Completed on 21 June, 1870 and identical to No.6, but with wheels one inch larger. This received a new boiler in 1898, and was further rebuilt at New Yard in 1917 including a new boiler. It was finally disposed of after July, 1949. However, its final destination is not known, but it was probably scrapped on site shortly after the NCB vesting day.

Running No. / Name	Wheels	Cylinders	Builder	Works No.	Date Built
No.2	0-6-0ST	IC	Lilleshall	341	1886

This was built to replace the earlier number 2 (Neilson 64 of 1854) and was completed on 30 June 1886.. It was rebuilt twice at New Yard, in 1903 and in 1925, on which dates it received a new boiler (per the 1915 and 1937 Valuations). According to Mr. E. Owen, boiler pressure was 150 lbs, and the weight was 25 tons. However, the 1915 and 1937 Valuations record the boiler pressure as 140 lbs. As for the previous locomotive, its disposal around 1948 is not documented.

Running No. / Name	Wheels	Cylinders	Builder	Works No.	Date Built
No.8	0-6-0ST	IC	Peckett	856	1900

Board approval for purchase was given on 27 July 1900, and the order was placed by 31 August 1900. Delivered new on 22 October 1900, this was a standard 'X' class engine. Per the Lilleshall loco foreman, the weight was approximately 30 tons, and the working boiler pressure was 160 lbs per square inch. Its residual value of £161-9s-9d was written off in 1932, and it was believed to have been scrapped on site in May 1932.

Running No. / Name	Wheels	Cylinders	Builder	Works No.	Date Built
No.9	0-6-0ST	IC	Robert Stephenson	1800	1866

Delivered new to John Bowes & Partners Ltd., Marley Hill Colliery, County Durham in 1866, where it was their No.14. It was sold to Carron & Co., Carron Ironworks, Falkirk, Stirlingshire around 1880. Acquired around 1900 or 1901, but possibly not until 1904, as the 1915 Valuation records that it was 'bought second-hand in 1904', although this may once again refer to the boiler which was renewed in 1904. The 1937 Valuation states that it was sold in February 1929 to the Victoria Coal & Iron Co. Ltd. for £145. This is confirmed by an entry in the Impersonal Ledger dated 28 February,1929 and the sale value suggests that it was sold as a working loco, rather than as for scrap. IRS Handbook G records it as being scrapped on site around 1935, but no further details of its final disposal have been traced. As conjecture, it may have been purchased for possible sale or hire to a third party, and thus remained on site, as it is known that the purchaser did not have a rail connected site. Failure to find a suitable home for it would then have sealed its fate.

Running No. / Name	Wheels	Cylinders	Builder	Works No.	Date Built
(10)	0-4-0ST	OC	Peckett	883	1901

Board minutes dated 26 April 1901 record that the order had been placed at a price of £1,050. Delivered new on 10 July 1901, this was a standard 'W4' class engine. Board minutes dated 26 July 1901 record that 'the locomotive is working satisfactorily'. Per Mr. E. Owen, the working boiler pressure was 160 lbs, (140 lbs in 1915), and the total weight was 21 tons. It was loaned to Joseph Sankey & Sons Ltd., at nearby Hadley Castle Works during the Second World War, being returned in 1943. Per IRS records it was subject to a rebuild in 1945, but according to the Lilleshall loco foreman, it received a new boiler and firebox at Peckett in August 1956. This seems rather strange, as it was scrapped only two years later, at the New Yard Works in 1958 by Bell of Doncaster.

Running No. / Name	Wheels	Cylinders	Builder	Works No.	Date Built
(11) MERCURY	0-6-0ST	IC	Manning Wardle	995	1886

This was a Manning Wardle 'Special K' Class with 12x17in cylinders and wheels of 3ft 1½in diameter, delivered new on 30 September 1886 to contractor T. A. Matthews working at Hartlepool headland protection works. Purchased from them at an unknown date, it was given the running number 11, which was later removed, although it's original name stayed in place. The Company offered it for sale by advertisement on 21 February 1908, and presumably it moved shortly afterwards, but its destination is unknown. However, an advertisement in 'Machinery Market' of 17 March, 1911 by T.W. Ward listed a number of locomotives, including 'Standard gauge six wheeled coupled saddletank MERCURY, inside cylinders, 12' x 18' (*sic*), by Manning Wardle.' A similar list appeared in the issue of 19 May, 1911 and it also appeared in a list on 6 October 1911. (Details per 'Extracts from Machinery Market, 1879 – 1970', F. Jux, 1985.) No further details of its history or eventual disposal have been traced.

Former Barry Railway 'B1' class 0-6-2T No.60 (later GWR No.251) became the Company's No.5. It is seen here in the mid-1950s at the New Yard locomotive shed in very poor condition. [A. J. B. Dodd]

Ex-GWR 0-6-0PT No.12, still carrying its GWR 2794 numberplate, stands outside the locomotive shed at New Yard Works in the 1950s. [A. J. B. Dodd]

Running No. / Name	Wheels	Cylinders	Builder	Works No.	Date Built
3	0-6-0T	OC	Andrew Barclay	1392	1914

A Board Minute dated 25 September, 1914 stated that 'authority was given to purchase a locomotive from Messrs. Andrew Barclay & Sons of Kilmarnock on deferred payment terms'. Delivered new on 9 January 1915 , to replace the aging 'Phoenix' loco which had been laid aside. The approximate weight was 30 tons, and the working boiler pressure was 150 lbs per square inch, according to the Lilleshall loco foreman. The 1932 Valuation records that it was condemned in that year and its residual value of £184-12s-2d written off. It was scrapped on site in June 1933.

Running No. / Name	Wheels	Cylinders	Builder	Works No.	Date Built
No.11	0-6-0T	OC	Andrew Barclay	1486	1916

Approval was given by the Board on 28 January 1916 to 'purchase a new locomotive of a suitable size', which decision was revised in a Board Minute dated 25 February 1916 'that an 18in locomotive be purchased'. Delivered new on 27 December 1916, this engine incorporated slightly larger cylinders than the preceding Barclay engine, Mr. E. Owen stated that the boiler pressure was 160 lbs and the weight was 38 tons. It was rebuilt in 1930, when it received a new boiler (per the 1937 Valuation). Following the 1930 rebuilding, it carried the painted legend 'LILLESHALL CO. LTD.' and 'No.11' in cream or gold lettering on its side tanks. It survived until the closure in July 1959, when it was scrapped on site by Bell of Doncaster.

Running No. / Name	Wheels	Cylinders	Builder	Works No.	Date Built
No.12	0-4-4T	IC	Hudswell Clarke	612	1902

Ordered on 10 January 1902 and delivered to John Best & Co. Ltd., of Broughton, Peeblesshire on 25 April 1902 at a cost of £2,300 as their No.19 EDINBURGH for their contract at Talla Reservoir and Works for the Edinburgh & District Water Board . This contract had started in 1896, and was originally awarded to James Young & Sons, who went into liquidation in September, 1899. The contract was re-let to Best in December, 1899, who also undertook the working and maintenance of the railway. The inauguration ceremony was held on 28 September, 1905 (see article in SLS Journal, October,1966). Afterwards it was used at Pateley Bridge (here by December,1906 per SLS Journal, October 1966) on the Lofthouse and Angram Reservoir until around 1919, when it is said to have gone to the Elswick Works of Sir W.G. Armstrong Whitworth & Co. Ltd. However, there is some doubt as to whether or not it did go there, and if it did, then it's stay was a short one, as in 1919 it arrived at Samuel Fox & Co. Ltd.'s Stocksbridge Ironworks, South Yorkshire. The name was certainly retained at Angram.

The wheel arrangement was unusual for an industrial locomotive, more commonly being found on locomotives for local passenger work. Nonetheless, other examples were found on this type of work. For example, James Manson's '266' class of six such engines were built for shunting work on the Glasgow and South Western Railway in 1906, and were successful, the last one being withdrawn by the LMSR in 1932. This loco would probably have found favour on the longer runs to Priorslee from the pits around Donnington Wood. The inside cylinders were 18' x 26', the driving wheels were 4'6' diameter, bogie wheels were 2'9' and the weight was 39 tons 8 cwts. When new, it was painted blue, with a white lining, although this livery is not likely to have survived through to its days at Lilleshall. No date has been traced for its arrival at the company, although it is recorded that it was withdrawn from service around 1932, and in 1933 there were only six months remaining on its boiler certificate. It was sold for scrap to an unknown bidder for £52-10s-od in 1932, and its residual book value of £455-13s-7d written off, giving a recorded book loss of £403-3s-7d. It was finally scrapped on site in 1934.

Running No. / Name	Wheels	Cylinders	Builder	Works No.	Date Built
No.1	0-6-2T	IC	West Yard Works, Cardiff	305	1895

A former Taff Vale Railway Riches 'O' Class loco (TVR number 190), this was built in May, 1895 and acquired by the GWR in October, 1922 at a cost of £1,993 and renumbered 581. In May, 1922 it was allocated to Treherbert shed, but was withdrawn from traffic in August, 1930 at Radyr shed. It received a new boiler in May, 1923 and a general overhaul at Caerphilly Works in September, 1926 which cost £821, including new cylinders .Its total mileage when sold in May, 1932 to the Company was 555,715 . Per the 1932 Valuation the cost was £236-13s-7d, inclusive of delivery. The inside cylinders were operated by Stephensons valve gear, and the rigid wheelbase was 14' 5'. The weight was 56 tons 6 cwt, water capacity was 1,400 gallons, coal capacity was 2 tons, boiler pressure was 140 lbs per square inch, and tractive effort of 17,380 lbs. It eventually was scrapped on site at the New Yard Works in August 1958 by Bell of Doncaster.

Former Taff Vale Railway 0-6-2T No.1 stands out of use at the New Yard Works around 1957. The Barclay 0-4-0ST behind is believed to be ALBERTA, similarly out of use at this time. Note the 'balloon' water tank, similar to the one at the Priorslee Furnaces. [A. J. B. Dodd]

Another of the former GWR locomotives was this Dean '2721' Class 0-6-0PT No.2794, seen here outside the running shed at Priorslee Furnaces on 19 June 1954. It was originally built as a saddle tank and converted to a pannier tank in March 1916. After acquisition from BR in October 1950 it retained its cabside numberplates, but also bore the painted legend 'Lilleshall Co. Ltd. No. 12' on its tank sides. [F. W. Shuttleworth]

Andrew Barclay 0-6-0T No.11 (1496/1916) newly rebuilt and posing for its photograph outside the New Yard Works in 1930. [Ironbridge Gorge Museum Trust]

Running No. / Name	Wheels	Cylinders	Builder	Works No.	Date Built
No.3	0-6-2T	IC	Vulcan Foundry	1442	1895

Also a former Taff Vale Railway engine, this was one of Riches 'U' class engines (TVR number 72) which differed from the above in having 8 ½in larger driving wheels. Other less noticeable differences were a higher boiler pressure at 160 lbs, weight of 63 tons and tractive effort of 17,190 lbs. It was completed in October, 1895 to Vulcan's order no. 402. By May, 1922 it was allocated to Cathays shed, Cardiff (when it is recorded as having achieved 661,744 miles) but was withdrawn from the former TVR shed at Coke Ovens (Pontypridd) in December, 1930. It had been acquired by the GWR in September, 1922 at a cost of £2,148 and was given their number 589. It received a new boiler at TVR's West Yard Works in November, 1923 and a general overhaul at Caerphilly Works in September, 1927 costing £780, including patching the tank. It too was purchased in May, 1932 and per the 1932 Valuation, the cost was £311-8s-5d, including delivery. This was passed on vesting day, 1 January 1948 to the NCB for use at Granville Colliery. It is known to have been finished in a light green livery, although rarely cleaned. Lilleshall were obviously keen to retain the best engines for themselves, as this engine is not thought to have worked much whilst in NCB ownership. It was certainly dumped out of use by December 1951, and was eventually scrapped on site by Cox and Danks between November 1953 and February 1954.

Running No. / Name	Wheels	Cylinders	Builder	Works No.	Date Built
No.5	0-6-2T	IC	Vulcan Foundry	1342	1892

Designed by Hosgood, this was originally Barry Railway 'B1' class number 60, with inside cylinders operated by Stephenson valve gear, and a rigid wheelbase of 14' 5'. The total weight was 55 tons 3 cwt, the boiler was pressed to 160 lbs and the tractive effort was 20,825 lbs. It was delivered in April, 1892 having been part of the Vulcan Foundry build order no. 290, and remained allocated to Barry shed for its working life in South Wales. In September, 1921 it was rebuilt with a Barry Railway Type 3A boiler, and had amassed 509,517 miles at 20 May 1922. At the Grouping, it was allotted GWR number 251, and was given a new boiler during a general overhaul at Swindon in April, 1925 which cost £1,253 –9s-0d. At this time it had run 61,036 miles since its previous overhaul. It was acquired by Lilleshall in July, 1934 at a cost of £308-1s-1d inclusive of delivery, and became one of the more active engines, lasting until around January 1957 before being scrapped on site.

Running No. / Name	Wheels	Cylinders	Builder	Works No.	Date Built
2794 LILLESHALL No.12	0-6-0PT	IC	Swindon	1900	1901

A Dean '2721' Class 0-6-0PT, this retained its GWR (and BR) numberplate, as well as receiving its Lilleshall running number after acquisition. It was outshopped at Swindon under Lot 129 as a saddletank loco in February, 1901 having cost £1,528 and was fitted with a Swindon S4 saturated boiler, and piston valves. However, the boiler was exchanged for a superheated B4 Belpaire boiler in December, 1915, although the superheat was later removed. New pannier tanks of 1,200 gallons capacity were fitted in place of the saddletank in March, 1916 for which no cost is recorded. The first general overhaul was at 72,962 miles and was completed on 29 April, 1921, having cost £1,490-12-5, including a new boiler. Subsequently it received a light overhaul at Swindon in March, 1925, which was not costed. Its final general overhaul at Swindon was in October, 1927 at 109,860 miles, costing £1,205- 4-11, including new cylinders. As the piston valves on this class proved unsatisfactory and were replaced by slide valves, this work may have been incorporated into this overhaul.

The original tractive effort was given as 16,885 lbs, but this was amended to 20,260 lbs after the fitting of pannier tanks. The working boiler pressure was 165 lbs per square inch, the wheelbase measured 15' 6' and the final weight was approximately 46 tons. By May, 1922 it was working out of Pontypool shed, but was withdrawn by BR from Ebbw Junction shed, Newport in November, 1949 having been allocated there since prior to nationalisation. The boiler was tested at Swindon Works on 15 August 1950, prior to delivery to Lilleshall in October of that year. These were well known engines in the exchange sidings at Hollinswood, and may well have been hired in during times of motive power shortages, so it made sense to acquire something with a known capability. It was finally scrapped on site in September 1958 by Bell of Doncaster. It is appropriate to mention at this time that all of the surviving locomotives (except those passed to the NCB in 1947) were transferred to the new subsidiary company, Lilleshall Iron and Steel Co Ltd as from 31 December 1947 along with the locomotive sheds and railways. This eventually became a nationalised company on 15 February 1951. This was subsequently denationalised and returned as a subsidiary as from 2 October 1954 but the locomotives and railways remained in its ownership.

Running No. / Name	Wheels	Cylinders	Builder	Works No.	Date Built
(5) ALBERTA	0-4-0ST	OC	Andrew Barclay	1349	1913
(4) PRINCE OF WALES	0-4-0ST	OC	Andrew Barclay	1484	1916

No photographs are believed to have survived of the four locomotives supplied by Neilson & Mitchell in the 1850s. However, as this firm was a very early proponent of the standard product, it is thought that they would have looked very much like this locomotive. This is one of the box tanks supplied to the West Somerset Mineral Railway in 1856/57. [F. Jones Collection]

Lilleshall inside cylinder 0-6-0ST No.2 (341 of 1886) and outside cylinder 0-6-0ST No.7 (135 of 1870) standing out of use at the New Yard locomotive shed in 1948. [Ironbridge Gorge Museum Trust]

Lilleshall's venerable 0-4-0ST No.4 CONSTANCE of 1865 poses with its crew and shunters some time between 1945 and 1955. [Ironbridge Gorge Museum Trust]

Lilleshall 0-6-0ST No.6 (90 of 1869) still going strong, at the New Yard Works around 1935. [Ironbridge Gorge Museum Trust]

Left. Lilleshall 0-4-0ST No.4 CONSTANCE (89 of 1865) at the New Yard Works around 1948. [Ironbridge Gorge Museum Trust]

Below. Peckett 0-4-0ST 883 of 1901, once numbered 10 in the company sequence, standing at Priorslee, probably in the early 1950s. [Industrial Railway Society: Ken Cooper collection]

These two final engines were purchased via the dealer, Bell of Doncaster on 12 October 1956 from Lever Brothers Ltd., Port Sunlight, Cheshire (to whom they had been supplied new on 27 November 1913, and 22 October 1916, respectively). They were allocated the numbers 5 and 4, but do not seem to ever have carried these running numbers. They were identical, with a working boiler pressure of 160 lbs, the approximate weights were 29 tons and wheelbase was 6 feet.. They were in fine condition, and lasted until the end of the system, being scrapped on site in July 1959 by Bell of Doncaster (per Jim Rollason).

Old Lodge Furnaces
The furnaces at this location were laid out with a narrow gauge line for the charging of the furnaces, which were finally blown out in 1888. However, the narrow gauge system had fallen into disuse some years earlier. The gauge of this line per IRS records is given as 2'4'. Whilst this was a common gauge for many of the tramways and plateways in the area (including those of the Coalbrookedale, Horsehay, and Lilleshall Companies) it has now been established that this system was actually of 3'0' gauge. Two sources within the 1876 Valuation specify this measurement.

The locomotives listed below were identical, each featuring 7' x 12' cylinders, although the TH lists gives the bore for two of them as 6'.

0-4-0T	OC	Lilleshall	137	1869
0-4-0T	OC	Lilleshall	138	1869
0-4-0T	OC	Lilleshall	139	1869

It has been suggested that these locomotives carried the running numbers 1, 2, and 3. However, no confirmation has been traced. Two of these locomotives are believed to have been sold around 1881, but their subsequent history and that of the third one, are unknown. However, the 1937 Valuation records in the section for Priorslee Furnaces a note as follows: '3 slag shunting engines. Broken up. One boiler removed and sold 1927.' There is no indication of any value, and this note has all the appearances of having been added from some other record, probably in order to indicate that these were no longer in existence. Unfortunately, this note creates more problems than it solves. Firstly, if this refers to the above three locos from the Lodge Furnaces, then it solves the question of the disposal of these locos. But we cannot be sure that these were not three additional locos, not previously recorded. The next earliest Valuation, from 1915, regrettably does not go into the same detail, so that it is not possible to determine if these were in use at Priorslee at that date, or simply stored there. The next earliest detail is in the 1876 Valuation, where of course the three were recorded as in use at Lodge, and there is no mention of any such locos at Priorslee. They may have been used on the slag bank at Priorslee after their retirement from Lodge, but they would have required major overhauls after nearly twenty years hard use in the harsh conditions of the Lodge Furnaces. Furthermore, the gauge of the Priorslee slag bank tramway is given as 2' 8" in the detailed report from the Company to Earl Granville dated 29 March 1899. Although the 1915 Valuation gives the 'cinder incline' as having a gauge of 33in (2' 9") and also lists a steam winch, indicating rope or cable haulage. So these locomotives, if used here, would have needed to be regauged as well. But the possibility remains that these were three further locomotives not previously recorded.

CHAPTER NINE
OPERATING THE RAILWAY

As we have seen, the railway was almost certainly developed on a piecemeal basis, to provide access between the various mines, furnaces, brickworks and main line connections. The total route mileage was given in various Company records as being 11¼ miles of running lines and 14¼ miles of sidings. It is interesting to record the detail of the Company railway as given in the 1941 Valuation: '38,655 yards *(21.96 miles)* of standard gauge railway, 218 points and crossings, 10 crossover roads, one diamond crossing, 13 buffer stops, 10 gates and 6 signals.' That there were only thirteen buffer stops on the entire system suggests either that some had gone unrecorded, or that other, perhaps simpler arrangements had been installed at the end of many sidings!

The northern mines and Lodge Furnaces connected together, and had access to the LNWR exchange sidings at Donnington, whilst the southern mines around Priorslee had access to that furnace, and to Snedshill, as well as to the exchange sidings at Oakengates on the Coalport branch, and to the GWR at Hollinswood. Traffic to and from the New Yard Works was worked to either of the three exchange sidings. The railway continued to function in this way, never being used as a complete line from one end to the other. Nonetheless, it is useful to describe the line from one end to the other, giving the opportunity to detail the working practices along the way.

From Donnington to Hollinswood
Starting in the exchange sidings at Donnington, adjacent to the LNWR Stafford to Wellington line, the Company railway faced eastwards and passed the access lines to the Midland Ironworks of C.&W. Walker Ltd. on the left, then swept round to a southwards direction, and crossed Wellington Road at an ungated level crossing. Here trains would be controlled by the crossing keeper, then after around 200 yards halted just before the gates of the next level crossing, over School Road, whilst the crossing keeper closed the gates to road traffic. This was originally the only gated crossing on the system, although gates were installed at the Wellington Road crossing at a later date. The crossing keeper also had responsibility for a further ungated crossing, of a minor road towards the old Freehold Pit, and therefore his shelter was sited just to the south of the School Road crossing, adjacent to the coal wharf or landsale yard. This yard comprised a loop and one siding, used by local coal merchants, reached from a north facing junction. The northernmost points of the loop were removed some time after 1914, creating two sidings instead of one. The 1876 Valuation records that a 15 ton weighbridge was in use here. Trip workings to supply this landsale yard were made from the various collieries in production over the years on this northern section of the line.

Traffic to and from the Donnington exchange sidings was subject to considerable care, as the main line company may have its own locos working in the sidings. The Company Rule Book specified the procedure to be used here:

(1) When approaching level crossing near Donnington coal wharf engine driver shall give 4 (four) whistles.

(2) On engine arriving at Donnington Exchange Sidings engine driver shall give 4 (four) whistles.

When practicable, Lilleshall Company's locos, when delivering

The former Taff Vale Railway 0-6-2T No.1, hauling internal wagons from the exchange sidings with Granville Colliery in the mid-1950s. [A. J. B. Dodd]

Former GWR '2721' class 0-6-0PT No.12 climbs through the wooded area around The Nabb, and passes beneath the 'metal bridge' in the mid-1950s. It appears to be hauling one wagon and the Barclay 0-6-0T No.11. [A. J. B. Dodd]

Andrew Barclay 0-4-0ST ALBERTA (1349/1913) approaches the level crossing at The Rookery with the return leg of the final railtour of the system on 26 September, 1958. [A. J. B. Dodd]

Andrew Barclay 0-6-0T No.11 (1486/1916) with a trainload of mostly wooden bodied coal wagons heading away from Granville Colliery exchange sidings towards Priorslee in the 1950s. [A. J. B. Dodd]

outward traffic, must draw their trains into the Middle Road, and return through Humber Arms [sic] Road.

In taking the train into the siding, every care must be taken to prevent the train from striking any wagons which may already be in the siding. The L.M.S. will do all possible to keep the siding clear, but, however, locos must travel cautiously and be prepared to stop at any obstruction.

The Humber Arm Road was the southernmost of the Donnington exchange sidings, and originally gave direct access to the Humber Arm Railway, subsequently being used primarily as an engine release road, unless other sidings were full.

The first part of the line from the exchange sidings through the level crossings had been fairly level, but from beyond the landsale yard it gradually steepened, and passed over a couple of minor lanes on its way past Freehold Pit, and onwards to Muxtonbridge Pit. 'Whistle' boards were placed either side of these and other minor lanes as a warning to vehicular traffic, as the line wound its way uphill through a basically rural setting. At Muxtonbridge, trains requiring to travel further south were put into one of the two reception roads, with the locomotive at the rear of the train, which then propelled the train up the grade to Waxhill Barracks Pit, or to the sidings adjacent to Granville and Grange Pits.

Wagons for Freehold Pit were similarly propelled back down the gradient to reach the north facing junction for this pit. In later years, wagons for the asphalt works were also worked via the reception sidings at Muxtonbridge, the trackwork here being revised from that originally laid to service Waxhill Barracks Pit.

The area now changed from rural to industrial, with the spoil heaps and remains of the numerous pits dotting the landscape. Housing in this area was limited to a few scattered workmen's cottages, apart from the basic terraced housing provided by the company at the appropriately named Waxhill Barracks. However, the small village of Granville was located beyond Granville Pit, on its eastern side, and contained a noted Methodist church, now preserved at Blists Hill Open Air Museum.

The elevated position of the sorting sidings adjacent to Granville and Grange pits was actually on the site of the original Lodge Bank Coke Works, and this later became a tipping site for spoil from Granville Pit, and was located alongside a landsale yard. A watering column was installed at this location, which was also furnished with a wagon or two of locomotive coal from Granville Pit, and the locomotives were coaled directly from these wagons for many years. It is not known when the practice started, but it certainly continued well into the days of the nationalised collieries.

This site was also used after the Second World War, for the dismantling of surplus military equipment brought from the nearby Ordnance Depot at Donnington, the hard standing making it particularly suitable, as was the use of former Italian prisoners of war from the nearby camp at Sherriffhales. Unbelievably, much of the dismantled equipment was dumped as 'infill' down the shaft at the old Freehold Pit, which had closed in 1928. Both Len Jones and his wife can recall many of the artefacts 'liberated' at this time, when many goods were, of course, still on ration. It is recalled that one particular person managed to salvage sufficient parts, on a piecemeal basis over a period of time, that enabled him to build himself a car! Not bad at this time in post-war Britain, when you would have been hard put to even buy one at any price.

From here, various lines disappeared: eastwards to Granville Pit, northwards to the site of the Lodge Furnaces, and southwards to Grange Pit. Originally, this latter line had also permitted direct running from Grange to the Lodge, so this was a complex junction, which was controlled by signals, shown on the Ordnance Survey maps of 1881 and 1902. In fact, several signal posts are shown on these early maps but their method of operation is not known. They were evidently discontinued some time after the beginning of the 20th century and were certainly not in use in the living memory of any Company employee interviewed. Continuing our journey in a south and west direction, after a further quarter mile we arrive at the triangular junction for Donnington Brickworks. This was laid in to provide for the supply of coal from any of the pits we have already passed, and also to facilitate the shipment of finished brick products through the exchange sidings at Oakengates and Hollinswood. In addition, a certain amount of refractory products were used by the company within the iron works at Priorslee. Actually, the locomotive department was also supplied with firebricks for the brick arches by this brickworks, as the Donnington Works Day Book records this supply in 1925 in 'small and large Loco Centres and Ends.' However, rail traffic to this brickworks diminished rapidly after the Second World War, most traffic being by road.

A short distance further on, a short siding branched off northwards to the site of the original Cockshutts Pit, used afterwards as a further tip for waste from the furnaces. Less than half a mile later, and after the line crossed Gower Street by the only underline bridge on the system, a facing junction gave access to the New Yard Engineering Works at St.Georges and at around this point, the line had reached his summit, and then began a descent southwards. Also known as the Phoenix Foundry, this works contained the main locomotive running shed and repair shop, at the entrance to the works yard. This running shed operated in an 'auxiliary role' after the running shed was opened at Priorslee in the 1930s. The building is described in the 1876 Valuation as a 'brick building, 90 feet long by 31 feet wide with double pits. Covered with a corrugated galvanised iron roof and fitted with smoke troughs and chimneys. Gas fittings throughout.' It was valued at £300.

As indicated, only two of the three roads in this shed had inspection pits. The third road, on the eastern side was purely for stabling purposes. This shed was enlarged at a later date by an extension to the two inspection roads, and was described in the 1937 Valuation as '122 feet by 30 feet, brick building, corrugated iron roof, part glazed, wood swing doors, brick floor, two engine pits.' It was valued at £1,000 in 1941. The running shed was stated to contain a sand screen for dry sand, a light 2 ton crane and a brazing hearth. Outside were a pair of shear legs with 20 ton grab, and a 20 feet by 6 feet overhead water tank on cast iron columns. In the 1950s the Company locomotives were scrapped in this area, in front of the running shed.

Immediately to the east of the running shed was the Locomotive Repair Shop, with two roads. This building was originally built as the Wagon Repair Shop, and was described in the 1876 Valuation as 'one brick building, 90 feet long by 24 feet wide with three blacksmiths fires. Covered with a galvanised iron roof and gas fittings throughout'. It was valued at £250 at this time. It is not surprising that such facilities for the maintenance of the Company's wagon fleet were required, as that fleet numbered 757 wagons in 1876, and further details of this fleet, which was used both externally and internally can be found in Appendix 5. However, around the turn of the century, this building was converted into the Locomotive Repair Shop, and is described in the 1937 Valuation as '87 feet by 24 feet, brick building, corrugated iron roof, part glazed, wood swing doors' and the value given as £550 in 1941. Wagons were thereafter serviced in an extension to the main New Yard Works, logically cited adjacent to the sawmill, and erected around 1901/2. This building was 76 feet 6 inches by 60 feet, and after the cessation of wagon repairs was also allocated to the locomotive department, being valued at £920 in 1941. It is not known what use was made of this building in later times.

North of these buildings, and therefore nearer to the 'main line' was the Wagon Paint Shop. This was 27 feet long by 15 feet wide with the conventional 'corrugated galvanised iron roof resting on cast iron columns' and valued in 1876 at £80. This too became the property of the locomotive department, and in 1941 was described as an 'engine shed' and valued at £35. In later years this building was extended and used by the permanent way staff to house their collection of wagons and recovery gear.

Returning to the 'main line' journey, the line now curved almost directly southwards, and ran through the pleasant woodland area of The Nabb. As the line was descending steeply from

Above and opposite. Further views of the railtour of 26 September 1958, with Barclay 0-4-0ST ALBERTA. In the first photograph the members of the party are being 'loaded' into the open wagons at Priorslee Furnaces. In the second, the train is at the Rookery siding, which was the furthest extent of the tour. Note that no brake van was used. [A. J. B. Dodd]

Peckett 0-4-0ST No.10 shunting wagons apparently loaded with wodden pit props, probably conveyed from the saw mill at the new Yard Works. The date is 27 May, 1947 and the location seems to be one of the collieries. [A. Glover/F. Wycherley]

this point, it also ran in a shallow cutting, being crossed by the locally known 'iron bridge' carrying a footpath, which itself ran on the trackbed of one of the original tramways. A short distance further on, another footpath crossed the line on the 'wooden bridge'. In this area the line passed a number of houses, and thus entered into an area of concentrated habitation. As it continued southwards, the cutting on the right hand side diminished, revealing a view towards the west, overlooking the Oakengates area.

Approaching the eastern side of Oakengates the line crossed Station Hill where the crossing keeper closed the gates to control road traffic, though the next several busy road crossings were ungated. The unusual aspect at these locations was the keeper's 'watch box' or 'cabin' that was provided for his shelter. This was a conical shaped structure resembling a beehive, about seven feet tall, and around six feet diameter at the base, constructed entirely of brick, with a separate brick chimney. This was furnished with a single window, with steel plates bolted across the window when out of use, and a strong door so that when unoccupied, it would not prove an attractive 'residence' to undesirables. Such persons are not solely a feature of modern times. Inside there was a large fireplace, and seats were provided along the sides.

Crossing keepers were invariably men who had been injured in their previous Company positions, not necessarily on the railway. There are thought to have been seven of these shelters; the northernmost was as already mentioned, at Donnington. The others were at Station Hill, Oakengates, then also at Canongate, Holyhead Road (also sometimes referred to as 'The Greyhound crossing' on account of the nearby public house of that name), Hollinswood Road, Shifnal Road at Snedshill, and at The Pigeon Box on the Priorslee Road. The shelter at the Shifnal Road crossing was also known as 'Ford's Box', and was under the control of Jabez Rushton in the 1920s. Jack Hassall was also occasionally a flagman at this crossing, but normally worked as a ganger for the permanent way department. A Mr. Williams was the flagman at Hollinshead Road just after the Second World War. Coincidentally, similar structures were built for crossing keepers on the Pensnett Railway, which predated our railway, opening from 1829 onwards.

Crossing keepers or 'flagmen' were required to halt road traffic in favour of rail traffic by alerting them with a red flag, and after dark by an illuminated red lamp. The flagmen generally only worked a day shift from around 7am to 5pm, even though the traffic department usually worked shifts from 6am to 2pm and 2pm to 10pm, and sometimes had to keep going later into the night, in order to ensure a continuity of supplies to the furnaces, etc. In such circumstances, the Company's Rule Book specified: *If no gateman is visible, the driver must send the fireman or shunter forward to investigate, and in (the) gateman's absence protect the crossing until the train has passed over; any absence of gateman must at once be reported ... At night, when no gateman is on duty, before passing over any crossing the driver must send his shunter or fireman to protect the crossing. Before giving the signal to pass over the shunter must satisfy himself that the crossing is clear, and must remain on the crossing exhibiting a red light until the whole train has passed over, and then rejoin his train.*

It appears that certain crossings were considered to have the right of way automatically in the favour of the railway, as the Company Rule Book required that for the purposes of warning crossing keepers that trains were about to pass over the crossings: *Drivers must give 3 short whistles and be prepared to stop unless the crossing is duly protected:-*

Oakengates Hill Crossing [Station Hill], *Corfields Crossing* [Holyhead Road] *and Canteen Crossing* [Hollinswood Road].

Still descending, the line crossed the minor road known as 'Hydraulic Bank', then divided. The 'main line' went to the left, and divided into several reception sidings, whilst the line on the right went through the site of the original Snedshill Ironworks. This later served, firstly a landsale yard with its own wagon weighbridge (of 25 ton capacity in 1876) then dividing again to serve the Concrete Works, locally known as the 'Flag Plant'. The right-hand of these two lines carried on after the Concrete Works across Canongate by an ungated level crossing to provide access to the

Divergence of the lines, looking north-east near to the Rookery, 19 June, 1954. The left-hand line goes to the Lodge Tip, the centre line carries on to the exchange sidings for Granville Colliery, and the line verging off to the right is part of the triangular junction serving Donnington Brickworks. The tall signal is interesting, but its function and means of operation are unknown. [F. W. Shuttleworth]

foundry of J. Maddock & Sons Ltd. (formerly the Snedshill Forge), mainly for pig iron and coal deliveries. The left hand line passed on the other side of the Concrete Works, and after passing under Canongate, descended on the other side of the valley to reach the exchange sidings with the LNWR Coalport branch, just after passing beneath the Holyhead Road and running alongside the LNWR line, albeit at a slightly higher level. From these exchange sidings, a further line climbed southwards directly to the sorting sidings alongside Priorslee Furnaces, thus creating, in effect, a 'loop' line, and giving direct access from Priorslee to these exchange sidings.

Meanwhile, the 'main line' continued southwards, also crossing Canongate on the level, and now running on the bed of the original Shropshire Canal. After about another quarter of a mile, a branch to the left led directly into the Snedshill Brick and Tile Works, just before the 'main line' crossed the Holyhead Road (formerly the A5) again by an ungated crossing on the level. After the Second World War, virtually no shunting ever took place at the Snedshill Brick and Tile Works, as most traffic was already coming and going by road. Its location adjacent to the old A5 road no doubt contributed towards the change. Nonetheless, its two sidings remained in place until closure of the railway system. Immediately on the south side of the A5 crossing was yet another landsale yard, for the benefit of local customers. In the years between the two World Wars, benzole was on sale here produced at the nearby Distillation Plant. Just beyond there were stacks of pig iron on both sides of the line. The line once again divided, this time into several running lines, so that by the time it reached Hollinswood Road, this was crossed by no less than seven running lines, none of them gated. Then on the right was a large slag heap, that gradually disappeared over the years, as it was used for its road building properties. Now on the left was the main Priorslee Furnaces, which were subject to much change over the long years. At the rear of the furnaces was the Distillation Plant and Coking Furnaces, and overlooking the whole industrial area was St. Peter's Church, much rebuilt in 1836.

After passing the furnaces, the running lines divided into two groups. To the right, the lines continued past the Asphalt Works and into the GWR exchange sidings at Hollinswood, which were immediately adjacent to the GWR's own Hollinswood Sidings. To the left, the lines continued directly eastwards to the Lawn and Stafford Pits, near to Priorslee Hall. Almost immediately, at the level crossing of the Holyhead Road, this branch generated a further one mile branch, that turned north-westwards and ran across Priorslee Road at The Pigeon Box to Woodhouse Pit. This line ran on the site of an earlier tramway, and passed the now legendary 'Oily Pool', whose water was usually warm and of a green/yellow colour, but nonetheless much favoured by the local youths for swimming. Before reaching Woodhouse, the line turned westwards and climbed around the base of the prosaically named 'Hangman's Hill', passing another pool known alternatively as 'The Flash', 'Hangman's Pool' or 'Rough Rozzer'.

Working the Line

As mentioned briefly above, the importance of the locomotive running shed at the New Yard Works was reduced from some time in the 1930s. Locomotives working the southern section of the line were stabled in a single road shed at the northern end of the Priorslee Furnaces, capable of holding only two or three of the locomotives. This may have been an enlargement of an earlier small shed, listed in the 1919 Fire Insurance Schedule, for which no further details or precise location are available. Servicing and repair of the locos was undertaken in a bay of the main rolling shop at the northern end of Priorslee Furnaces. Only those working the northern section continued to stable at the New Yard, plus those out of use and stored. In later years, it also became

Peckett 0-4-0ST No.10 (883/1901) and 0-6-2T No.3 (former GWR No.589) are assisting during 1936 with the demolition of the 98 ft. high coal bunker, as part of the more general demolition of the former steelworks site seen in the background. [Ironbridge Gorge Museum Trust]

the site of the scrapping of the final fleet of locomotives. This division of the locomotive fleet reduced the amount of light engine running, and track capacity on the single line section. Two of the fitters employed here were originally employed by the LNER at Kings Cross shed, thus attracting considerable regard. These fitters also serviced the small Peckett 0-4-0ST loaned to Joseph Sankey and Sons Ltd. at Hadley Castle during the Second World War, as well as travelling to Ironbridge Power Station to regularly attend the small fleet of Peckett saddle tanks there.

Locomotives were able to take on water at six locations around the system: at Freehold Pit (30ft tank); near Waxhill Pit (30ft tank); at the main locomotive shed (23½ft tank); at Furnace Crossing, near Lodge (27½ft tank); at Snedshill, adjacent to the Concrete Plant (13ft tank) and at Priorslee Furnaces (30ft tank).

The Priorslee stabling facility was shared by the steam cranes used in the rolling mills and for loading raw materials into the furnaces, and for removing the slag and ash deposits. Mention of the steam cranes in the various Company Valuations unfortunately give no details until the 1937 and 1941 Valuations. However, the incomplete surviving Board minutes do give us some idea of their introduction towards the end of the nineteenth century, as follows:

27 September 1893: Provided a special locomotive for the Engine [sic] Shop be dispensed with, the board agreed to sanction the purchase of a steam travelling and shunting crane at cost not exceeding about £800.

27 October 1893: With reference to the sanction given to obtaining a Steam Crane for the Engineering Department, the Managing Director, after explaining that the railroads were not in a suitable condition for such a Crane, was instructed to deal with the question of getting the roads into proper condition as he thought best.

A gap of four years then follows before anything more is reported on this subject:

31 March 1897: The Managing Director reported that a Steam Travelling Crane had been ordered for the Engineering Shops, in accordance with the authority given by the Board previously.

28 May 1897: The Directors are informed that the alterations to the Engine [sic] Shops were practically completed, and that a Loco Travelling Crane had been purchased and was at work.

28 October 1898: The purchase of a Steam Crane for the Steel Rolling Department at a cost of about £700 was approved.

STEAM CRANE FLEET

Running No.	Capacity	Maker	User and disposition
No.1	4 ton	Smith	Steel Rolling Dept.
No.2	4 ton	Smith	Bessemer Shop until 1928, then Steel Rolling Dept.
No.4	15 ton	Cowans Sheldon	Bessemer Shop. For sale 1930, possibly never sold.
No.5	5 ton	Wilson	Steel Rolling Dept.
No.6	5 ton	Wilson	Bessemer Shop.
No.7	1½ ton		Bessemer Shop until 1928, then Constructional Shop.
No.8	10 ton	Smith	Purchased 1918. Bessemer Shop. Sold to J.Cashmore, 1928.
No.9	5 ton	Wilson	Purchased 1919. Bessemer Shop until 1928, then Steel Rolling Dept.
No.10	5 ton		Bessemer Shop. Sold to Victoria Coal & Iron Co. Ltd 1928.

28 November 1898: The Board confirmed the order placed with Messrs. Wilson & Co. [sic] for a new steam crane at a cost of £700 for the Steel Rolling Department.

Thus there is evidence for the purchase of only two of the steam cranes. The later one was evidently obtained from John Hayes Wilson & Co. Ltd., of Sandhills, Liverpool. Other makes subsequently represented were Thos. Smith & Sons (Rodley) Ltd., Old Foundry, Rodley, Leeds and Cowans Sheldon & Co. Ltd., St. Nicholas Works, Carlisle. The steam cranes came under the responsibility of the individual user department rather than the locomotive department. Examination of the 1937 and 1941 Valuations reveals the following cranes in use (see previous page).

There is no trace of a No.3 in the surviving Company records. As the second locomotive crane purchased above in 1898 was by Wilson, it is possible that the earlier ones had already gone by the time this numbering system was in use, or that some renumbering had already taken place. No.4 is believed to have become derelict by the 1950s and was scrapped when the railway system closed. The remainder are also presumed to have lasted until the cessation of rail traffic in 1958.

Interestingly, correspondence relating to alterations at Donnington Brickworks during 1919, included a quotation from A. Roberts & Co., Machinery Merchants, of 15 Queen Street, Leeds for 'one second-hand steam propelling crane by Rushworth of Colne for £850 in Liverpool.' However, there is no evidence that any order was placed for this machine.

The Company Rule Book for Railwaymen specifically forbade dangerous practices by all classes of railwaymen, and in particular, by shunters: *No person must ride on a locomotive or wagon by means of a coupling pole or other appliance, not upon the buffer of a locomotive or wagon unless there is secure handhold, or stand there unless there is also a secure footplate.*

Nonetheless, Len Jones, who was a shunter from 1949 to 1952, can well recall that in the early 1950s such dangerous practices were routinely performed. Shunters rode on the headstock of the wagon buffers when wagons were being propelled, so that they could jump off and guard level crossings without stopping, or switch points, uncouple wagons, or pin down or release brakes. Everyone concerned were apparently quite philosophical about the possibility of being injured, accepting that it was perhaps inevitable. It is possible to understand the pride that such men had in performing their duties in what they saw as the most efficient manner, even if they did not appreciate that any injuries would completely negate their enthusiastic 'efficiency'.

However, Ernie Wood was not quite so sanguine about such performances, as he recalled that one day he was working up a ladder at the side of a building, that required the ladder to be placed in between the rails of a siding leading into the building. In accordance with the Company rules, he had placed a red flag between the rails to ensure that no shunting took place on that line. He was less than happy to see a shunter casually remove his red flag, and prepare to shunt some wagons into his ladder. The shunter was, I believe, made very well aware that this behaviour and lack of awareness could be very dangerous to his own health in future!

The Company Rule Book was equally fastidious in its requirements for the safety of the platelayers and their responsibilities towards other members of the Traffic Department. In particular, it required that: *Each foreman or leading man must walk over his length every morning and tighten up the keys and other fastenings that may be loose, and inspect all points and crossings.*

The numerous gradients around the system were the subject of particular concern, and no doubt as the result of unfortunate experiences, the following rules were applied.

Explanation is necessary for some of the terminology given above. 'Water Engine' is taken as being in the area of the Pigeon Box road crossing, 'Priors Lee Machine' is the site of the furnaces, 'Main Line Points' is the triangular junction from the Donnington Brickworks on to the company main line, and the 'Highways Co. Works' relates to either of their asphalt works at Priors Lee or Waxhill, as appropriate.

The Rule Book was also equally fastidious in its requirement for the use of lamps at night, and their use as shunting signals, as well as hand signals. A detailed description of these can be found in Appendix 6.

A final comment in this section must be that an interesting Minute was discovered dating from a Board Meeting of 1 April, 1931, in which 'it was reported that the LMSR company and the GWR company had declined to take over the working of the Company's railways'. Evidently, the Company was disillusioned with its own capability to handle its internal traffic at that time. It is probably no coincidence that it obtained the two more powerful ex-Taff Vale Railway locos from the GWR early in the following year.

Shunting at Priorslee

Iron ore for smelting was imported from Spain and Sierra Leone, as well as a certain amount from the Oxfordshire Ironstone Co. Ltd., near Banbury. Mostly this arrived at the GWR sidings at Hollinswood, and was worked to the

Gradients on the Lilleshall Railways where, in addition to Engine Brake Power, Shunters must peg down wagon brakes to ensure safety:-

From	To
Woodhouse Empty Wagon Siding	Water Engine
Priors Lee Wharf (approaching)	Priors Lee Machine
Dark Lane Siding	Stafford Pits
Priors Lee Siding	G.W. Sidings and Highways Ltd. Works
Priors Lee Sidings	L.M.S. Sidings
Snedshill Forge Machine	L.M.S. Sidings or Works Sidings
Nabb Bridge	Lodge Sidings
Donnington Brickworks	Main Line Points, both routes
Grange	Lodge Sidings
Granville	Lodge Sidings
Lodge Sidings	Muxton Bridge
Main Line Points	Highway Co.'s Works
Muxton Bridge	Donnington, L.M.S.

furnaces by any of the locomotives, even the smaller ones. The smaller, four coupled engines worked mainly around the furnaces, moving pig iron from the beds to the store on the Snedshill Forge site, loads of coal, coke and ash around the furnaces, and also on the slag bank, taking ladles of molten slag in the side tippers for disposal. The 1941 Valuation records that there were '16 side tip ladles and carriages, plus 3 end tip ladles and carriages' available for use, with a total value of £8,550. The larger engines were used on the runs from either direction on the gradients to the LNWR exchange sidings at Oakengates (and Donnington), as they had greater braking power. This would be for the outgoing shipments of coal, rolled steel, pig iron, or fabrications, and the corresponding empties. Either large or small engines would be used for the occasional shunt at the New Yard Works, which gradually lessened into the 1950s.

After the Second World War, much scrap was received from the south of England for the furnace and as it often contained armour plate, contributed to the quality of the pig iron produced. However, a notable source at Portsmouth contributed tin cans, which also produced a favourable metallurgical content. Unfortunately, on at least one occasion the tins contained fish, which when fed into the furnaces created a most disagreeable odour over that part of Oakengates! The

Peckett 0-4-0ST No.10 (883/1901) and Barclay 0-6-0T No.11 in the yards at the south end of Priorslee Furnaces, some time between 1933 and 1939. [Ironbridge Gorge Museum Trust]

Ministry of Food also sent animal carcasses for incineration in the furnaces (but not with the iron production) if they were deemed as unfit through disease or whatever.

The Coking Plant at Priorslee was part of the Coal Distillation Plant. It was located on the higher ground behind the actual furnaces, so that the coke produced simply cascaded by gravity down a concrete chute to the furnaces. The shunting of the coking coal up to this position involved working a severe gradient, but because of some severe curves, was almost always performed by the smaller engines propelling only two or three wagons at a time. Eventually, after the Second World War the Company ceased to make its own coke, preferring to obtain coke produced from a softer, more suitable coal, notably from the North Staffordshire coalfield. The site was given over to a new plant for concrete products, the former site at Snedshill being demolished. Later, in the 1950s, the Company went over to oil firing of the furnaces, which was supplied by road from Esso at Stanlow. However, much trouble was experienced in keeping this rather thick fuel in a liquid state during the winter months. Later still, some of the plant was converted to gas firing.

The remainder of the Coal Distillation Plant was originally set up to produce benzole, ammonium sulphate and various other chemical by-products. However, the distillation works was closed in 1927, after which time the remaining plant was absorbed into the main Priorslee Furnaces complex, acting purely as a Coal Washing Plant. Coal from the Company's pits was washed here until nationalisation of the pits, after which the plant was used to wash coal for local power stations, notably that at Ironbridge.

The main part of the plant comprised a huge bunker, some 98 feet high, from which the coal was dropped into the washing plant. To get coal into the bunker, wagons were propelled up an incline for about 500 yards, then the line levelled where it ran over the chambers from where the coal was hoisted into the bunker. The rake of wagons were left beyond the unloading point, and individual wagons were 'pinched' back over to the bottom discharge point and emptied. After emptying, the wagons were 'pinched' to the next position along, but because of the gradient, it was often difficult to operate the wagon brakes fully or in time, so that runaways were frequent. Because of the complex and potentially conflicting movements around Priorslee Furnaces, an audible warning system was installed at this location, which became known as 'Priorslee Machine'.

One of the features of the system was to warn of runaways from the bunker road. Along the walkway adjacent to the bunker road four poles were installed

---

Code of Signals for working Electrical Siren between Furnaces, Washery and Priors Lee Machine:-
Wagons leaving out of control	1 long (Danger)
Requiring Fuel or Loco	1 short
Line clear to Washery or Furnaces	2 short
Trains (or loco) leaving Washery	3 short
Trains (or loco) leaving Furnaces	4 short

The same signals must also be given by the Engine Whistle.

Code of signals to be used for working electrical Siren between Priors Lee Machine and Priors Lee Wharf:-
Trains (or locos) about to leave Priors Lee Machine	2 long

This signal must be given by fireman on four man locos and by head shunter on other locos. Drivers must also give the same warning on the engine whistle.

at intervals, each with a push button that activated a siren to warn other rail workers of any runaways. This siren could also be used for other purposes, and similar activating buttons were installed at strategic positions in the yard around the furnaces.

It was generally arranged that one siding below the washery road would be kept empty so that runaways could be switched into it in any such emergency. In 1936 the 98ft high bunker was demolished, after which coal was loaded into the washing plant via separate hoists, that did not involve the previous steep rail incline.

Oakengates Exchange Sidings
Semaphore signals were provided to control access to and from the LNWR exchange sidings at Oakengates, operated by LNWR (later LMSR, then BR) men from a ground frame in their Priors Lee Signal Cabin. Thus only trains authorised by the railway company could be admitted to the sidings. The Company Rule Book specifies that trains approaching from the northern (Snedshill) direction and requiring admittance were required to give two distinct whistles, asking for the signal to be cleared. In the event of the signal not being taken off, the driver or head shunter had to give two rings on the electric gong, fixed on the signal post, to call attention of the railway company shunter.

Trains on the southern (Hollinswood) line were required to give three distinct whistles for acceptance. When the railway company shunter cleared either signal, he was required to set the points for the opposite incline, until the train had come to a stop at his cabin. In this way, any runaway would be confined to the Company property and not endanger traffic on the Coalport branch. Similarly, 'Cease Shunting' indicators were provided at the cabin to indicate the approach of a train from either direction on the Coalport branch. Should either the up or down indicator point to 'train on line' for a passenger train, all shunting movements on lines adjacent to the main running line were to come to a stand until the train had passed, or the indicator released from the 'train on line' position.

Out of the normal working hours, when no shunter was present at the Priors Lee cabin, the signal for the northern incline was fixed at danger, whilst that for the southern incline was left in the 'off' position. Company employees were then responsible for the safety of all movements during such periods, which were generally between 5pm and 8am (Monday to Friday), and 6.30pm to 7am (Friday to Monday). For some unaccountable reason, Company locos were not allowed to enter the exchange sidings between 7pm and 8pm and between 9pm and 10pm on any day.

The 1905 LNWR Working Timetable shows four weekday goods workings calling at Priorslee sidings. One of these was the morning daily branch goods to Coalport while another morning goods was worked on Mondays, Wednesdays and Fridays only, as far as Priorslee. In both cases, the engine and brake van returned to Hadley Junction without load. Two afternoon mineral trains were scheduled to arrive at Priorslee at 4.30pm and 5.30pm, and to return to Hadley Junction at 5.20pm and 6.05pm respectively. These services provided empty coal wagons inwards, and full trains outwards. This pattern of services continued until after the Second World War, but with the addition of a further afternoon goods working from Stafford arriving at Priorslee at 2.15pm and returning at 2.45pm.

However, after the transfer of the Coalport branch to the Western Region of BR as from 2 April 1950 the services were recast to take into consideration that the nationalised mines at Grange and Granville would use Donnington as their exchange point. This left incoming traffic to Priorslee principally coke and limestone with outgoing pig iron, bricks, tiles, concrete products and engineering products. One diagram sufficed for this traffic, 'Target 69'; it originated with a light engine from Shrewsbury shed (Coleham) at 5.10am, then from Shrewsbury (Abbey Foregate) at 5.35am with a goods working to Coalport. This returned at 11.10am to Wellington (arriving at 1.05pm), then at 2.20pm to Priorslee Siding, and at 3.53pm to Hadley Junction. The generous schedule allowed the next leg of this diagram to work to Donnington at 5.15pm, departing there at 6.10pm back to Hadley Junction, then finally leaving there at 7.50pm for

Barclay 0-4-0ST ALBERTA about to depart from the Priorslee Furnaces at the start of the final railtour of 26 September 1958. [Edgar Meeson]

Looking north around 1956, with the Coalport branch curving away to the left towards Oakengates. An unidentified WR '94XX' 0-6-0PT is shunting in the Snedshill Sidings. [A. J. B. Dodd]

ALBERTA after running round the wagons at the Rookery, in the woods of The Nabb, at the entrance to the New Yard Works, where it went to take on water. [Edgar Meeson]

Shrewsbury, arriving at 8.28pm at Harlescott Sidings. Interestingly, this entire working was often the responsibility of a Burton engine, usually a 4F 0-6-0, that had worked into Shrewsbury on the 9.30pm Burton to Swansea class 'F' goods, arriving at 3.15am. This engine returned the next day at 2.30am to Burton on another class 'F' goods.

Following the closure and dismantling of the Company railway and its link at Priorslee Siding, the southernmost section of the branch from Coalport to Stirchley was closed, with effect from 5 December 1960. The daily goods continued as working 9T69, leaving Shrewsbury (Coton Hill) at 5.30am, pausing at Priorslee Siding from 8.15 until 8.25am and reaching Stirchley at 8.45am. This left at 9.00am, pausing again at Priorslee Siding from 9.10 to 9.20am, and returning to Coton Hill. The remainder of the branch, including the line past Oakengates survived until 6 September 1964 at which time the entire branch from Hadley Junction was closed and subsequently lifted. Some of the sidings and running lines at Hadley Junction were retained for wagon storage for several years thereafter.

Locomotives used on the branch goods are known to have included the ubiquitous Ramsbottom 0-6-0 'DX Goods' in the early days and later the various Webb 0-6-0 and 0-6-2T classes, such as his 'Cauliflowers' and 'Coal Tanks'. In LMS days Shrewsbury was supplied with former Midland Railway 3F and 4F 0-6-0s which became frequent visitors, as did the Bowen-Cooke LNWR 'Super D' 0-8-0s. These continued into BR days but after the transfer to the Western Region former GWR '57XX' and '94XX' 0-6-0PTs became increasingly common. It is believed that a BR 204hp 0-6-0 diesel was tried on the line around 1961/62, but no regular use was made of this more modern form of traction.

GWR Hollinswood Exchange Sidings

A stop signal was erected by the gate, which similar to Oakengates, was worked by the main line company's men to control admission and reduce the risk of conflicting movements in the sidings. Company engine drivers were required to give one long whistle to request the signal to be set to 'off', and the railway company staff were then required to clear the sidings so as to be able to accept such traffic before setting the signal. The railway company was at all times to ensure that sufficient space was available to Company trains arriving in the sidings, and that the main line locomotives would not be

Above. Believed to date from 1898, this view down Station Hill clearly shows the company's level crossing in the foreground, with the beehive-shaped crossing keeper's hut just left of centre. The bridge over the erstwhile Shropshire Canal is still there at that time. [Shropshire Archives]

Right. A later view down Station Hill, this time thought to date from the 1920s. The canal bridge has gone, and trees now fill its course. The crossing keeper's hut is partially hidden by an advertisement hoarding, but the level crossing is more evident from this angle. [Shropshire Archives]

about to make any conflicting movements.

An examination of GWR Working Timetables reveals that few goods workings actually started from or terminated at the GWR Hollinswood Yard, and that most of these were local trip workings between Wellington or down to the Severn Valley routes. As will be seen in the next chapter, even the limestone trains from the Company's quarries at Presthope were trip worked from Wellington to Hollinswood. The incoming loads of iron ore are therefore also presumed to have been incorporated into more general train loads, or those proceeding onwards to other destinations. After the opening of Ironbridge Power Station in 1932, coal from Granville and Stafford pits was forwarded directly via these exchange sidings. This amounted to, on average, only one (fairly short) train load per week, as other Midlands pits also supplied the power station.

Consequently, Hollinswood Yard would have seen the whole range of GWR freight motive power over the years in which it operated, and probably quite a few BR and even former LMSR types in the later years of steam activity. As the extent of the yard was gradually reduced after 1960, only a limited number of diesels are believed to have frequented the yard before its final closure in 1970.

Donnington Exchange Sidings
As we have seen, the exchange sidings at Donnington in the period before the end of the Second World War were principally used for the transfer of traffic to and from the Lodge Furnaces and the northern pits of the company. For the purposes of the Company administration, these pits were grouped together as the 'Donnington pits' and are listed in Appendix 1.

Such traffic involved incoming limestone and iron ore for the Lodge Furnaces and outgoing coal from the pits. This was not too substantial as much of the limestone came by canal, most of the iron ore for Lodge was produced at the Company pits, and a great deal of the coal produced was for Company consumption. Nonetheless, a considerable amount of coal was shipped out via the LNWR at Donnington, mostly in wagon loads to individual customers, although a lot of it also went to the various Company wharves at a number of locations, including one, for a number of years, as far away as London. These wagon loads were picked up by the freight trains calling at Donnington and proceeding

```
THE LILLESHALL CO., LTD.,
SUPPLY AT THEIR WHARVES AND DEPOTS:—
   BEST HOUSE & STEAM COALS,
 COBBLES, NUTS, AND SLACK
        OF ALL DESCRIPTIONS,
    DIRECT FROM THEIR COLLIERIES; ALSO
 FIRE CLAY AND BRICK GOODS,
   DRAINING PIPES AND LIME
  FOR BEST HOUSE PURPOSES THE
            FAMOUS
      MARQUIS AND TOP COAL
          ARE RECOMMENDED.
      LIST OF WHARVES AND DEPOTS:—
   PRIORSLEE WHARF,
   SHIFNAL WHARF (Rail),
   DONNINGTON WHARF,
   TRENCH WHARF (Rail),
   NEWPORT WHARF (Rail and Canal),
   EDGMOND WHARF (Canal),
   STAFFORD WHARF (Rail),
   SHREWSBURY (Rail and Canal),
   MARKET DRAYTON WHARF (Rail and Canal),
   LONG LANE (near Wellington) WHARF (Canal),
   CRUDGINGTON WHARF (Rail),
   LONGDON WHARF (Canal),
   BERWICK WHARF (Canal),
   MUCH WENLOCK WHARF (Rail),
   PRESTHOPE WHARF (Rail),
   ALBRIGHTON & CODSALL (Rail),
   WESTBURY WHARF (Rail),
   MINSTERLEY WHARF (Rail),
   POCKLETON WHARF (Rail).
```

The Company advertised its coal for sale locally, as well as through its agents, as per this advertisment from the 'Wellington Journal & Shrewsbury News' of September, 1899.

```
MARQUIS' COAL AND TILERY WHARF,
LONDON AND NORTH-WESTERN GOODS STATION, WELLINGTON.
                                    At the Wharf.    Delivered in the Town.
LILLESHALL COMPANY'S Best FUNGOUS COAL.... 13s 9d per ton...... 14s 2d per ton
    ,,         ,,       TOP COAL.............. 13s 4d per ton...... 13s 9d per ton
    ,,         ,,       FLINT and DOUBLE COAL 11s 8d per ton...... 12s 1d per ton
    ,,         ,,       Ditto ditto COBBLES... 9s 2d per ton...... 9s 7d per ton
    ,,         ,,       FUNGOUS SLACK......... 8s 5d per ton...... 8s 10d per ton
SLATES, BRICKS, TILES, QUARRIES, GLAZED SANITARY PIPES, CHIMNEY TOPS,
                    &c., always on hand.
LIME from the PRESTHOPE LIME-WORKS delivered at LIGHTMOOR, HORSEHAY,
KETLEY, SHIFFNAL, and WELLINGTON RAILWAY STATIONS.
FOUNDRY LOAM supplied direct from the Stanton Loam Bank, Shiffnal.
Also a Stock of Lilleshall Company's COALS of every description kept for Sale at the Great
Western Railway Station, Shiffnal. Prices upon application to the Agent, at the Wharf, to whom,
also, orders for Loam should be forwarded.
                    JOHN MILLINGTON, Agent.
```

A local coal merchant advertised the Company coals and lime in this extract from the 'Wellington Journal' of 26 October, 1867.

eastwards or westwards towards the eventual customers.

The frequency of such freights varied over the years, but there were never less than two per day in each direction, as there were additional local calls to be made at Trench sidings (for the Wombridge branch), at Hadley Junction sidings (for the Joseph Sankey works) and at Haybridge, as well as the additional traffic in Wellington at the LNWR Queen Street Goods Depot. Only after the nationalisation of the remaining northern pits did the exchange sidings at Donnington take on a more important role, as then all of their output was transported via these exchange sidings, as we shall see in Chapter 11.

Over the years probably the whole range of LNW and LMS freight motive power (with the exception of the Beyer-Garratts) would have been seen calling at Donnington, from the tanks, 0-6-0s, 0-8-0s and others already noted through to Fowler 2-6-4Ts, 'Crab' and Stanier 2-6-0s, 8Fs and Ivatt Moguls.

Traffic

One of the principle design features for the working of full trains from quarries and mines was that they should be generally helped by the gradient, so that only empty trains had to work against any gradients. This was achieved at all the mines, with the sole exception of the line to the Lawn Pit.

An example of a contract for the supply of coal is one of May 1892, when the Company signed a contract with the LNWR to supply 50,000 tons of locomotive coal at 7s 6d per ton. A later contract was awarded, in May 1896, to supply a similar amount at the reduced rate of 6s 9d per ton. The Company's 'Double' and 'Flint' coals were recommended as locomotive and steam coals. The Company also supplied hotel coal to the LNWR and locomotive coal to the GWR, the Great Central Railway, the Cambrian Railways and the North Staffordshire Railway.

Under the terms of the transfer of the railway, engine sheds and locomotives to the Lilleshall Iron and Steel Co Ltd in 1947, all shunting and other rail movements for the remainder of the Company's works (i.e. engineering, concrete products, bricks and tiles, by-products) would be undertaken by the new subsidiary. This meant that the charges for such services would of course, after the nationalisation in 1951, be imposed on these businesses by the nationalised concern. This arrangement continued after the denationalisation of the iron and steel industry in 1954.

Industrial Unrest

It goes without saying that labour disputes would occasionally interrupt the flow of traffic on the Company railway. The economic and political upheavals in the 19th and 20th centuries were inevitably reflected at the Company through its miners and ironworkers. Occasional disputes sometimes escalated into local strikes and national strikes had their effect in this corner of Shropshire. The following are the only known instances where the railway was affected.

An early view of Priorslee, with the steelworks furnaces prominent in the centre. The locomotive is clearly a Manning Wardle 0-6-0ST, so this is the only known photograph of No.11 MERCURY (995/1886) which worked here from probably 1903 until 1908. [Shropshire Archives]

1873

The following report is extracted from the 'Colliery Guardian' of 22 August, 1873:

THE LILLESHALL COMPANY AND THEIR COLLIERS

Four of the chief coal pits of the Lilleshall Company remain standing, to the inconvenience of the ironmaking and engineering departments of that concern. The stoppage is due to the alleged determination of the colliers in Shropshire, as well as elsewhere, to work only by weight. They decline to accept the terms of their employers, which are day work. The Company are equally resolved not to be driven to what they deem to be the unnecessary expense of putting down weighing machines at all their numerous pits – for that is what they will have to do if they should yield to the men who are now striking. The colliers who are out are understood to derive their support from the union to which they belong, and there is reason to believe that only the company's three pits [sic] have struck; because for all the men to have ceased, would be to have thrown upon the union so great a mass of unemployed members that capitulation must have been inevitable. On account of the Lilleshall Company having found it desirable to

Peckett 0-4-0ST No.10 (883/1901) and Barclay 0-6-0T No.11 in the yards at the south end of Priorslee Furnaces, sometime between 1933 and 1939. [Ironbridge Gorge Museum Trust]

Former GWR 0-6-2T No.5 and its crew pause between shunting operations at Priorslee in the 1930s. [C. E. G. Budd/ Ironbridge Gorge Museum Trust]

make some alterations at their lodge, the strike has not been of so much importance as would otherwise have been the case. Now that these furnaces are again ready to be put into work, the Company are making the requisite arrangements for supplying themselves with fuel as well as stone from other markets. These arrangements are likely to make them independent of the men for a period, which the Company may make long or short as they please.

This report is of interest because it reveals that the Company continued with its iron making activities by obtaining coal supplies from elsewhere. However, it does not give the whole story. The dispute arose from the introduction of the Coal Mines Regulations Act, which required that as from 1 August, 1873 miners must be paid either by day work or by weight, unless the employer was exempt. A tribunal decided that the Company was not exempt. At three of the Company's mines, the men had traditionally been paid by measurement (of the coal face). In line with the new legislation, the men wanted to be paid by weight, but the Company did not want the expense of installing weighing machines, and preferred the men to be paid by day work. The men felt that they would lose money if paid by day work, and so collectively gave their notice. The Company took this as being on strike, but the men insisted that they had been 'locked out'.

The strike began on Thursday, 24 July 1873 and affected the Company's four largest pits: Woodhouse, Stafford, Grange and Granville. The 'Wellington Journal and Shrewsbury News' reported weekly on the progress of the dispute, and of each of the miners' meetings. It continued, becoming increasingly acrimonious, for 12½ weeks. Work eventually recommenced on Monday, 20 October after the Company agreed to the men's demands.

1911
A very bitter and in some cases, extremely violent, shipping strike was in progress in 1911, when the trade unions attempted to spread their militancy and to involve other transport workers. The railway workers gave 24 hours notice to strike as from Thursday, 17 August, ostensibly over the slowness of a conciliation scheme introduced in 1907, which also forbade strikes until 1914. However, the railway workers were slow to react to the strike call, and in some areas there was barely any effect on rail services. In any case, a settlement was concluded within two days, and the entire strike was officially terminated as from midnight on Saturday, 19 August. The government agreed to reorganise the conciliation procedures so as to speed up its processes. No reports have been traced in any of the local newspapers to indicate any particular effect on the Company.

1919
The inflationary effects of the First World War on the wages of many workers, including railway workers, led to a disastrous post-war deflationary situation when the then unrealistically high wages in some parts of the nation's economy caused an imbalance in earnings. At the same time, the price of goods was actually falling. The railway companies were amongst those employers seeking to reduce the wages of many of their workers. In particular, the average railway workers weekly wage before the war had been 25 shillings, but during the war a special 'War Bonus' was awarded, which by the end of the war amounted to 33 shillings over and above the normal weekly wage. The railways now wanted to eliminate this bonus. But the men stood to lose around 13 shillings per week, and wanted to have their wages settled at around 60 shillings.

The first such national strike on support of their claim started on Friday, 26 September, 1919, although farm workers had already been on strike for a considerable period, and the ironfounders had been out since 20 September, causing around 100 workers to be laid off at the Company. The following extracts from the 'Wellington Journal and Shrewsbury News' illustrates the local effect of this strike:

29 September, 1919
The Snedshill steel works and steel rolling mill belonging to the Lilleshall Company have, it is understood, closed down. Something like 600 men are idle.

4 October, 1919
OAKENGATES
The railway strike has caused great dislocation in the locality owing to the stoppage of several works. The Lilleshall Co.'s Steel Works, Steel Rolling Mill, and Snedshill department closed down at midday, Saturday 27 September, owing to the inability to get materials essential to the carrying on of such works. The cessation of work in these departments has automatically caused a reduction in the traffic department's staff. The other departments still at work have had issued to them a notice by the managing director stating that owing to the uncertain condition of affairs in the country, work will be carried on in those departments from day to day.

The strike ended on Sunday, 5 October, 1919 so that normality began to resume on the following day.

1920
An unusual local dispute arose in January 1920 over the amount of coal allowed to the Company's railway footplate staff. It is unclear from local reports whether the Company wished to reduce the amount, or whether the men wanted it increased. The 'Wellington Journal and Shrewsbury News' reported as follows, on 17 January, 1920:

A LOCAL STRIKE.
SERIOUS SITUATION.
On Wednesday morning the local members of the National Amalgamated Union of Engineers and Firemen, who are employed by the Lilleshall Company, ceased work owing to a dispute between the men and the company, over the question of the workmen's allowance coal. As all the locomotive men, shunters, enginemen and most firemen and electricians are members of the above society, they hold the key to the Lilleshall Company's various activities, and as a result a most serious situation has arisen, for it means that the whole of the

Former GWR 0-6-2T No.5 engaged in the demolition work of the coal bunker at Priorslee in 1936. [C. E. G. Budd/ Ironbridge Gorge Museum Trust]

'Wellington Journal and Shrewsbury News' of 8 May 1926 as follows:

In the Lilleshall Co's coalfield with the exception of the safety man, all the miners are out. The steel rolling mills department ceased work on Tuesday 4 May and the coking department stopped work on Wednesday. The engineering works at New Yard, St. Georges are still carrying on, but the local slag crushing works, of which there are several, are closed down. The works normally employ several hundreds of men.

The General Strike came about through widespread unrest in the coal mining industry and despite its early collapse miners stayed out on strike during most of the remainder of the year, though there was a gradual return to work. Miners at the Company pits had mostly returned to normal working by 25 September, according to the local press. What is not clear is the effect this had on the Company's production and local newspaper reports do not shed any light on this. The unions officially called off the coal strike on 20 November, although the bitterness arising during the previous months meant that in certain areas, notably in South Wales, men still refused to return for some time.

Accidents

We have seen how some of the operating practices of the railway, and in particular, that of the shunters, were not only foolhardy but downright dangerous too. This would not be so bad if it only involved their own safety, but inevitably the safety of others was often endangered by such acts of carelessness.

In January 1858 an unusual accident took place at Priorslee, although contemporary accounts do not specify whereabouts in this complex. A locomotive was hauling coal wagons to the furnaces there, and approaching a level crossing, the driver stopped to wait for the crossing keeper to control the road traffic, and to give him right of way across the road. However, the keepers were away at lunch, so he decided to open the gates himself. Having dismounted from his engine, he operated the gates, but somehow managed to get himself in front of his moving engine, and was run over by it and killed. Evidently he had left the engine in gear, without ensuring that the brake was properly applied. It is unlikely that he had left his engine in the charge of the fireman or shunter, as it would have been their job to clear the road.

Another early accident was recorded by the 'Wellington Journal' of 31 October, 1868 unfortunately without too much detail, as follows:

COLLISION

On Monday week [19 October 1868] a

Company's departments have closed down, and over 3,000 persons will be thrown out of employment. It is hoped that a settlement will soon be arrived at, for the life of the Oakengates district largely depends upon the works which are now closed down.

At a Board meeting on 29 January 1920 the managing director reported on the strike, and the Board passed the resolution that *'his action in dealing with this matter (was) wholly approved'*. A further report from this newspaper on 31 January revealed that the situation was pretty well unchanged:

THE LOCAL STRIKE.
A DEADLOCK.

The local strike of enginemen and firemen of the Lilleshall Company over the question of workmen's allowance coal still continues and is in its third week. The hopefulness of last week's negotiations has not materialised and at present there seems to be a deadlock.

The continuance of the strike has caused a serious shortage locally. There is an acute shortage of coal in the district as all the collieries are closed down, and many families will experience great hardship as nearly all the wage earners are out of employment. It is sincerely hoped by everyone that negotiations will be immediately reopened and an amicable settlement made and thus bring to an end one of the most serious strikes that has taken place in the locality. The firm of John Maddock and Co. Ltd., Great Western Works, Oakengates, have had to put their workmen on short time owing o the lack of fuel, which is usually obtained from the Lilleshall Company's collieries.

The strike was finally settled after four weeks on 11 February, 1920 and the managing director reported this to a Board meeting held on that day.

1926

The General Strike started on Tuesday, 4 May 1926 and was called off on Wednesday, 12 May. The national effects are generally well known, but the local effects here were reported in the *collision happened between two locomotive engines belonging to the Lilleshall company; a truck was between them, which was smashed to pieces, but fortunately no loss of life ensued.*

Len Jones recalls one incident just prior to his joining the Company in 1949, when a bogie bolster wagon that had been placed at the entrance to the New Yard Engineering Works was not sufficiently braked. These wagons had only one brake wheel, and this was evidently on the 'wrong' side of the wagon for the person responsible to be bothered about applying it. Steel girders had been loaded on the wagon. From its position at New Yard, the line drops away towards the site of the Lodge Tip (formerly Furnaces). Inevitably, the wagon moved off slowly at first, across the points giving access to the Company 'main line' which had been left open in its favour and gradually accelerated towards the Lodge.

At the Lodge a locomotive taking on water and coal was standing with its cab towards the approaching wagon. Fortunately for the locomotive man, he was concentrating on the fire of his locomotive and so never saw the impending impact. The wagon hit the locomotive with such force that the steel girder was launched from its position on the wagon, straight between the legs of the engineman and into the firebox, completely wrecking the boiler. The engineman, astonishingly, was relatively unhurt but not so the locomotive. This was apparently never repaired. From the circumstantial dates, the locomotive involved must have been either Company built No.2 or No.7, both of which disappeared around 1948. Evidently the practice of coaling from a wagon brought from Granville pit to this site had continued after the National Coal Board vesting day of 1 January 1947.

There are several legends of suicides occurring on the line, but the only verifiable one happened on 14 April, 1950 and was reported in the Wellington Journal and Shropshire News of 22 April, following the inevitable request. Fifty-eight year old Stanley Ernest Airey had been having mental problems arising from his domestic situation and on this day had been drinking heavily in the Fighting Cocks pub and the Caledonian Hotel, both in Oakengates. A friend tried to console him, and took him for some fish and chips at nearby Owen's chip shop, but he became agitated and ran off, shouting that he was going to 'do himself in' at Dark Lane. A little while later, just beyond Maddock's Pool, Oakengates a Lilleshall train was approaching at around ten miles per hour, with shunter Leonard Jones riding on the footplate. He saw a man walking alongside the track, until they were about four or five yards away, when he half turned and appeared to kneel on the track right in front of the engine. Jones shouted to the driver, John Thomas Pritchard, who immediately applied the brakes. However, the train took about 100 feet to stop as it was hauling three wagons loaded with steel. The man had been killed instantly.

Ex-GWR 0-6-2T No.5 at work in the yards at Priorslee, some time between 1933 and 1939. [C. E. G. Budd/ Ironbridge Gorge Museum Trust]

Final Railtour

A final railtour, just ahead of the complete closure of the rail system, was made on 26 September 1958. Passengers were carried in three open 10 ton wooden bodied wagons, hauled by Barclay 0-4-0ST ALBERTA. The tour commenced at Priorslee Furnaces, and proceeded via Snedshill and The Nabb to the New Yard Engineering Works. After taking water there, it continued on to the sidings at the Rookery, where ALBERTA round round its train. Consequently, the tour did not embrace all of the then existing system, as it did not visit the Oakengates and Hollinswood exchange sidings.

On the footplate of the locomotive were the driver, J. Beddall of Hayward Avenue, Donnington, foreman A. Ashton and brakesman H. Davies. On the return from the New Yard, the Company Managing Director, E. Bruce Ball took over the regulator.

Lasting Reminders

The Severn Valley Railway is host to the immaculately restored GWR Collett 'Manor' 4-6-0 7802 BRADLEY MANOR. Close examination will reward the enthusiast with a glimpse of the Company's past, for the vertical part of the running plate, from over the cylinders to the cab, is manufactured from 'Lilleshall Steel' (actually only rolled at the Company). This name is embossed into the steel plate forming this component of the locomotive.

Another reminder exists in Oakengates. The wrought iron girder bridge carrying the Wolverhampton to Wellington line, over the junction of Bridge Street and Church Street, was originally supplied for the Shrewsbury and Birmingham Railway by the Company. A plate recording its manufacture is still plainly visible stating: LILLESHALL COMPANY FECT. 1848.

Beehive-shaped crossing keeper's hut at the Rookery, one of the few surviving by the 1950s. [Edgar Meeson]

NANTMAWR QUARRIES (1902)

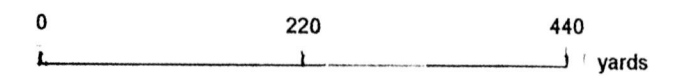

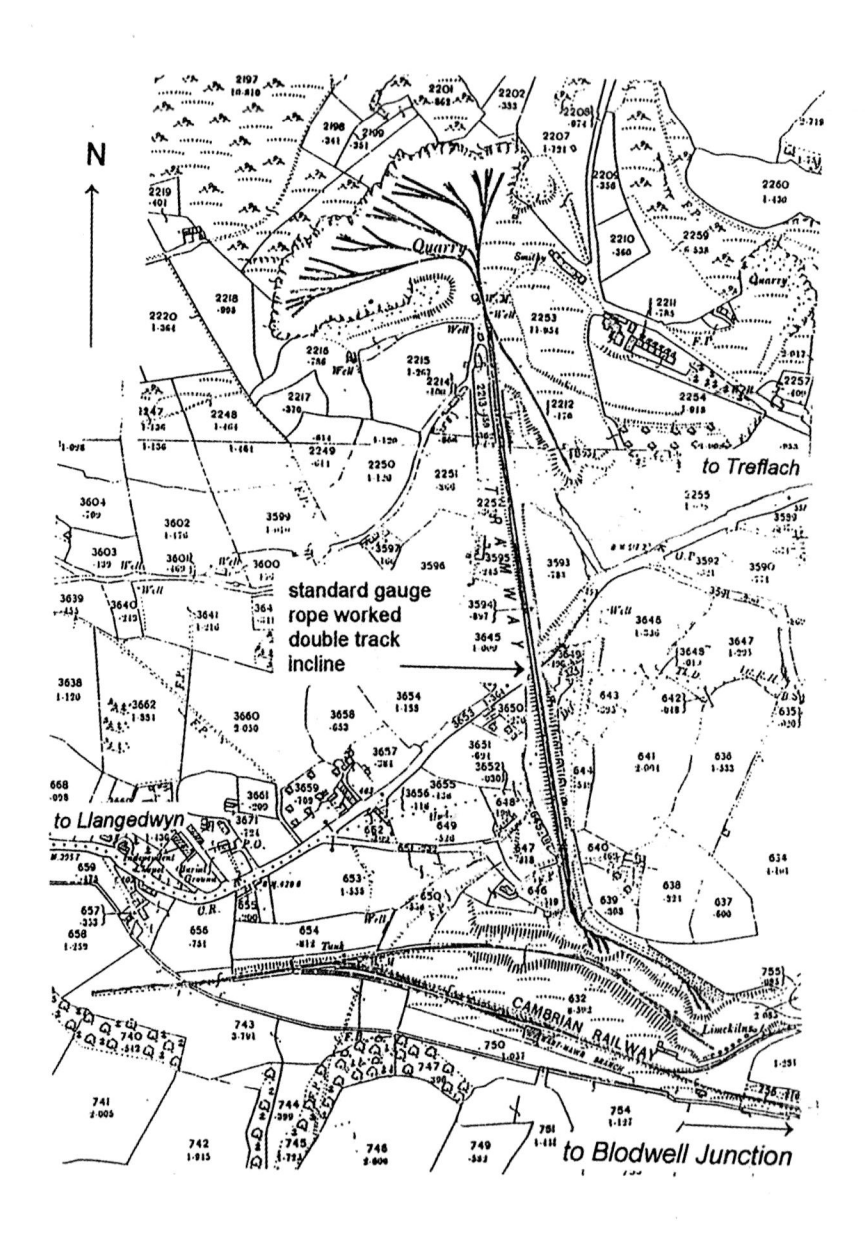

CHAPTER TEN
LIMESTONE QUARRIES

Although the various limestone workings detailed below did not form part of the Lilleshall Company's railway system, they did generate traffic that fed on to that system. These operations were researched in some detail to ascertain the extent of their own internal railway systems, and whether or not they may have used Lilleshall-built locomotives. Regrettably, none were found to have used any Company locomotives. Nonetheless, details of these operations are included for the sake of completeness, and to further illustrate the extent of the Company's self sufficiency.

Lilleshall village

Limestone had been quarried and kilns established here by a variety of persons using leases from the Leveson-Gower family from the 16th century. However, the family business became involved during the 18th century; certainly by 1767 it was operating its own quarries and kilns. Some time after 1860 this quarry became flooded and was abandoned. None of the limestone quarries in this area were rail connected. Instead, they were either served by short tramways to nearby canal wharves, or directly by local canals, and thence to the company furnaces.

Church Aston (near Newport)

Limestone also quarried in this area from the 16th century on the same basis as above. In 1880 the Company employed thirty men here, who produced 7,000 tons annually, but by 1882 all activity had ceased. It would appear that limestone from the Presthope and Nantmawr quarries was of a much better quality, as well as being in much greater abundance. Once again, there was no direct rail access to the quarry, the local canals providing adequate direct routes to the various furnaces.

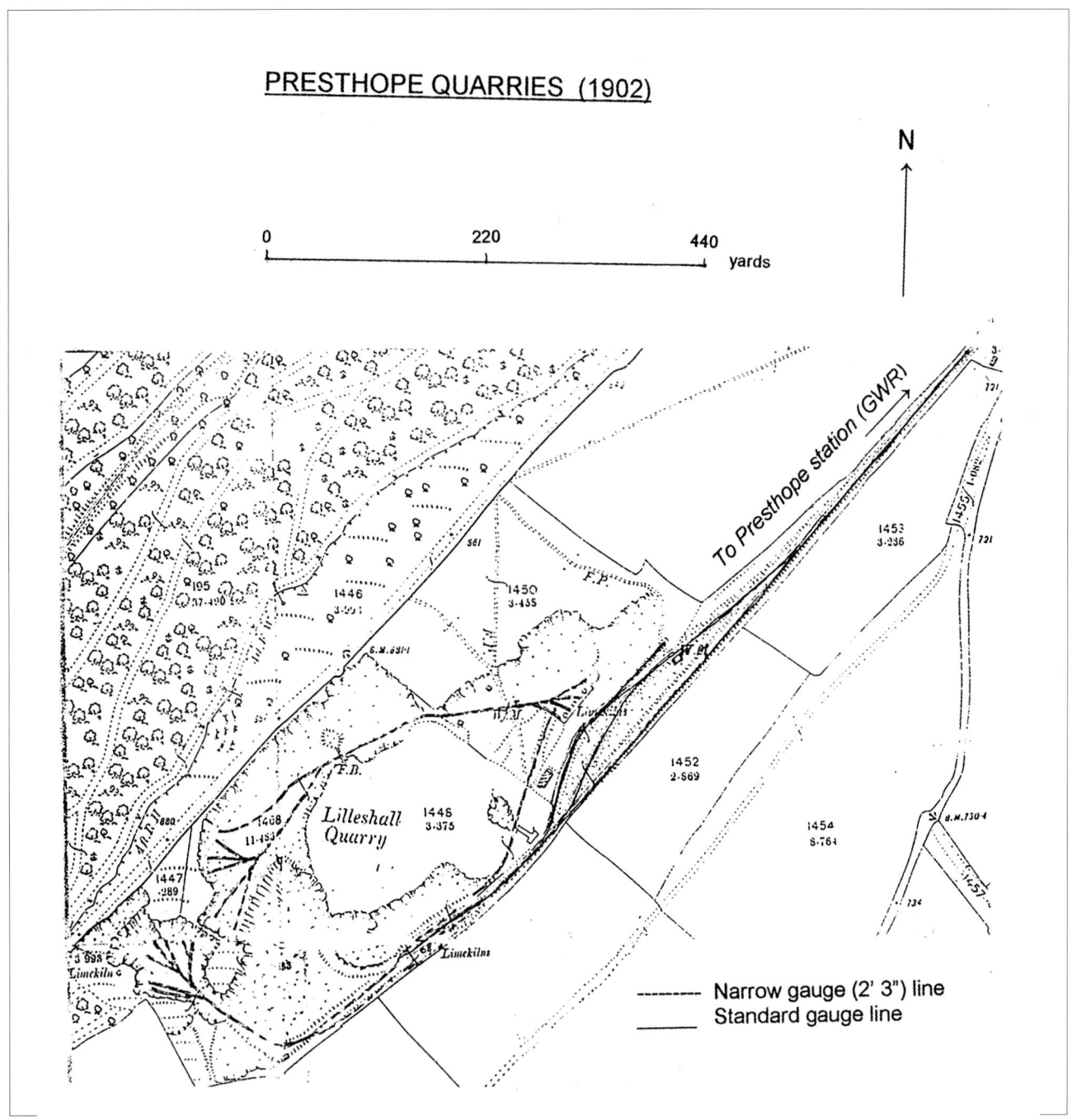

Following the closure of the Lilleshall village quarries, alternative supplies were obtained from the Llangollen Lime and Fluxing Stone Company Limited. These were shipped via the Shropshire Union Canal to the Lubstree Wharf, where they were transhipped into railway wagons for the journey along the Company's Humber Arm railway and then via their main line to the Lodge Furnaces and to the Snedshill and Priorslee Furnaces. However, although this source became secondary, as the company embarked upon further quarry activities as detailed below, a new agreement was signed for the supply of fluxing stone from Llangollen as late as 27 September 1895.

Nantmawr (near Oswestry)
Quarries were leased for fifty years here firstly by Richard Samuel France from the Earl of Powis on 25 December 1869, this lease being subsequently taken over by Mr John Parson Smith. An agreement dated 24 July 1885 between Smith and the Cambrian Railways provided for the restoration of the Nantmawr branch, whose permanent way had apparently become somewhat dilapidated. He agreed to pay £800 towards the costs of restoration, and a traffic charge of 3d. per ton on all goods carried over the line (i.e. in both directions from Llanymynech to Nantmawr) to offset the costs of maintenance of the track.

Limestone was extracted and transported down a double track standard gauge rope worked incline from the quarry faces to the kilns, where after firing it was transhipped to the branch line for the trip to Llanymynech. From here the journey onwards was via the Cambrian Railways main line to Welshpool, and thence via the LNWR/GWR joint lines to Shrewsbury and Wellington, finally reaching the GWR exchange sidings at Hollinswood. The Nantmawr branch line had originally been built by the Potteries, Shrewsbury and North Wales Railway (PSNWR) opening on 13 August 1866 but was closed at the same time as the 'main line' of the PSNWR in June 1880. In January, 1881 the Cambrian Railways leased the Nantmawr branch and continued to work the line, even after the short-lived Shropshire Railway had purchased the old PSNWR (including the Nantmawr branch) in 1888. The initial annual rental of £555 had risen to £886 by 1939, as the branch remained in the official ownership of the Shropshire Railway after the entire railway was put into receivership on 11 November 1891 (where it remained) right through to nationalisation in 1948. However, the opening of the nominally independent Tanat Valley Railway on 5 January 1904 entailed new construction from the Porthywaen branch through to Llanginog, to which the Nantmawr branch was joined just east of Blodwell Junction. Thus, northbound trains from Nantmawr could now eliminate the circuitous route southwards to join the Cambrian main line south of Llanymynech. Nonetheless, although the journey was shortened, this now entailed a reversal outside Blodwell Junction in order to gain the direct northbound line past the Porthywaen and Whitehaven Hill quarry branches.

Board minutes note that the lease of the quarry was assigned to the Company on 28 December 1899. In anticipation of this transfer, John Parson Smith (or more likely, the Company) had arranged a new agreement with the Cambrian Railways, dated 15 November 1899, whereby the tonnage rate would be reduced from 3d. to 2d. However, the opening of the Tanat Valley Railway gave the Company further reason to request a reduction in this charge, as they not unreasonably pointed out that their traffic was no longer the sole user of the line, running all the way round from Llanymynech, but was a common user of the line to Blodwell, and only from there to Nantmawr used the line exclusively. The correspondence relating to these negotiations continued for the best part of 1904, and latterly the Company pointed out that they could obtain their limestone requirements from the Froghall quarries in North Staffordshire. The Cambrian Railways were most put out that the Company should use this threat to move their sources elsewhere, as a lever in their bargaining position. The Company was immediately at some pains to deny that this was ever intended as a threat. But it most certainly was. Eventually, the Cambrian Railways agreed in a letter dated 10 April 1905, that the rate should be reduced to 1½d. per ton, with an allowance of 2 cwts per truck for 'wastage' (i.e. seepage) as long as the Company agreed not to obtain lime from Froghall. But this is exactly what they eventually did do, for with the changing demands for lime, it became more economic not to engage in quarrying operations of their own.

On 13 April 1911 Colonel H.F. Stephens reopened the former Shropshire Railway (one-time PSNWR) from Llanymynech to Shrewsbury, now rejoicing in the name of the Shropshire and Montgomeryshire Railway (SMR). During 1919 he twice contacted the Company in an attempt to gain traffic for the SMR. Finally, in May of that year the Lilleshall directors agreed to allow Colonel Stephens to examine the books of the Nantmawr quarry to determine whether he could compete with their present arrangements for the transport of limestone. The records are silent as to the outcome, but other evidence survives that at least part of this traffic was awarded to the SMR. Such traffic then eliminated the reversals in Llanymynech and Welshpool, travelling directly from Nantmawr via Llanymynech to Potteries Junction, Shrewsbury, where it joined the joint line to Wellington. After closure of the SMR, such rail traffic reverted to the route via Welshpool, Shrewsbury and Wellington.

The quarry lines were laid out in standard gauge, to feed the rope worked double track compensating incline, which fed the crushing plant and lime burning kilns situated adjacent to the Cambrian Railways branch. No evidence has come to light that locomotives were used in the quarry system, and so the inference is that horses were used to move the wagons to the incline head, as even seven ton wagons would have been beyond the use of manpower on a regular basis. The incline itself is still in situ, bridging one of the small lanes in the area and providing an interesting reminder of the industrial past of this locality.

The Company's lease of the Nantmawr quarry was renegotiated as from 25 December 1919 for a further period of twenty-five years, with contract breaks every five years requiring six months notice by either party. This new lease was sealed on 2 September 1920.

It appears that all was not well at the quarry by 1927, as the amount of limestone taken by the Company was insufficient to keep the quarry in full production. As we have seen, the production of steel ceased in 1925 and pig iron production was considerably reduced from this time. At a board meeting on 29 February 1927, the Lilleshall Managing Director stated that 'the attempt to work the quarries and lime kilns *(at Nantmawr)* had resulted in an increased loss owing mainly to the lack of demand, though strenuous efforts had been made to obtain orders. It was resolved that the quarries and kilns be closed down.' The Company's Annual Inventory disclosed a total value of stocks at Nantmawr on 30 June, 1926 of £1,165-9s.-3d. A year later this value had reduced to £685-2s.-5d., at which level it stood for a further year; a further year on this value was given as 'nil'. The implication is that production ceased prior to 30 June 1927 and the remaining stocks took over a year to clear.

The Company's direct involvement with Nantmawr ceased with a report at the Board Meeting of 3 May 1929 that the quarries and limeworks had been sold for £5,000 to the Chirk Castle Lime & Stone Co. Ltd., including leasehold interest, railways, incline and all plant and machinery. However, photographic evidence suggests that the Company continued to source some of its limestone requirements from Nantmawr at least until 1934.

Presthope (near Much Wenlock)
In 1862, Moses George Benson of Lutwyche Hall leased a parcel of land totalling some 28 acres to the Company.

The terms of the lease specified an annual rental of £500 per annum, with additional royalties of 4d. per 2,640lbs of limestone extracted, and 12d per cartload (56 bushels) of burnt lime produced. A single line railway with a total length of 69 chains and 35 links (a little over 1,500 yards) was constructed by the Company to link the quarry to the GWR's Wenlock Railway then under construction. It is presumed that the Resident Engineer for this line, Joseph Fogerty, was responsible for the construction of the quarry line. The line ran uphill from the GWR exchange sidings at Presthope along the side of the Wenlock Edge at a gradient of 1 in 76 for the first 17 chains, then at 1 in 129 for the next 11 chains, during which the line crossed two minor lanes on the level. For the final 41 chains, the line ascended at 1 in 49. Thus the gradients favoured loaded trains from the quarry to the exchange sidings. There was a slight curve between the two road crossings, otherwise the line was completely straight. The total length of the standard gauge line, including runround loops was given in the 1876 Company Valuation as 1,708 yards, with a value at that time of £1,100-4s-0d. The lease was renewed by the Company in 1896 for a further 14 years, at the very much reduced rate of £200 rent per annum, although the royalties remained unchanged.

As can be seen from the plan, there was a double runround loop at the quarry terminus of the line. At the Presthope end, there was a storage siding, and a runround loop giving access to the main line. GWR locomotives provided the motive power along the quarry line from the outset, this being operated on the 'one engine in steam' principle. The GWR Working Timetable specifically states that 'no two engines are permitted in the sidings *(sic)* at any one time'.

A narrow gauge system served the quarry faces and the running kilns. It is likely that the standard Shropshire tramway gauge of 2ft 3in was used for this system, as the 1876 Company Valuation describes the lines as being '810 yards of tramroads with wood sleepers, one yard apart in quarry and on kiln bank, with wrought iron bridge rails. (value £141-15s-0d.)'. The tubs were hauled by horses from the quarry faces to the kilns, but manually powered barrows seem to have been the main form of transport around the kiln areas. Reference to the 1876 Company Valuation again tells us that there were:

'3 coal tipping wagons
16 limestone wagons
12 limestone barrows
6 lime barrows'

In addition, there was a 15 ton weighbridge, which is thought to have been located on the standard gauge line.

There were two sets of lime kilns, the larger kilnbank comprising four running kilns of some 60 feet in height, and the smaller bank of six pot kilns of around twelve feet in height near to the headshunt of the standard gauge line.

The line from Presthope to Much Wenlock opened for mineral traffic only on 5 December, 1864. So it is presumed that the quarry had not been operational prior to this date, as there was no other means of hauling the lime or limestone out from the quarry. Certainly, by 1864 there were two goods trains booked to arrive on weekdays at Presthope: at 1.30pm (from Buildwas), and at 5.05pm (from Much Wenlock). These returned at 2.00pm and 5.30pm, both running through to Buildwas. Later, the 1869 Working Timetable shows a daily train departing from Hollinswood at 11.40am and travelling via Madeley Junction to arrive at the quarry at 2.15pm. This train presumably carried coal for the kilns, as well as returning the empty lime wagons, which for many years were of 8 ton capacity. The return working left the quarry at 2.20pm, arriving back at Hollinswood at 4.20pm. The five minute turn around at the quarry seems a little sharp, and presumably reflects the use of horses for shunting after the GWR train had departed. The timing had changed a little by 1898, when the outward train left Hollinswood at 12.05pm, again via Madeley Junction, arriving at 2.50pm. The return working left at 3.00pm (thus doubling the turn around time at the quarry!) but travelled back via Ketley to arrive in Wellington at 6.00pm. Lime for Hollinswood was worked forward on the next available trip working.

Production of lime had reached around 1,000 tons per week by 1900, but that seems to have been the height of production. It was agreed at the Board Meeting of 22 December 1910 that the lease should be renewed for a further seven years at a further reduced annual rental of £140. The conclusion is that the productivity of the quarry and limeworks was being called into question at that time. The next Board Meeting, on 27 January 1911 confirmed that the lease had been renewed as agreed. The malign influence of the First World War was almost certainly behind the decision at a Board Meeting on 29 January 1915 that 'the lease would be surrendered on 25 March 1916 and that due notice was ordered to be given to the lessor'. There is a distinct possibility that the lack of available manpower at this time hastened the closure of this operation.

Motive power on the branch line for the limestone traffic was invariably a Dean 0-6-0ST (most of which were rebuilt as pannier tanks) of either the '45', '655' or '2021' classes, supplied by Wellington shed or its sub-shed at Much Wenlock.

The standard gauge line from the quarry to Presthope was lifted, it is believed, during 1917 in order to assist with the requirement for steel for the war effort. Subsequently, a new quarry was operated for a number of years from 1926 by Knowle Lime Ltd., linked by a narrow gauge tramway to the truncated remains of the original quarry line. This company also operated another nearby quarry, at Westwood, until after the Second World War.

Hunslet 18in 0-6-0ST No.3 (3789 of 1953) stands between duties outside the running shed at Granville Colliery on a very hot 21 August 1967. It had only arrived some two months earlier from Cannock Wood Colliery, and was in superb condition. [Allan C. Baker]

Hunslet 18in 0-6-0ST No.8 (3776 of 1952) shunting empty hopper wagons in the upper yard at Granville Colliery on 20 March, 1969. [Allan C. Baker]

CHAPTER ELEVEN
THE COLLIERIES UNDER NCB OWNERSHIP

Upon nationalisation of the coal industry on 1 January, 1947 the Company's surviving Grange and Granville Collieries were initially placed in the NCB's Area No.3 (South Staffordshire) of the West Midlands Division. From 1 June, 1962 this became part of the Area No.2, which was retitled the Cannock, South Staffs & Shropshire Area. A further reorganisation occurred as from 26 March, 1967 when these collieries were placed in a newly formed Staffordshire Area. Finally, the Staffordshire Area amalgamated with the North Western Area as from 1 April, 1974 to form a new Western Area.

Grange Colliery
As mentioned earlier, Grange Colliery (located at grid reference SJ 721115) was connected underground to Granville, this work being completed in April, 1952. Thereafter, Grange effectively ceased to operate as a separate colliery, although the shafts were retained for pumping and ventilation until the closure of Granville. Thus all mining activity and the related rail traffic was concentrated at Granville for the most part of the NCB ownership.

The attached map (page 105), dating from 1954 shows the rail connections to the screens still in place, and these must surely have been retained for several years, in case of any problems arising at Granville. It is not known when these were removed, although they had certainly gone by the early 1970's. The pithead winding gear still remains, however, as a local landmark and part of a commercial site. Many persons visiting the nearby council refuse site mistakenly believe this to be part of the Granville Colliery buildings.

The rail exit from Grange Colliery originally went directly into the Lodge Furnaces. Later, a connection was made to the 'main line' towards Oakengates. However, this still meant that any traffic that was bound for the exchange sidings at Donnington had to reverse at this point. The angle of the Grange line was such that it was not possible to put in pointwork to give direct access to the Granville sidings. This inconvenience must have been at least one of the reasons for the decision to link the two pits underground.

Granville Colliery
The colliery was located at grid reference SJ 727120. Output from the mine arrived in narrow gauge (2ft 3in) tubs at the pithead, where a hydraulic ram pushed the tub out of the cage, and sent it running by gravity down to the rotary tippler. Here, a 'banksman' braked the tub, using the time honoured method of a shunting pole through the spokes of the tub's wheels. The tippler rotated the tub, so that the contents were discharged into the washery, and the tub then continued its journey by gravity round a curve. It was finally moved into position for returning underground by the arrival of the next tub behind it.

There were various other narrow gauge lines connecting the pithead to the stores, engineering workshops, etc. and originally to the spoil heap on the north western side of the mine. It is interesting to reflect that the traditional Shropshire gauge for tramways from a very early time had been 2ft 3in, and that its use was perpetuated at Granville, not only on the surface, but underground too. Although there were latterly several small flameproof battery electric locomotives employed underground, none are believed to have been used on these surface lines. However, they did come to the surface for occasional

This 18in Hunslet 0-6-0ST was built in 1943 (works number 2895) and originally supplied to the War Department. It arrived at Granville still bearing its WD number, 75046, around the middle of 1947. Subsequently it bore no running number. It is shunting an internal user wagon in Granville Colliery sidings on 20 March, 1969 after it had been fitted with a Giesl oblong ejector. [Allan C. Baker]

Hudswell Clarke 0-6-0ST THE COLONEL (1073/1914) at Granville Colliery around 1964. [F. Jones]

Hunslet 0-6-0ST HOLLY BANK No.3 (1451/1924) in the colliery sidings at Granville during 1966. It appears to have lost its nameplate by this time. [F. Jones]

Hunslet 0-6-0ST GRANVILLE No.5 (3771/1952) poses in the Granville exchange sidings some time in the late 1950s, before it was fitted with a Giesl oblong ejector. [A. J. B. Dodd]

maintenance and so may have been used on these lines, if only when testing or running in after overhaul. The majority of the narrow gauge surface lines here linked the screens to the spoil heaps; being of 2ft 6in gauge they would not have been compatible.

In steam days, the engine arriving with a string of empties from Donnington exchange sidings would stop on the level just past the engine shed, and uncouple. The loco shunting Granville washery would take its place, and take the required number of wagons over the weighbridge road, then reverse back over the weighbridge, weighing each one in turn. When complete it would then be positioned so as to get a good push up the gradient to the washery road. Here the empty wagons would be labelled as to the required grades of coal, and then pass singly over the traverser at the rear of the washery. They would be routed to one of the three lines under the screens for filling with the grade of coal that they had been designated. These wagons were under the charge of shunters who controlled them in rakes by gravity and the judicious use of their shunting sticks into the 'full' siding.

When sufficient wagons had accumulated here they were taken back down to the weighbridge, for weighing in their 'full' capacity, then stabled until a trainload was ready for taking down to Donnington. Any wagons that had previously contained slack were either limited to being refilled with slack, or were washed out, as otherwise customers complained about getting excessive amounts of slack in their consignments. Any wagons that had been in common usage on the main line would be examined, as these often contained remnants of scrap metal that required to be removed. A similar procedure was adopted in diesel days, except that the loco arriving from Donnington would be employed to propel the wagons to the washery.

Spoil continued under the NCB to be deposited on the heap on the northwestern side of the mine, but during the 1960s this practice was gradually discontinued. Instead, a heavily reinforced concrete roadway was laid from the washery down to the site of the former Lodge Furnaces, near to Rookery Road. Thereafter, massive Euclid earth moving trucks were used to transport the rocks and other debris from the screens and washery for dumping at this site. There was also a landsale yard adjacent to the spoil dump at the Rookery. This was used by local coal merchants, until the landsale yard was opened adjacent to the Wellington Road crossing in Donnington.

The line to the landsale yard turned northwards off the original 'main line' to Oakengates, which remained in situ until the closure of the Company's railway in 1959. Right up until this time, the Company had running powers (granted under the nationalisation agreement) through to the exchange sidings at Donnington. It seems unlikely that these powers were ever used, although it has been recalled that occasionally steel wagons for the Company turned up in the exchange sidings at Donnington. There was a certain amount of exchange traffic in coal being sent from Granville to the Priorslee Furnaces and to the New Yard Engineering Works. Generally, such traffic was exchanged in the sidings adjacent to the Rookery, but on occasions it is recalled that NCB locos took coal down into the New Yard Works. It is therefore likely that any steel wagons would have been worked through on the same basis.

Donnington to Granville
The exchange sidings at Donnington were somewhat simplified around 1970, with the introduction of block trains for power stations and diesel traction, as the accompanying maps reveal. This also coincided with the removal of track from the Stafford-Donnington BR line, which had closed to all traffic in August 1966 and the singling of the Wellington-Donnington section in 1971. The lines connecting to C.&W. Walker Ltd. at their nearby Midland Ironworks had been removed in the late 1950s after they had ceased using rail traffic.

The line to Granville and the exchange sidings were situated on a sharp curve ending in a south-easterly direction, then immediately passed over Wellington Road on a gated level crossing, followed shortly afterwards by a further gated crossing over School Road. Thus the length of trains was limited by the distance between these two crossings, because the crossing attendant had to open one gate to allow the train into this section, then close this gate and walk to the other end of the train and open the other gate. This practice was adopted regardless of the direction of travel at this time. The section could only accommodate thirty wagons of the old 16 ton or 20 ton steel and wooden bodied type, plus the engine. With the introduction of the 27 ton air-braked 'merry-go-round' (MGR) wagons, these were, at first, brought down in rakes of 12 or 13, until working arrangements were changed to permit the through working of rakes of these wagons over both crossings. In this way, up to 20 wagons could now be handled on each train, although the diesels would often be double headed. There was a single (originally double) refuge siding on the south side of the Wellington Road crossing, which during NCB days continued to be used as an additional landsale yard. Slack for the Ordnance Depot at Donnington was loaded here by a local contractor (Billy Tar, of Dawley) who transported it to the Depot's main boiler house, which was locally known as the 'Queen Mary',

Barclay 0-4-0ST 2246 of 1948 was supplied new to the NCB at Granville colliery, but never received a running number. Here it is shunting a rake of wagons at the Granville landsale yard, around 1957. [A. J. B. Dodd]

Hunslet 0-6-0ST GRANVILLE No.5 (3771/52) stands in the Lodge Sidings at Granville colliery while a similar locomotive shunts spoil wagons, around 1960. At this time, it had not yet been fitted with the Giesl oblong ejector. [A.J.B. Dodd]

because of its four chimneys. Other grades were also sold here, such as Bakers Nuts, DS nuts, and improved slack. The landsale yard was serviced by special workings from Granville.

The line then climbed steeply up to the site of Muxtonbridge Colliery, where there were two headshunts, and all trains reversed direction. The NCB locomotive practice was the reverse of the Lilleshall Company practice, in that it was usual to have the locomotive propelling empty trains from Donnington to this point, from where they would be hauling the trains up to Granville sidings. Loaded trains would have the locomotive at the rear of the train down to Muxtonbridge, then at the front for the journey past the level crossings, so as to protect against individual runaway wagons and to provide the maximum amount of braking power over this crucial section.

Around 1956, the line was reconstructed to eliminate the reversal at Muxtonbridge, and this can be seen on the accompanying maps. This also had the effect of reducing the distance from Donnington to the Granville sidings adjacent to the engine shed (just over two miles) by about 600 yards. Thereafter, the northernmost line to Muxtonbridge was taken up, and the southernmost line was used for wagon storage. At this time, the line into the former Shepherd slag crushing works was also removed. In the immediate years following nationalisation, traffic from this plant, which recycled the mine spoils and the former Lodge Furnace slag heaps, had been sufficient to require separate workings down to the Donnington exchange sidings. This line had been considerably simplified over the years and immediately prior to removal only consisted of a single line dividing into two sidings. The plant continued to function into the 1970s, albeit on a much reduced scale and utilising road transport.

With the advent of the new direct line working practices were again revised so that all trains were worked with the locomotive at the head of the train. Full trains were assembled in the yard at Granville, and the shunters pinned down the brakes of sufficient wagons until the driver was confident that he had adequate braking power. However, there was a notable runaway of a full train some time after 1974, when one of the diesels was unable to control the train, which became derailed on the curve near to the site of the old Freehold Colliery. A steam crane was called out from Bescot BR shed, and took a week to clear the debris, during which time the colliery was closed as the output could not be despatched. The track was eventually relaid by Grant Lyon Eagre from Cardiff.

Working the Line
Little was wasted from Granville Colliery; besides the recycling of the

An unidentified Hunslet 0-6-0ST propels wagons at the Lodge Tip during the late 1950s. [A. J. B. Dodd]

Gangers are re-laying some of the sidings at the Lodge Tip, as Hunslet 0-6-0ST GRANVILLE No.5 busies itself in the background. [A. J. B. Dodd]

Hunslet 0-6-0ST No.8 (3776/1952) pounds up the grade near Muxtonbridge with a mixture of 16, 20 and 21 ton empty mineral wagons bound for Granville Colliery in the mid-1960s. [Ironbridge Gorge Museum Trust]

GRANVILLE COLLIERY (1954)

0 — 220 — 440 yards

N

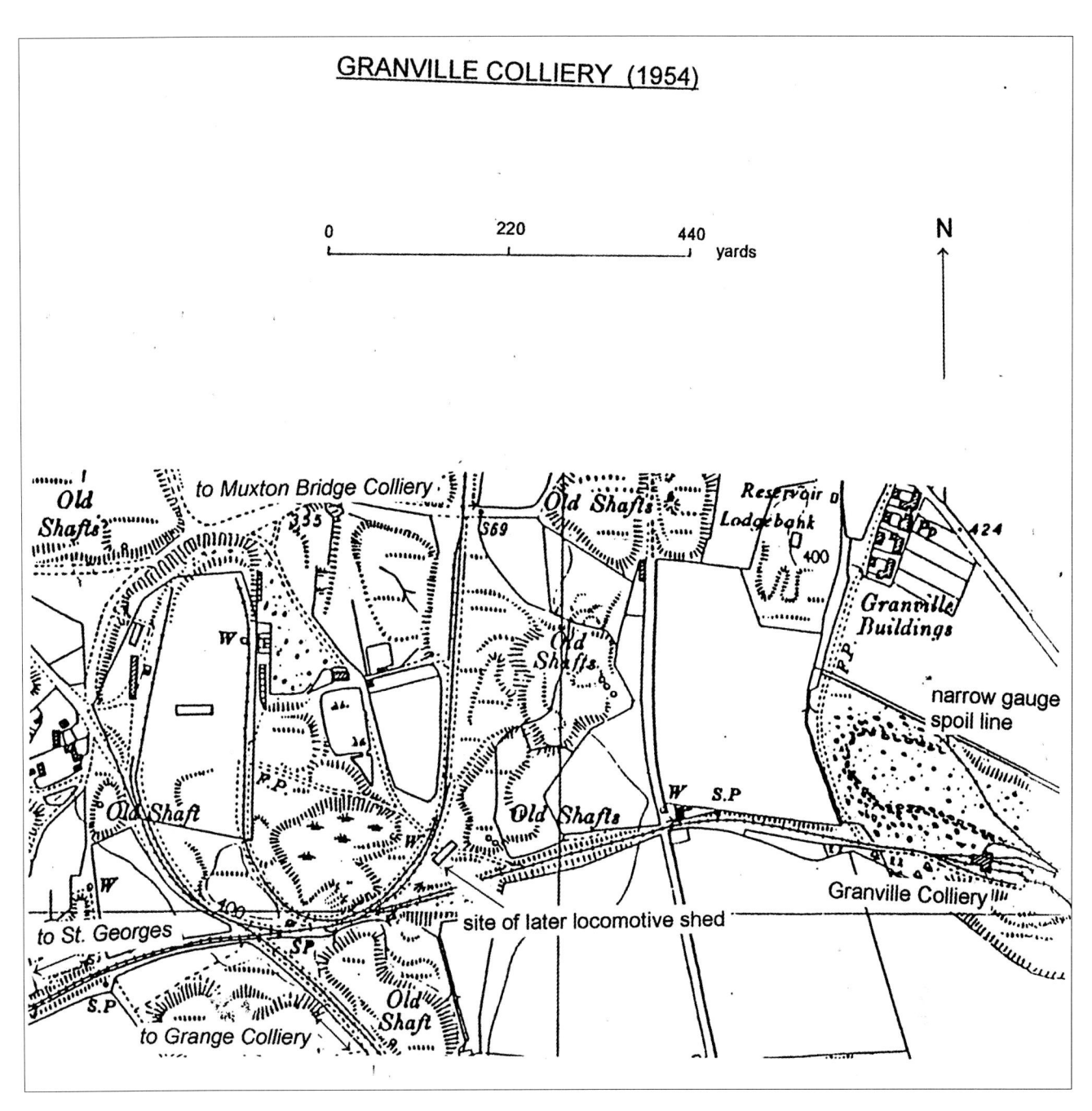

Map labels:
- Old Shafts
- to Muxton Bridge Colliery
- Old Shafts
- Reservoir Lodgebank
- Granville Buildings
- narrow gauge spoil line
- Old Shafts
- Old Shaft
- Granville Colliery
- site of later locomotive shed
- to St. Georges
- to Grange Colliery
- Old Shaft

Hunslet 16" 0-6-0ST HOLLY BANK No.3 shunts 21 ton hopper wagons at Granville Colliery around 1967. [P. ward]

Top. A study of Hudswell Clarke THE COLONEL, paused during shunting operations adjacent to the weighbridge, at Granville Colliery around 1966. [P. Ward]

Middle. GRANVILLE No.5 heads through the countryside near to the site of Muxtonbridge Colliery with empties to Granville Colliery around 1969. [P. Ward]

Bottom. A charming study of Hunslet 0-6-0ST HOLLY BANK No.3 in high summer at Granville colliery, probably during 1967. [P. Ward]

rocks from the mine spoil, the main line was ballasted using red shale produced by the washery and the sidings used ash from the colliery boilers and locomotives. However, the sidings often became covered in slack dust from passing wagons, sometimes up to rail level. In wet weather, the area around the washery became the morass so familiar to those readers who have ventured into such areas at collieries all over the world. In the later NCB days the main line from the engine shed to Donnington was properly ballasted (especially after the major accident) for it was recognised that the increased weight of the MGR wagons required a more stable trackbed. Nonetheless, resleepering was limited to replacing one in three, even though many were rotten through. When replacement rails were required, the new rails were taken to the appropriate position by the simple expedient of dragging them behind the loco in the 'four-foot'.

Derailments were fairly commonplace and became part of the daily routine of the colliery line. Rerailing was generally achieved by packing and jacking, or by the use of shackles and snatch lines secured to a convenient nearby object, such as a tree, or other rail lines. But sometimes the wagons (especially internal user) were treated very roughly, being either towed by a loco and chain back on to the track, or pushed by a tractor or bulldozer into place.

During NCB days, only two locos were required at any one time. One for the trips to the exchange sidings at Donnington, and one shunting the washery, the upper landsale yard, and the storage sidings leading down to the old Muxtonbridge Colliery site. One shift was worked by two engine crews, normally 5.45am to 1.45pm, although these often extended until 4.00pm or 5.00pm. At 'peak' times an additional night shift was worked, with additional engine crews being rostered from the fitters and shunters. Such working was more the result of the necessity to clear traffic from the colliery sidings and exchange sidings, and not necessarily the result of coal production at the pit. Consequently, the shifts of the pitmen, including nightshifts, did not affect the operation of the railway.

Maintenance at the shed was limited to essential repairs, rather than any programmed maintenance schedule, other than boiler washouts. Such repairs often included rerolling the tube ends, which regularly became distorted, sometimes so much so, that water poured out like a fountain. Washouts were generally performed each weekend, when the engines were off duty. Engines were not kept in steam continuously, but had their fires dropped at the end of each day. An outside locomotive maintenance contractor (believed to have been M.A. Mudd of Stoke-on-Trent) was used for major repair work such as renewing boiler stays, rewheeling after tyre replacement, attention to hornguides, etc. To even out tyre wear, the steam locos were sent behind BR locos to Shrewsbury for turning on the triangle there.

None of the locos were assigned to specific duties but the 18in Hunslets were the obvious choice for working the trips to the exchange sidings, and the 16in Hunslet and Hudswell Clarke for the washery shunts. However, it is recalled that the Barclay 0-4-0ST was even used on one occasion for the trip to Donnington, even if it did not take a full load. The diesels in later years, being of identical power, were used on any duty.

The NCB drivers obviously did not undergo BR style training. As a result, most of them treated the reverser as a 'forward/reverse' control, and did not understand how to 'notch-up' through the reverser, to control the engine's performance. However, Peter Bushell had been trained on BR in the 1950s and treated his engines with more care. The arrival of the diesels did go some way to making an improvement, as intensive training was initially required to familiarise the running crews with their controls. After this time, shunters were rarely allowed to drive the modern traction.

Hunslet 0-6-0ST HOLLY BANK No.3 (1451/1924) receiving attention inside the shed at Granville Colliery on 21 August, 1967. [Allan C. Baker]

STANDARD GAUGE
0-6-2T   IC   VF   1442 1895

Under the terms of the nationalisation agreement, this locomotive was taken over from the Lilleshall Company along with the collieries on 1 January, 1947. At this time, it was still painted an overall mid-green colour, with no lining, and seems to have lost its original running number '3'. This locomotive does not appear to have seen much use by its new owners, and it is eminently possible that the Lilleshall Company selected this engine as being the one that they could do without the most, from its fleet of engines. By December, 1951 it was stored out of use, and was finally cut up on site by Cox & Danks Ltd., of Birmingham between November, 1953 and February, 1954.

The earlier history and dimensions of this locomotive may be found in the 'Lilleshall Company Locomotives' section.

(75046)   0-6-0ST   IC   HE   2895 1943

One of the Second World War 'Austerity' saddle tanks, based closely on the Hunslet '50550' class. The inside cylinders measured 18" x 26", the driving wheels were 4' 3" diameter, and weight was 48 tons. The tractive effort was 23,800lbs, and the wheelbase was 11' 0". Originally supplied new to the War Department, and delivered to the Longmoor Military Railway, Hampshire on 1 January, 1944. It does not appear to have seen much use there, as it was next noted in April of the same year at the Swindon Engineer Store Depot in Wiltshire. This depot had been erected on the site of the First World War Ministry of Munitions Stratton Filling Factory. It was noted as still at this location in March, 1945 and again in May, 1946. Purchased by the NCB, it was recorded at Reading GWR locomotive shed on 21 May, 1947 and first reported at Granville on 23 August, 1947. A popular engine, it latterly acquired an all over blue livery, but without any lining or running number, although it operated in its WD livery until it was repainted. It lasted until the end of steam on this system, finally being transported to John Cashmore Ltd., of Great Bridge, Staffs. for scrap in April, 1970.

0-4-0ST   OC   AB   2246 1948

Supplied new by Andrew Barclay in 1948. It was fitted with 16" x 24" cylinders, 3' 7" diameter wheels, with a wheelbase of 6' 0" and a tractive effort of 19,430 lbs. It was finished in a plain black livery, without lining, and never carried a running number. Rather too small for the intensive traffic from Donnington up to the Granville sidings, it was nevertheless a popular engine for the lighter duties to the Shepherds Hill Slag Crushing Plant, shunting the disposal site at the Rookery, taking a few wagons down to the landsale yard by the School Road crossing, and shunting the upper yards and colliery screens. It was scrapped on site between August, 1967 and March, 1968.

No.6   0-6-0ST   IC   Lill   1869

This came from the Lilleshall Company sometime between May and September, 1950. It was finished in a plain black livery, with no lining, but had previously carried the lettering 'Lilleshall Co. Ltd.', which was almost certainly removed by its new owners. The transfer of this engine at this time gives credence to the belief that the former Taff Vale Railway 0-6-2T above was found to have been something of a liability, and that this loco was supplied as a palliative. However, it too did not last long, being scrapped between August, 1955 and May, 1956, although it was admittedly 86 years old by this time! Again, the earlier history and leading dimensions may be found in the 'Lilleshall Company Locomotives ' section.

GRANVILLE No.5   0-6-0ST   IC   HE   3771 1952

Supplied new, the name reflects the fact that there were five locos at the colliery at the time of its delivery. The design was Hunslet's post-war development of the 'Austerity' design, which it followed very closely. It was equipped with the usual 18" x 26" cylinders and 4'3" wheels, weighing in at 48 tons. As far as is known, this loco carried a plain, unlined black livery for the whole of its life. It was a very strong locomotive, whose performance was enhanced by the fitting of a Giesl oblong ejector some time prior to 1969, and was particularly favoured for the climb up from Donnington. One of the last steam locos here, it was scrapped on site in April, 1970.

Hunslet 0-6-0ST No.8 (3776/52) at work in the sidings at Granville Colliery on 20 March, 1969. [Allan C. Baker]

Hunslet 0-6-0ST GRANVILLE No.5 restarts a train of empties, made up of wooden and steel bodied wagons, over the level crossing at Wellington Road, Donnington on a snowy day in the winter of 1968. The gasometer in the background was in the premises of the Midland Ironworks of C. &. W. Walker Co. Ltd., manufacturers of gasometers. [P. Ward]

Hunslet 0-6-0ST 3789 of 1953 on 27 August 1967. It carried 'No.3' but this disappeared following a repaint and afterwards it had no identification. [Allan C. Baker]

On the trips to Donnington, the crew would consist of the driver and fireman in steam days (only a driver required in diesel days), plus two shunters. In the early days, the shunters usually rode in the last wagon of the train. On the empties, they would lower the end door of the last wagon, so that when being propelled they had a fine view of the road ahead. When the brake vans were introduced, the shunters rode in these. At the Granville sidings, the shunters would pin down the brakes of the first six wagons, then the engine would couple up and take the slack out of the couplings. The shunters would then go along the wagons, pinning down the brakes of additional wagons until the driver was satisfied that the number pinned down had given him control of the train, as he otherwise only had his steam brake to rely upon. The driver would whistle when he reached this point, and the shunters would stop pinning down wagon brakes. The train would proceed down the grade to the School Road level crossing, where the shunters would release all of the wagon brakes, except for the two next to the engine, as the line was more or less level from thereon to the exchange sidings.

In a further change to Lilleshall Company practice, the 'Arm Road', (so called as this had previously led to the Humber Arm railway) was kept free for full wagons. The loco at the head would pull its train towards this road, then a shunter would uncouple the engine whilst on the move, the engine would accelerate into one of the other roads, and the points would be changed behind it for the wagons to go into the 'Arm Road'. The other shunter would uncouple the brake van (when used in later years), and controlling the brake, would switch this into another road, ready to be coupled up to the next load of empties to go up. Complications often arose when most of the roads were occupied by empties. In such cases, it was not unusual for a loco to work light down to Donnington, in order to clear the empties from the exchange roads. On the other hand, there were occasions when the loco had to wait for an incoming train from BR for another load of empties.

It was not unusual at many collieries for there to be internal passenger workings for the benefit of the pitmen going on shifts. However, there were no such workings here. The only other type of traffic other than coal was the occasional stores vans, but most types of stores, pit props, and so on came in by road during NCB days.

Andrew Barclay 0-4-0ST 2246 of 1948, out of use beside the locomotive shed at Granville on 21 August, 1967. [Allan C. Baker]

Wagon repairs were also the responsibility of an outside contractor (believed to have been from Cannock), who used the fitters' workshop facilities at Granville. However, the use of outside contractors ceased with the introduction of MGR wagons in the early 1970s.

A former Midland Railway 'Scenery Van' (designed to transport stage scenery for travelling theatrical companies) had originally been used as a tool van by the permanent way gang, and by the fitters when out on the line.

In the summer of 1968, No.8 is once again pictured at the Granville Colliery locomotive shed. Another, unidentified Hunslet can be seen in the left-hand shed road. [P. Ward]

The body of this van was subsequently removed from its wheels at an unknown date, and positioned adjacent to the locomotive shed, where it was afterwards used as a mess room and workshop. This van was subsequently donated to the Telford Horsehay Steam Trust, and is presently mounted on a six wheel underframe, and awaiting restoration. However, restoration may not be an easy task, as the wooden body has not only suffered from the effects of 20 years of British weather, but was damaged when being lifted. The van is believed to date from 1885, although despite considerable research the builder has not been determined.

The two brake vans that were introduced following the major derailment came from the NCB's Rawnsley Depot which served various collieries on the Cannock Chase. These are believed to have been built for the original Cannock & Rugeley Colliery Co. Ltd., but could also have been acquired second-hand from one of the main line companies. They featured single veranda ends. One of these has been acquired and restored by Reg Stanley, and is kept at Horsehay. It has been restored in grey livery, carrying the legend 'C.R.C. No.1' on one side and 'Granville Colliery' on the other. Considerable research has again failed to disclose its origins, although from its wooden chassis, and 'open' spokes, it is believed to date from at least 1880. The other brake van, which carried the running number 'C.R.C. No.4' was scrapped along with many of the internal user wagons when Granville closed in 1979.

A final vehicle from Granville has also been restored at Horsehay, being one of the internal user standard 5-plank 10 ton open wagons. This was built by Charles Roberts of Horbury, West Yorkshire, and is presently sporting the lively red livery of Spillers pet foods. Unusually, it has been fitted at some point in time with Southern Railway axlebox covers.

The internal user wagons were all wooden bodied and were used for the transfer of coal to the two landsale yards, which included bagging of some grades of coal at the screens for certain customers. When the landsale yards closed, the wagons were piled into one great heap and set on fire. When the wood had burned away, a firm of scrap metal merchants took away all that they wanted.

Hunslet 325 hp 0-6-0DM No.1D (6663/1969) arrives at Granville Colliery with a load of empties from the Donnington exchange sidings in the snows of 6 January 1970. [Allan C. Baker]

Diesel No.2D (Hunslet 6664/1969) passing loaded wagons over the weighbridge at Granville on 6 January 1970. The locomotive shed can be seen on the left. [Allan C. Baker]

THE COLONEL   0-6-0ST   IC   HC   1073 1914
The inside cylinders measured 16" (later 16¼") x 22", wheels were 3' 10" diameter, and the laden weight was 40 tons. The wheelbase was 11' 0" and the tractive effort was 18,000lbs. The order for this locomotive was placed by Houghton Main Colliery Co. Ltd., Yorkshire on behalf of William Harrison Ltd., of Brownhills, Staffordshire. It was delivered on 22 June, 1914 to their locomotive shed at Grove Colliery for use on their system, linking this, and their various pits at Brownhills, to the LNWR exchange sidings and canal wharves. It passed to the NCB on Vesting Day, 1 January, 1947 and remained at Grove Colliery shed until some time between May, 1960 and June, 1961 when it was sent to the Cannock Central Workshops at Chase Terrace for a major overhaul. This was completed by 11 July, 1963 when it was sent to nearby Coppice Colliery, at Norton Canes. However, rail traffic ceased here very shortly afterwards, on 27 September, 1963 and so it was moved to Granville on 17 October, 1963. In its later years, it wore an attractive livery of royal blue, lined out in pale blue. Peter Harris recalls that it had a patch under the boiler, near to the firebox, and was constantly leaking water. On one occasion, the boiler inspector was due to visit, so Peter added a bag of bran to the water, which effected a convincing temporary seal, and the boiler passed its test! However, it was scrapped on site between October, 1966 and March, 1967.

HOLLY BANK No.3   0-6-0ST   IC   HE   1451 1924
This locomotive had 16" x 22" cylinders and wheels of 3' 9" diameter. The livery was royal blue with pale blue lining. It was delivered on 15 May, 1924 to the Holly Bank Coal Co. Ltd. at their locomotive shed adjoining Holly Bank Colliery, although it was purchased to work the line from their newly opened Hilton Main Colliery to the LNWR exchange sidings. It continued in this work, right through the change of ownership upon nationalisation, until being moved to nearby Littleton Colliery on 13 January, 1959. However, it must have been found wanting, as it was moved to the Cannock Central Workshops at Chase Terrace for overhaul between May and June, 1959, finally returning to Littleton in June, 1961. In June, 1966 it was moved to Granville, although it was only a little over two years later, in July, 1968 that it was cut up on site.

No.3   0-6-0ST   IC   HE   3789 1953
Another of the standard post-war Hunslet 'Austerity' designs, with 18" x 26" cylinders, 4' 3" wheels and a weight of 48 tons. The livery was plain black with no lining. It had been delivered new on 25 August, 1953 to the NCB's Rawnsley Locomotive Shed, near Hednesford which was responsible for the workings to many pits served by the former Cannock Chase Railway. However, a new loco shed was opened at Cannock Wood Colliery in October, 1964 and Rawnsley shed closed as a result in February, 1965. This loco was transferred accordingly, staying until June, 1967 when it moved to Granville. Once again, it succumbed in two years, being cut up on site in August, 1969.

No.8   63000326 0-6-0ST   IC   HE   3776 1952
Another identical post-war 'Austerity' design, this too was given an unlined plain black livery when new and retained this for most of its NCB service. The eight digit 'asset number' was applied during the 1960s. It was delivered new on 30 September, 1952 to Baggeridge Colliery, Sedgley where it stayed for fifteen years, apart from a visit to the former GWR Stafford Road Locomotive Works, Wolverhampton, for repairs during 1960. It moved briefly to Hilton Main Colliery, near Featherstone, Staffs between August, 1967 and February, 1968 until around 24 August, 1968 when it was noted at the former GWR Tyseley locomotive shed for tyre turning, on its way to Granville. Its stay here was for less than two years, as it moved to Cannock Wood Colliery in either May or June, 1970 then on to nearby West Cannock No.5 Colliery at Hednesford in January, 1971. Next it moved out of the area altogether, going to Bickershaw Colliery, near Leigh, Lancashire on 9 February, 1977 and becoming one of the much photographed stalwarts at this location. While there, it was repainted in July 1978 in an unlined green and renumbered 'No.7'. Happily it moved into preservation at the East Lancashire Railway, Bury on 26 June, 1984 where it was restored to full working in a tastefully lined crimson lake livery, and acquired the name 'SIR ROBERT PEEL'. Subsequently, it has visited several other heritage railways around the country for varying loan periods, and at the time of writing can be found at the Embsay and Bolton Abbey Steam Railway in North Yorkshire.

The Locomotive Shed

Under the Lilleshall Company, locomotives working at the collieries adjacent to Granville, and down to Donnington were stabled at the main locomotive shed at the New Yard Works in St. Georges. Obviously, under the new order, the NCB would have to make its own arrangements for locomotive stabling and servicing. It is believed that watering facilities had already been established in the sidings adjacent to the line up to the Granville washery, and so this point seemed a logical place to position the locomotive facility. A metal framework was erected, and covered with a rather primitive form of metal cladding, so as to provide some sort of protection for the engine crews, and their steeds. Unfortunately, the chosen location was rather exposed, and it was not long before the primitive building had collapsed from the onslaught of the prevailing westerly winds. No particular date has been attributed to this demise, but it must have been in the early 1950s.

Around 1954 a new building was erected, this time in a substantial and modern manner, from brick and with plenty of glazing to facilitate repair work. This two road structure, at grid reference SJ 719121, remained in use throughout both the steam and diesel eras but was demolished some time after the closure of Granville Colliery.

The Locomotives

The following locomotives were the property of the NCB for the periods indicated, and are known to have worked from Granville Colliery (and initially also to Grange Colliery). A similar system to that for the 'Lilleshall Company Locomotives' is adopted for the description of each locomotive, where the running number and/or name is given in column 1, the wheel arrangement in column 2, the disposition of cylinders in column 3, the maker in column 4, maker's works number in column 5, and year of manufacture in column 6.

The following abbreviations have been used:
IC: inside cylinders
OC: outside cylinders
AB: Andrew Barclay, Sons & Co. Ltd., Caledonia Works, Kilmarnock, Ayrshire
EE: English Electric Co. Ltd., Dick Kerr Works, Preston
EES: English Electric Co. Ltd., Stephenson Works, Darlington

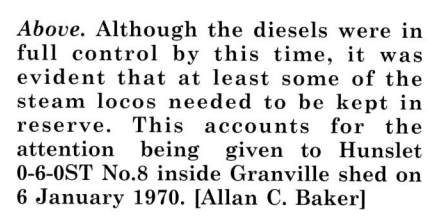

Above. Although the diesels were in full control by this time, it was evident that at least some of the steam locos needed to be kept in reserve. This accounts for the attention being given to Hunslet 0-6-0ST No.8 inside Granville shed on 6 January 1970. [Allan C. Baker]

Left. 21 August 1967 was evidently a bright summer day, as Hunslet 0-6-0ST 2895 of 1943 propels wagons into the yard at Granville Colliery. [Allan C. Baker]

AB: Hunslet-Barclay Ltd., Caledonia Works, Kilmarnock
HC: Hudswell, Clarke & Co. Ltd., Railway Foundry, Leeds
HE: Hunslet Engine Co. Ltd., Hunslet, Leeds
Lill: Lilleshall Co. Ltd., Oakengates, Shropshire
RSHD: Robert Stephenson & Hawthorns Ltd., Darlington
RSHN: Robert Stephenson & Hawthorns Ltd., Newcastle-upon-Tyne
VF: Vulcan Foundry Ltd., Newton-le-Willows, Lancashire

Main Line Movements

The 1954 London Midland Region Working Timetable gives a good illustration of the workings through Donnington exchange sidings. The first movement was a local pick-up goods leaving at 10.10am for Newport, which returned at 11.30am for Hadley Junction. Another local goods arrived at 2.00pm and left at 3.00pm for Shrewsbury as part of diagram 117. Then at 4.12pm a class 'H' freight from Hadley Junction arrived, departing at 4.19pm for Stafford. At 5.20pm a light engine and brake van arrived as part of diagram 69 from Hadley Junction, and left at 6.10pm, eventually reaching Harlescott Sidings, Shrewsbury at 8.28pm. In addition, during the weekdays, three 'up' and two 'down' freights were scheduled to call at Donnington, although not necessarily at the exchange sidings.

While the local goods workings and passing freights moved occasional loads of coal, and deposited some empty wagons, the majority of traffic from the NCB was handled by the 4.19pm to Stafford, and the 6.10pm Shrewsbury working. By 1962 the principal workings for the NCB coal traffic was the 5.10pm Donnington to Shrewsbury (Coton Hill) and the 4.05pm from Coton

Top. One of the former underground locos from Granville has survived into preservation, and is shown here on 27 September 2003 at the Red Rose Steam Society's premises at the former Astley Green Colliery, near Manchester. It is a four wheel flameproof battery locomotive, built by English Electric (works No.2417) and Robert Stephenson & Hawthorns (works No.7936) in 1957. The spare batteries on their carrier can be seen on the right in the lower photograph). [Author]

Middle. The much rebuilt and modernised pithead at Granville, on 19 July 1980, not long after closure. [Allan C. Baker]

Left. Hunslet 325hp 0-6-0DM 2D (6664/69) positions wagons on the weighbridge, which can be seen behind, during shunting manoeuvres on 6 January 1970. [Allan C. Baker]

No.1D 63000329 0-6-0DM HE 6663 1969

Delivered new in 1969, this 325 hp locomotive along with its twin (below) represented the incursion of modern traction at Granville, and both proved to be successful. These locos were turned out in a smart unlined royal blue livery, and remained here until after closure of the mine. This one first went to the Walkden Central Workshops in Manchester for overhaul on 15 November, 1979 moving on to Bersham Colliery, near Wrexham on 19 June, 1980. Whilst at Walkden it lost its running number '1D' when repainted, but retained its asset number. On 4 July, 1987 it was noted as having been transferred to Holditch Colliery, near Newcastle-under-Lyme, Staffs. Around February, 1990 it was transferred to the Kilmarnock Works of Hunslet-Barclay Ltd. for a major overhaul. The overhaul was actually classified as a rebuild and assigned the HAB works number 6586, being completed in 1999. It found a new owner at the Elf Refinery Ltd., Herbrandston, Milford Haven, Pembrokeshire, where it moved on 30 July, 1999 and where it remains in use today.

No.2D 63000328 0-6-0DM HE 6664 1969

Identical to the loco above, this loco stayed at Granville two days longer than its twin, leaving also for overhaul at the Walkden Central Workshops on 17 November, 1979 (where it too lost its running number) then also on to Bersham Colliery, but somewhat earlier, on 10 January, 1980. However, it parted company with its twin on 4 March, 1980 when it was transferred to Point of Ayr Colliery, near Prestatyn. After a further five years active life, it was sold on 21 March, 1985 to Marple & Gillott Ltd., of Sheffield who scrapped it the following month.

6D 63000322 0-6-0DM HE 7017 1971

Delivered new in September, 1971 to West Cannock No.5 Colliery, near Hednesford this was a 400 hp locomotive, fitted with a Rolls Royce C8TFL engine, 3' 9" wheels, and sporting the familiar royal blue livery. No precise date is available for its transfer to Granville, but it was during the period February, 1977 and June, 1978. After closure of Granville pit, it went to William Pit, near Whitehaven, Cumbria between July, 1979 and June, 1980. Here it was used on duties at the Haig Colliery Coal Preparation Plant. After closure of this operation, it was acquired for preservation by the Derwent Railway Society, and moved on 4 November, 1986 to their premises in Workington. On 25 January, 1989 it moved again, to Steamtown, Carnforth, where it remains preserved.

Hunslet 0-6-0ST No.8 stands outside the locomotive shed at Granville Colliery between duties in the winter of 1968. [P. Ward]

At Donnington down exchange sidings in 1966, Wellington shed's '57XX' 0-6-0PT No. 9630 shunts the wagons of a recently arrived string of empties, while an unidentified '8F' 2-8-0 waits to depart with a loaded train. [P. Ward]

Below left. Hunslet No.8 near to Muxtonbridge with a haul of empties from Donnington exchange sidings, winter 1968. [P. Ward]. *Below right and opposite page top.* Hunslet No.8 passing over the Wellington Road level crossing at Donnington on its way to Granville colliery with empties from the exchange sidings around 1968. The line can be seen stretching ahead to the next level crossing (just out of sight) over School Road. [P. Ward]

Hill to Stafford. Coal for Ironbridge power station at this time was conveyed to Wellington, before being tripped back along the Wolverhampton line and the Madeley branch to Ironbridge. However, in 1964 the 'B' station at Ironbridge was opened, and shortly afterwards, block trains were introduced from Donnington, which also involved running round in Wellington.

In 1970 there were two daily block coal trains, formed of 27 ton air braked 'merry-go-round' hopper wagons, normally in rakes of around 25 wagons. In addition, there were two daily freight services, which also contained coal, but additionally picked up from the local factory sidings at COD Donnington, GKN Sankey and Hadley sidings. The movements to and from Donnington are given below:

08.27 MWFO Light engine arrives from Bescot.
09.08 MWFO Block coal train departs to Ironbridge Power Station, Buildwas (Train no 6G40)
10.02 Freight from Coton Hill, Shrewsbury (07.53) No 6G89) arrives
10.57 Freight for Coton Hill (13.00) departs, Train No 8J40
11.26 TThO Coal empties arrive from Buildwas, Train No 6G48
12.26 TThO Block coal train departs to Buildwas, Train No 6G40
13.02 MWFO Coal empties arrive from Buildwas, Train No 6G48
13.25 FO Light engine departs to Bescot
14.05 MWO Block coal train departs to Buildwas, Train No 6G41
15.59 Freight from Coton Hill (14.05) No 9G29 arrives
17.00 TThO Coal empties arrive from Buildwas, Train No 6G49
17.00 TThO Light engine departs for Bescot
17.10 Freight departs for Crewe, Gresty Lane and Middle Sorting Sidings, Train No 8K19

During BR days, the most ancient motive power to be seen in Donnington exchange sidings were Bowen-Cooke 'Super D' 0-8-0s, which trundled up and down this line well into the 1960s. Equally common were the Johnson 3F and Fowler 4F designs of the former Midland Railway, and their LMS variants. As during LMSR days, there would also be Hughes / Fowler 'Crabs', Fowler 2-6-4 tanks, and Stanier '8F' 2-8-0s and Class '5MT' 4-6-0s. The Class 4 Ivatt moguls also made appearances in the later days of BR steam plus locos of GWR origin. However, there is

An unidentified locomotive heads a string of empties from Donnington near to Granville Colliery around 1968, which can just be seen in the distance (top centre right). Note the use of an NCB brake van. [P. Ward]

2ft 3in GAUGE UNDERGROUND LOCOMOTIVES

As mentioned earlier, Grange mine was connected underground to Granville mine, by two 1,000 yard long tunnels, around 1953. Later underground improvements included a further 2,500 yard long tunnel beneath the existing workings as the main arterial roadway, and as an air intake for the mine. The existing method of underground haulage using a 'mane-and-tail' rope system, was gradually replaced by the introduction of new 12 ton 64 hp battery electric locomotives hauling 2½ ton capacity mine cars.

Each of these locos visited the Walkden Central Workshops, Manchester, for overhaul during the 1970s. The first loco went during 1973 and returned in September of that year. The second went some time prior to 25 August 1976, and returned in November of that year. The third went some time during 1970, and was returned in December, 1971, and went again during 1977, being returned during December of that year. The fourth was returned from overhaul in April, 1975, but it is not known when it went to Walkden.

Finally, upon closure of the mine, all were transferred to Walkden for assessment, (the first going in March, 1978, the second in July, 1979, and the final two in the following month) before being reallocated to other collieries. Each was regauged to 2' 6" at Walkden and their subsequent disposition is given below:

```
    4wBEF        RSHN      7935
                 EE        2416     1957
```
To Old Boston Training Centre, Haydock, on 13 December, 1979; moving to Parsonage Training Centre, Leigh between 5 and 12 September, 1986. Then it moved out of the Lancashire area to Trentham Training Centre, near Newcastle-under-Lyme between November, 1988 and February, 1989. Finally, it went for preservation in February, 1994 to Leicestershire County Council's Snibston Discovery Park at Coalville, where it remains today.

```
    4wBEF        RSHN      7936
                 EE        2417     1957
```
To Agecroft Colliery, Pendlebury on 19 January, 1981. It moved to the Red Rose Steam Society, Astley Green, Greater Manchester on 12 March, 1991, where it has been preserved.

```
    4wBEF        RSHD      8303
                 EE        3163     1961

    4wBEF        EES       8455
                 EE        3426     1963
```
These both also moved to Agecroft Colliery, the earlier one on 5 January, 1981, and the later one in September of that year. Upon the closure of this colliery, one of these, by now carrying the running number 'No.4', was moved to the Chatterley Whitfield Mining Museum, near Stoke-on-Trent in April, 1991. Although this museum site is closed at present, this locomotive remains there (although its identity has still not been determined), along with many other potential exhibits. The fate of the other locomotive is not known, and so is presumed to have been abandoned underground.

curiously no record of any of the BR Standard designs being engaged on such work.

The line from Stafford to Donnington was closed completely with effect from 1 August, 1966 although not officially until July, 1967. The track remained *in situ* until the early months of 1970. It is not believed that diesel traction was used on the freight traffic along this section, but it certainly was on the remaining section to Wellington, which was singled in 1971 and finally closed and lifted in 1991. BR Class 20, 31, 37, 40 and 47 diesels were all noted on coal workings during the intervening years. As mentioned earlier, Granville Colliery closed in May 1979 and, following clearance of stocks, the final train to Donnington exchange sidings ran on 2 October 1979.

'56XX' 0-6-2T No.5606 moves a string of loaded coal wagons out of the down exchange sidings at Donnington during 1966. The locomotive bears a painted '2A' shed code on its smokebox door, which signified its allocation to Tyseley at this date.[P. Ward]

'Jubilee' 4-6-0 No.45598 BASUTOLAND heads a lengthy coal train from Donnington exchange sidings to Ironbridge Power Station, near Hadley in January 1964. [P. Ward]

NCB, GRANVILLE COLLIERY SYSTEM (1970)

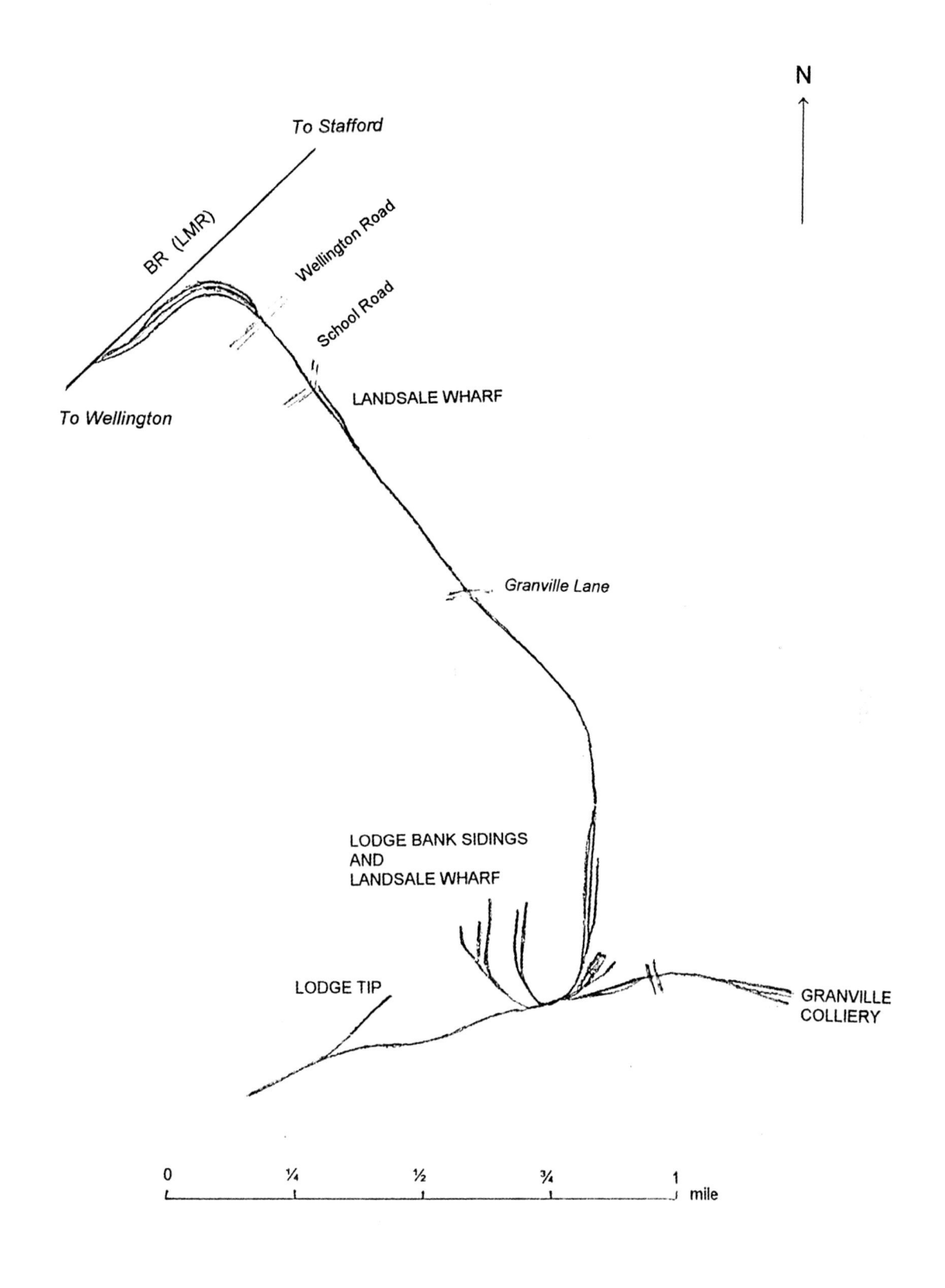

Appendices

Appendix 1

LILLESHALL COMPANY MINES

Priors Lee Pits

Albion	Horton	Slaughter
Dark Lane (alias Cage)	Hydraulic	Stafford
Fireclay	Lawn	Tarry
Furnace	Little Hayes	Top Spring
Hall	Lower Spring	Village
Hangman's Hill	Nelson	West Cliff
Hangman's Wall	Rickyard	Westcroft
		Woodhouse

Hadley Colliery
Nos. 1 – 7 Pits

Donnington Pits

Barn Pits	Granville	Nobby
Barnyard	Horton	Quarry
Blue Flat	Jervis Building	Rookery
Chimney	Langley	Sale
Drayton	Lodge Bank	Sour Leasow
Foundry	Lodgewood	Waxhill
Freehold	Meadow	White
Grange (Albert & Alexandra Pits)	Muxton Bridge	Woodfield

Chartermasters:

Bower	Gough and Limmers	Poppitt and Davies
Coopers	Griffiths	Stevens
Dainty	J. Humpherson	Tranter
Dorricott	S. Leeson	Wrockwardine
Ferridays	Overleys (Overton)	(Jiggers Bank)

Hope Colliery
Nos 1 and 2 Pits

Appendix 2

Lilleshall Company 0-4-0ST of 1862.

Extract from "The Colliery Guardian" of 1 November, 1862.
(Courtesy of the Ironbridge Gorge Museum Trust)

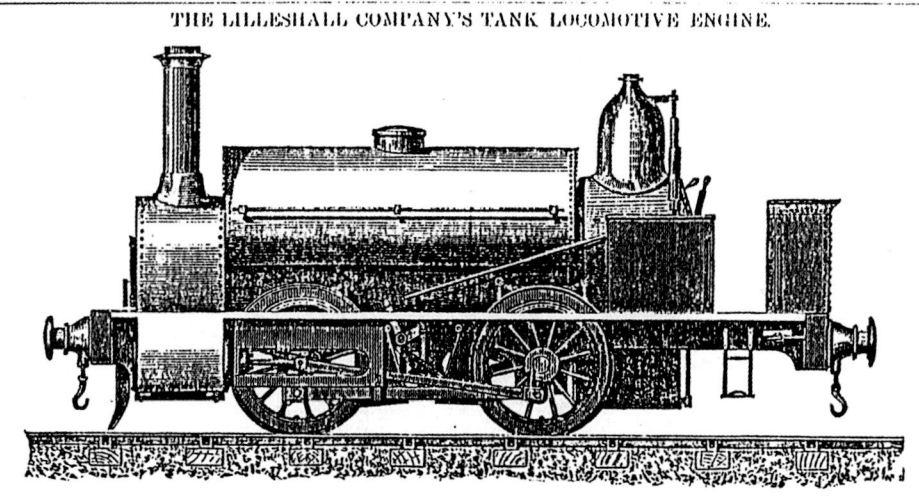

THE LILLESHALL COMPANY'S TANK LOCOMOTIVE ENGINE.

The Lilleshall Company of Shiffnal, Shropshire, having had four or five tank engines at work for the last twelve years, constructed by various makers, have succeeded, as will be seen by the above illustration, in producing an engine which is especially adapted for collieries, mineral traffic, and contractors' purposes; and where there are sharp curves and heavy gradients. It is built extra strong to resist the great wear and tear to which engines of this description are subject, and the severe strains and shocks which are occasioned by the traction of heavy loads over uneven roads. The cylindrical part of the boiler is ten feet in length and three feet in diameter, and is of 7-16 inch plates, riveted together, with three-quarter inch rivets. The boiler is fixed unusually low in the frame to avoid top weight. The outside fire-box is semi-cylindrical and eccentric with the boiler; it is of half-inch plate, and is 2·6 feet long, and 4 feet wide. The boiler and fire-box are covered with wood lining and a sheet iron case, bound with wrought-iron hoops. The inside fire-box is of copper; the top sides and front plate being quarter inch thick, and the tube plate three-quarter inch thick. The top of the fire-box is supported by six strong roof stays of flat iron; with bolts passing through the stays and top of box. The external and internal boxes are screwed together with hoops of copper studs, seven-eight inch in diameter 11, wire gauge next the fire-box, and 14, wire gauge at the smoke box end. The tank is semi-cylindrical, and is fitted on the back of boiler, and supported on four strong wrought-iron brackets. The coal-box is arranged behind the driver; the engine has outside cylinders, thirteen inches diameter and twenty inches stroke; and the metallic pistons, which are of very simple and durable construction, have two brass rings in each; and are self-acting by the pressure of the steam upon the valves. The valves work direct; and the regulator, which is in the smoke box, is easy of access, and can be examined without deranging any other part of the machine. The copper steam pipe passes through the entire length of the boiler, and being thoroughly screwed into the tube, into the plate of the smoke box, and into the front plate of the outer fire-box, it forms a good stay. The blast pipe is reduced in length, and a loose gland fitted in to allow the size of the muzzle to be varied in order to suit the quality of the coals. The length motion is of steel, hardened, and the arrangement is such as not to require balance weights, while, at the same time, admitting of being kept low on the bottom. The eccentrics are of cast iron; the hoops of brass; and there are four strong wrought iron wheels, three feet, nine inches, in diameter, hooped with low iron tyres, coupled; the coupling rods have brasses at each end; and the engine is fitted with Giffard's injector, blow-off cocks, and all the usual appliances for showing the level of water. One of the engines may be seen at the Company's works at Shiffnal.

In our impression of the 11th ult., we called attention to the Company's case in the Eastern Annexe containing specimens illustrative of their cold blast pig iron (and hot blast from the same material) castings, puddled bars, plates, malleable iron, and wire, made from the same. On the same occasion we drew attention to their specimens of blackstone calcined, argillaceous ironstone, Randle furnace coal, clod furnace coal, with several other varieties; and it only now remains for us to wish the Company the success that is due to their spirited enterprise.

Appendix 3

The Identity of 'Phoenix'

The question of the identity of the early Company locomotive 'Phoenix' has puzzled many researchers. This document looks at the available evidence, and at some of the theories put forward.

The IRS Handbook G gives PHOENIX as an 0-6-0T with inside cylinders, built around 1859 by the Phoenix Foundry of Stoke-on-Trent. This information is believed to have originated with either the late Ralph Russell or Selwyn Pierce Higgins, or possibly both. In the Higgins Archive (at the National Railway Museum), he has a note to the effect that a remark about PHOENIX being 'bought from the Potteries' was made to him by 'an old loco hand'. I believe that this casts serious doubt on the veracity of this locomotive's origin, even before further evidence is considered. There is a further comment that PHOENIX was an 0-4-2 tank, although this can be safely disregarded as both the 1876 and 1915 Valuations describe PHOENIX as 'six wheels coupled'.

Regarding the origin as being the Phoenix Foundry in Stoke-on-Trent, it is generally acknowledged that the only possible contender for this would have been the Phoenix Carriage & Wagon Works Ltd., but this was not formed until 1888. Consequently, this company can be eliminated. It is worthy of note that the first manager of the New Yard Engineering Works was one John Lloyd, who apparently came from Stoke, taking up his first appointment at the Old Yard, Donnington around the same time as PHOENIX is reputed to have been built. It can be seen how these two items possibly became confused, especially over the long years.

The word 'Phoenix' in the title of foundries was a very common, and entirely appropriate use of the word. The following businesses, producing locomotives at some time or another used this in their titles:

Cook & Deans, Phoenix Foundry, Little Bolton, Lancs.
Thos. Edington & Sons, Phoenix Iron Works, Glasgow.
Fawcett, Preston & Co., Phoenix Foundry, York Street, Liverpool.
Gilkes, Wilson & Co., Phoenix Iron & Brass Foundry, Shildon, Co. Durham.
Peel, Williams & Peel, Phoenix Foundry, Swan Street, Manchester.

However, none of these firms are known to have produced locomotives for the Company, although it may be that one of their products may have been obtained secondhand and rebuilt by the Company. Rebuilding of an earlier locomotive by the Company is a distinct possibility, especially as the New Yard Engineering Works was also known as the Phoenix Foundry, right up through the 20th century. We have already seen that this name was mentioned by Samuel Griffiths in his 'Guide to the Iron and Steel Trade' of 1873.

Taking this assumption a stage further, it has also been suggested that PHOENIX coming from the 'the Potteries' could also have meant that it came from 'the Potts', being the colloquial title given to the Potteries, Shrewsbury and North Wales Railway. This can be discounted, however, as this railway did not open until 1866, seven years after the alleged construction of PHOENIX.

Another interpretation of 'the Potts' may be that it was a Potts locomotive, i.e. built by Jones & Potts, at their Viaduct Works, Newton-le-Willows. This company was established in the early 1830s by John Jones, with partners William Turner and Richard Evans. However, this partnership was dissolved on 16 August, 1841, the second two partners being replaced by Arthur Potts, and the name changed accordingly. This partnership was in turn dissolved in 1851, and the Viaduct Foundry offered for sale in June 1851. The LNWR leased the premises from 1 March, 1853, and purchased it outright on 11 May, 1860 whence it became the Earlestown Wagon Works. This is indeed an intriguing possibility, as Jones & Potts had built Nos. 7 and 8 for the Shrewsbury & Chester Railway, supplying them in December, 1846 and March, 1847 respectively. These were long-boiler 2-4-0's with outside cylinders of 15" x 24". No.7 had a Gothic firebox, and No.8 had an ordinary raised one, with 'Crewe type' safety valves on this engine only. The most intriguing aspect of these locomotives is that they were both withdrawn in 1859, and their subsequent disposal and history is unknown. Taking the date and the name of their maker, along with the relative proximity of the Shrewsbury & Chester Railway (part of the GWR from 1 September, 1854) presents a strong case for one of these to have been the donor for rebuilding at the Company. Admittedly, there would not have been a great deal of the original locomotive left after rebuilding, particularly as PHOENIX had *inside* cylinders, and these were 16" x 21"!

The final, and probably most obvious contender as the 'donor' engine for a rebuild, must be Neilson & Mitchell No.50 of 1851. Firstly, both this engine and PHOENIX were given the running number '3'. Secondly, it seems to have been superseded by PHOENIX as the new number 3 in just eight years. Again, it would have required considerable reconstruction, but there is no record of its disposal.

The conclusion must be that a locomotive of uncertain origin was obtained by the Company and rebuilt using its acknowledged expertise of stationery steam engines, and experience of the requirements of industrial use. It probably underwent much development work before the Company decided to undertake the building of locomotives for customers from 1862 onwards. The naming of the locomotive as 'PHOENIX' almost certainly commemorates its rebuilding at the New Yard Works, or Phoenix Foundry as it was locally known.

Appendix 4

Lilleshall's 'Express Locomotive'.
This locomotive remains something of an enigma, as it represents the Company's sole attempt to break into the market for main line locomotives, and at the time of the 'Second Railway Mania' of the mid 1860s. As already mentioned in Chapter Seven, it was exhibited as first built at the Paris Exhibition of 1867 where it gained a silver medal. Details of the leading dimensions of this locomotive were given in 'The Engineer' of 1 November,1867 as follows:

Total grate surface, 18 square feet.
Length of tubes between tubeplates, 111ft. 2in.
Thickness of tubes, .062 in.
Heating surface of firebox, 96 square feet.
Mean diameter of boiler body, 4ft. 3.12 in.
Diameter of cylinders, 16 in.
Number of wheels, 6.
Distance between leading and trailing wheels, 16 ft. 5 in.
Diameter of driving wheels, 6 ft. 11 in.
Weight on leading axle, 10 tons 11 cwt.
Weight on trailing wheels, 8 tons 8 cwt.
Total weight of locomotive (empty), 27 tons 14 cwt.

Number of tubes, 186.
Internal diameter of tubes, 1.73 in.
Heating surface of tubes, 980 square feet.
Total heating surface, 1076 square feet.
Working pressure permitted, 9 ¼ atmospheres
Stroke, 21 in.
Number of coupled wheels, none.

Diameter of leading or trailing wheels, 4 ft. 2 ½ in.
Weight on driving axle, 12 tons 14 cwt.
Total weight of locomotive (working), 31 tons 13 cwt.

This engine was further described in Spon's Dictionary of Engineering (Volume III) of 1874 thus:
'Fig. 5207 is one of the Lilleshall Company's locomotives specially designed for services in India. It is a very pretty specimen of its kind, and is another good illustration of the pure English type. The mechanism is internal, with double lateral guides for the cross-heads of the pistons, but the cylinders have a slight upward inclination. The framing is double; the inner plates carry the oil boxes of the driving axle, the outer hold the end uncoupled wheels. The springs are all independent, and only those of the driving wheels are capable of being tightened at pleasure. The axles and tires *(sic)* of the wheels are of steel. The slide-valve is of the straight form known as Allen's. The firebox contains a brick arched roof, and an air deflector, to consume the smoke. The boiler is provided with self-acting lubricators, and with safety valves on Ramsbottom's system, and the general type of the engine is in accordance with that engineer's ideas. There is a complete plate-iron box over the footplate, to protect the driver.'

The illustrations and photographs attached reveal that the overall design has a considerable likeness to that of James Stirling for the Great Northern Railway, most particularly regarding the shape of the cab. Considering the Company's penchant for LNWR fittings, it is all the more remarkable that the design did not follow more closely those of Webb and Ramsbottom.

Following the Paris Exhibition, the locomotive was returned to Oakengates. No record of any main line trials have been traced, and although it has been suggested that this would have been a suitable express locomotive for the railways of India, no orders were forthcoming from that country, nor any other, unfortunately. This may, in part, be attributed to the collapse of the major bank of Overend & Gurney that followed the 'Second Railway Mania' of 1866. As a result, a financial panic ensued that stifled much fresh investment potential.

One other curiosity concerning this locomotive is that there is no record of a tender being built to accompany it. Descriptions of the 1867 Paris Exhibition do not mention whether it was shown with a tender or without one, and no photographic evidence survives of such a tender. Perhaps this was indicative of the level of expense that the Company was prepared to commit on such a speculative prototype.

As a result of its lack of acceptance, it was 'rebuilt' as an 0-6-0ST, with the following leading dimensions. Those of the original build are given in brackets, for comparison:
Driving wheels: 3' 7" diameter *(6' 11" driving wheels, other wheels 4' 2 ½")*.
Inside cylinders: 16" x 21" *(17" x 21")*
Frames : single, inside *(double)*
Weight in working order: 47 tons *(31.65 tons)*.
Overall length was 29 feet 6 inches *(not known)*.

As can be seen, there must have been only very little of the original locomotive incorporated in the 'rebuild', as the frames, wheels and cab could not be used. This really only leaves the boiler, and possibly some of the valve gear, assuming that the inside cylinders could be altered to their new dimensions.

Latterly it was equipped with Ross pop safety valves, and the cab had side windows fitted to further protect the crew on the exposed stretches of Cannock Chase. It was supplied 'as new' in its rebuilt form in July, 1873 to Cannock & Rugeley Collieries Ltd., Rawnsley, Staffordshire, its lengthy working life of 89 years finally terminating in March, 1962.

The express locomotive outside the New Yard Works, shortly after completion in 1967. The overall design is redolent of the 'Large Bloomers' designed by James McConnell, and built at Wolverton for the Southern Division of the LNWR from 1850 onwards. [Allan C Baker collection]

Interestingly, for this rear three quarter view, the locomotive appears to have been turned through 90 degrees, judging by the New Yard building behind. As there was no traverser or turntable there, this must have taken a considerable effot. This view emphasises the sizeable cab, not at all common on LNWR engines at this time, but bearing a striking resemblance to those fitted to the Great Northern Railway singles designed by James Stirling. There is no sign of a tender in either of these photos. [Courtesy: Ironbridge Gorge Museum Trust]

EXHIBITED AT PARIS.

LOCOMOTIVE BY THE LILLESHALL COMPANY.

Total grate surface, 18 square feet.
Number of tubes, 186.
Length of tubes between tube plates, 11ft. 2in.
Internal diameter of tubes, 1·73in.

Number of wheels, 6.
Ditto ditto, coupled, none.
Distance between leading and trailing wheels, 16ft. 5in.

The illustration from 'The Engineer' of 1 November, 1867 gives a good idea of the proportions of the locomotive, as well as the importance attached to its construction. However, the dome and chimney have been shortened to fit the space available for this illustration in the journal. Some principle dimensions are also given. [Courtesy: Ironbridge Gorge Museum Trust]

Appendix 5

Lilleshall Company Wagons

Wagon Inventory

At 30th June	Main Line	Works Wagons	On Hire Purchase
1915	325	660	78
1916	364	669	56
1917	334	694	56
1918	329	665	56
1919	309	620	56
1920	290	600	56
1921	345	576	-
1922	344	451	48
1923	346	420	48
1924	344	402	48
1925	351	439	-
1926	349	440	-
1927	349	440	-
1928	342	447	-
1929	340	409	-
1930	338	400	-
1931	317	418	-
1932	317	419	-
1933	310	426	-
1934	300	435	-
1935	295	436	-
1936	286	425	-
1937	267	438	-
1938	257	438	-
1939	183	489	-
1940	182	486	-
1941	182	485	-
1942	181	484	-
1943	181	483	-
1944	180	482	-

Types of wagons:
Main Line
Coal: 10T, 8T
Coke: 10T, 8T
Lime: 10T, 8T
Limestone: 10T, 8T
Hoppers: 10T

Works wagons
Coal: 10T, 8T, 6T
Coal hoppers: 10T
Limestone: 8T
Pig Iron: 10T
Basic Slag: 10T
Bar Iron: 10T
Flag Plant: 8T
Hoppers: 12T, 10T, 8T

The 1876 Valuation disclosed 372 6T wagons, 297 8T wagons and 74 10T wagons as well as 4 tipping wagons, giving a total of 747 wagons. These are not classified as to internal/main line use.

Hire purchase wagons: Midland Wagon Co Ltd
Coal 8T, quantity 26 (1915 to 1920)
Coal 8T, quantity 22 (1915)
Payable monthly from 1 March 1911 for five years

Gloucester Wagon Co Ltd
Limestone 10T, quantity 30 (1915 to 1920)
Payable monthly from 31 March 1914 for seven years

British Wagon Co Ltd
Coal 10T, quantity 48 (1922 to 1924)

Earlier hires were 20 wagons from W R Renshaw & Co Ltd of Stoke-on-Trent, per an agreement dated 20 November 1903. A further agreement was dated 7 February 1905 for 50 wagons from Hurst, Neilson & Co.

Appendix 6
CODE OF SIGNALS
To prevent confusion the following code of signals must be strictly observed:-
FIXED SIGNAL POSTS
Red is a signal of danger.
Green is an all right signal.
The fixed signals leading to railway junctions must not be passed at danger, unless verbally instructed to do so by the Railway Co.'s staff, or by receiving a hand signal to do so from the man in charge. When one or more engines are in the siding or junction at the same time, no engine driver must move unless instructed to do so by the person in charge.
HAND SIGNALS
A **Red Light** (or flag) is a danger signal (stop).
A **White Light,** waved up and down slowly, means move forward, i.e. go away from person.
A **White Light,** waved slowly from side to side across the body, means move back, i.e. come towards the person.
A **Green Light,** waved slowly up and down, means move forward slowly, i.e. go away from the person.
A **Green Light,** waved slowly from side to side across the body, means move back slowly, i.e. come towards person.
A **Green Light,** held steadily above the head, means go right away from one point to another.
SIGNALS IN THE ABSENCE OF FLAGS OR LAMPS.
Both arms raised above the head – Danger (stop).
One arm worked towards the body – come towards the person.
Two arms worked towards the body – come very steady towards the person.
One arm worked from the body – go from the person.
Two arms worked from the body – go very steady from the person.
One arm held straight out – go right away (one point to another).

During falling snow, or in foggy weather, or when the sight is intercepted the shunters may have by necessity to work by whistle code as under:-
One long whistle – go away from person.
Two long whistles – come towards person.
Three or more sharp whistles – stop – danger.
Drivers, when working to whistle codes, must work cautiously, and travel at reduced speed.
(Per the Company Rules and Regulations for Traffic Department Employees)

Appendix 7

Private Sidings Agreements

The exchange sidings with the main line railway companies were operated under Private Sidings Agreements, which were revised and extended as necessary over the years.

LNWR Snedshill Ironworks Sidings

These were situated on the LNWR Coalport branch, 36 chains (0.45 mile) south of Oakengates station. The sidings totalled 621 yards, and were maintained by the LNWR on its own land at its own cost. A further 92 yards of sidings, being nearer to the Snedshill Works were maintained by the LNWR on the Company land at the railway company's cost. This agreement was dated 26 May 1904 and remained in force until the closure of the Company's railway in December 1959.

LNWR Priorslee Siding

This group of sidings were further south than the above sidings, being 43 chains (0.54 mile) south of Oakengates. The first 126 yards of sidings were on LNWR land, and maintained by the LNWR at its cost. The next 363 yards were on the company land, but maintained by the LNWR at its own cost. The agreement (no.16465) was dated 11 November 1890. However, in April 1892 the Company pulled up 35 yards of sidings belonging to the LNWR, substituting their own materials and laying in an additional siding. The materials pulled up were taken possession of by the LNWR. This agreement also remained in force until the closure of the Company's railway in December 1959.

LNWR Trench Siding

This was located at Trench, some 55 chains and 14 yards (0.7 mile) east of Hadley station, and comprised the southernmost siding on the original Wombridge goods branch, just after its junction with the Stafford to Wellington main line. Being remote from the Company railway, it was worked entirely by LNWR locomotives. The siding totalled only 134 yards, and was maintained by the LNWR on LNWR land at the cost of the Company. The agreement was dated 4 September 1903 but the siding was subsequently taken over by Shropshire Associated Collieries from 1 July 1941 and its successor the National Coal Board, who terminated the agreement on 12 April 1949.

A further agreement was dated 22 July, 1903 for the use of wharf premises at Trench. This agreement was superceded by a further agreement dated 6 August 1916, but with effect from 1 July 1916 to continue the use of the premises at a monthly rental of 10 shillings. The agreement was open ended, but required six months notice to terminate by either party. The premises were presumably some form of office and store.

LNWR Donnington Siding

This siding was located 74 chains (0.925 mile) west of Donnington station. The sidings totalled 572 ½ yards, and were maintained by the LNWR on its own land at its own cost. This siding was the northernmost one of the group alongside the 'down' Stafford to Wellington running line, and this arrangement included the points and crossovers necessary to gain access to the siding from both directions of running lines. The LNWR Diagrams of Private Sidings do not give a date for the original agreement, but it was subsequently revised in an agreement dated 31 March 1927. W. Shepherd & Sons Ltd., who operated the asphalt plant at Waxhill were also permitted traffic from 1926, and their successors, Highways Construction Ltd. from 1938.

Following nationalisation of the coal mines, the agreement was taken over by the National Coal Board from vesting day, 1 January 1947 until closure of the Wellington to Donnington line on 2 October, 1979.

GWR Hollinswood Sidings

The earliest agreement discovered is one dating from 1 January 1872 permitting the working of traffic from the Company siding to the GWR Hollinswood sidings. Further sidings were laid on the north side of this group for W. Shepherd & Sons Ltd., who operated the asphalt plant at Priorslee, and were subject to a further agreement dated 7 September 1920 which was transferred to their successors, Highways Construction Ltd. from 1 September 1933 under an agreement dated 21 June 1933. This latter agreement was terminated as from 21 June 1934. The remainder of the agreement continued in force until the closure of the Company railway in December 1959.

Appendix 8.

COMPARISON OF LOCOMOTIVE DATA – LILLESHALL FLEET LOCOS

Locomotive	Cylinder dimensions	Driving wheel diameter
Neilson 46 of 1850	10" x 18" (WL)	
No.1 GRANVILLE Neilson 63 of 1854	12" X 18" (WL, IRS) 11" x 20" (1876V) 11½" x 18" (1915V) 13" x 22" (EO)	3' 0" (EO)
No.2 Neilson 64 of 1854	12" x 18" (WL, IRS) 12" x 20" (1876V)	
No.3 Neilson 50 of 1851	10" x 18" (WL, IRS)	
No.3 PHOENIX	16" x 21" (1876V, 1915V)	
No.4 CONSTANCE Lill, 1865	13" x 21" (1876V) 13¼" x 20" (1915V, 1937V, 1941V, HH, EO) 13" x 20" (TH, RR) 13" x 22" (EO)	3' 6" (1937V, HH, EO) 3' 5" (second EO)
No.5, Lill 1866	13" x 21" (1876V) 13¼ " x 20" (1915V, 1937V, HH) 13" x 20" (TH, RR) 13" x 22" (EO)	3' 6" (1937V,HH,EO)
No.6, Lill 1869	`13" x 21" (1876V) 13¼" x 20" (1915V, 1937V, 1941V, HH) 13" x 20" (TH, RR) 13" x 22" (EO)	3' 8" (1937V, TH,HH) 3' 6" (EO)
No.7, Lill 1870	13" x 21" (1876V) 13¼" x 20" (1915V, 1937V, 1941V, HH) 13" x 20" (TH, RR) 13" x 22" (EO)	3' 8" (HH) 3' 7" (1937V, TH) 3' 6" (EO)
No.2, Lill 1886	15 ½" x 18" (1915V,1937V,1941V, HH,TH,RR) 18 ½" x 18" (1941V) 14" x 22" (EO)	3' 6" (HH) 3' 5" (1915V, 1937V) 3' 2" (EO)
No.8, Peckett 856.	16" x 22" (IRS, 1915V, 1937V, HH, WL) 16" x 24" (EO)	3' 8" (EO) 3' 10" (1915V,1937V, WL,HH)
No.9, RS 1800.	14" x 20" (1915V, 1937V) 14" x 22" (IRS) 13 ½ " x 22" (EO)	3' 8" (1915V, 1937V) 3' 7" (IRS) 3' 6" (HH)
No.10, Peckett 883	14" x 20" (IRS, 1915V, 1937V, 1941V, HH, EO, WL) 14" x 22" (second EO)	3' 6" (EO) 3' 2" (IRS, WL, second EO) 3' 0" (HH)

No.11, MERCURY Manning Wardle 995	12" x 17" (IRS, WL)	3' 1$^{3/8}$" (IRS) 3' 1½"

No.3, Barclay 1392	16" x 24" (IRS, 1915V,
	    1937V, HH, EO)
		3' 7" (IRS, 1937V,
		    HH)
		3' 6" (EO)

No.11, Barclay 1486	18" x 24" (IRS, HH) 18" x 20" (1937V, 1941V) 18" x 26" (EO)	3' 9" (1937V, HH) 3' 7" (EO) 3' 6" (second EO)
No.12, Hudswell Clarke 612.	18" x 26" (IRS, 1937V, HH, EO)	4' 6" (IRS,1937V, HH) 4' 0" (EO)
No.1 (GWR 581)	17½" x 26" (IRS, EO, LG,GWR) 17½" x 28" (1937V) 18" x 26" (1941V)	4' 6 ½ " (IRS,LG, GWR) 4' 5" (EO)
No.3 (GWR 589)	17½" x 26" (IRS, LG,GWR) 18" x 26" (1941V, EO)	5' 3" (IRS, LG,GWR) 4' 8" (EO)
No.5 (GWR 251)	18" x 26" (IRS, 1941V, EO) 17 ½" x 26" (LG,1937V,GWR)	4' 4" (LG) 4' 3" (IRS,GWR, 1937V)
No.12 (GWR 2794)	17 ½" x 24" (IRS, GWR) 18" x 26" (EO)	4' 7 ½" (IRS, GWR) 4' 5" (EO)
No.4, PRINCE OF WALES Barclay 1484	16" x 24" (IRS) 16" x 22" (EO)	3' 7" (IRS, EO)
No.5, ALBERTA Barclay 1349	16" x 24" (IRS) 16" x 22" (EO)	3' 7" (IRS, EO)

Sources:

IRS	Industrial Railway Society Handbooks
1876V	Lilleshall Company Valuation of Assets, 1876
1915V	Lilleshall Company Valuation of Assets, 1915
1937V	Lilleshall Company Valuation of Assets, 1937
1941V	Lilleshall Company, independent Valuation of Assets, 1941
TH	Lists of Lilleshall built locos prepared by Thomas Hoggins, c1943 and 1956/7
RR	List of Lilleshall built locos prepared for Ralph Russell c1952
HH	List of Lilleshall loco fleet prepared by H. Hilton, New Yard Works Manager for the late Geoff Moore on 13 June, 1928.
EO	Lists of Lilleshall loco fleet prepared by E. Owen, Loco Foreman on 21 October, 1953
WL	Manufacturers works lists
GWR	Locomotives of the Great Western Railway, Parts Five and Ten (RCTS)
LG	Locomotives at the Grouping, Part Four ((H. C. Casserley & S. W. Johnston)

SOURCES

Published Material
The Dalmellington Company – Its Engines and Men, David L. Smith (David & Charles, 1967);

GWR Locomotive Allocations – First and Last Sheds, 1922 to 1967, J.W.P. Rowledge (David & Charles, 1986);

Hudswell Clarke & Co. Ltd. Locomotive Works List, Clive Hardy (Thomas Alexsandr, 1982);

Neilson & Mitchell, and Neilson Reid & Co. Ltd. Works List of Locomotives, Typescript, Unknown author, c1940s;

British Steam Locomotive Builders, J.W.Lowe (Guild Publishing, 1975);

Locomotives of the Cannock & Rugeley Colliery Co. Ltd. – The Locomotive, 15 February 1940;

Lilleshalls Flyer, C. Hamilton Ellis. – Railway Magazine, November 1979;

The Lilleshall Company – A History 1764-1964, W.K.V. Gale & C. R. Nicholls (Moorland Publishing);

The Glyn Valley Tramway, W.J. Milner (Oxford Publishing Co., 1964);

Canals of the West Midlands, Charles Hadfield (David & Charles, 1985);

Track Layout Diagrams of the GWR and BR Western Region: Section 32, East Shropshire, R.A. Cooke, 1994;

Bagnalls of Stafford, A.C. Baker & T.D.A. Civill (Oakwood Press, 1973);

Railways in and around Stafford, Edward Talbot (Foxline, 1994); *Canals of Shropshire*, Richard K. Morriss (Shropshire Books, 1991);

The Shroppie, Thomas Pellow & Paul Bowen (Landscape Press, 1994);

The Lilleshall Company Railway System, Estate of Moses Evans (Undated);

The Waggonways and Plateways of East Shropshire, R.F. Savage & L.D.W. Smith (Birmingham School of Architecture, 1965);

Stone Blocks and Iron Rails, Bertram Baxter (David & Charles, 1966);

Early Wooden Railways, M.J.T. Lewis (Routledge & Kegan Paul Ltd., 1974);

Priorslee Remembered, A. Frost, 1973; *Guide to the Iron and Steel Trade*, Samuel Griffiths, 1873;

Locomotives at the Grouping – Part Four – Great Western Railway, H.C.Casserley & S.W.Johnston (Ian Allan, 1974);

Spons Dictionary of Engineering (Vol.III) 1874;

The Chronicles of Boultons Sidings, A. Rosling Bennett (David & Charles, 1971);

The Wenlock Limestone Industry (An historical note) Glyn Williams (J.C.Williams, 1997);

The Industrial Archaeology of Shropshire, Barrie Trinder (Phillimore & Co.);

Industrial Revolution in Shropshire, Barrie Trinder (Phillimore & Co.);

Granville Country Park, Wrekin Council, 1997;

Images of England-The East Shropshire Coalfields, Ivor J. Brown (Tempus Publishing, 1999);

The Dictionary of National Biography, George Smith, edited by Sir Leslie Steven and Sir Sidney Lee (Oxford University Press);

The History and Locomotives of the Tees Engine Works, Fred W. Harman (Century Locoprints);

Contractors Locomotives – Part IV, F.D. Smith & D. Cole (Union Publications, 1970);

Contractors Steam Locomotives of Scotland, Russell Wear & Michael Cook (Industrial Locomotive Society, 1990);

Hudswell Clarke Works List, Clive Hardy (Thomas Alexsandr, 1982);

The Wrexham, Mold and Connahs Quay Railway, J.I.C. Boyd (Oakwood Press, 1991);

The Collieries of Denbighshire, G.G. Lerry (Wynn Williams, 1968);

The Geology of the country around Flint, Hawarden and Caergwrle, C.B. Wedd and W.B.R. King (HMSO, 1924);

The Ironstone Quarries of the Midlands – Part three – Northamptonshire E.S. Tonks (Runpast, 1989); *Cumberland Iron*, A. Harris (Bradford Barton, 1970);

Lilleshall Company History, W. Howard Williams, January 1973;

The Industries of the Oakengates Area (An Historical View), W. Howard Williams;

Trafalgar Colliery internet website, Forest of Dean Local History Society;

The National Portrait Gallery, Cassell, Peter & Galpin, c1900; *Shropshire Mines internet website*;

1911 Encyclopaedia internet website; *The Coalbrookdale Coalfield – Catalogue of Mines*, Ivor J. Brown. Shropshire County Library, 1968.

Newspapers and Periodicals
Wellington Journal, Wellington Journal and Shrewsbury News, Telford Journal, Shrewsbury Chronicle, Shropshire Magazine, Colliery Guardian, Iron & Steel Trades Journal, London Iron Trade Exchange.

Primary Documentation
Archive material of the Lilleshall Company, comprising board meetings minutes, ledgers, day books, stock books, inventories, financial records, staff records, drawings, maps, plans, agreements, contracts, deeds, correspondence, and other records (Ironbridge Gorge Museum Trust);

Selwyn Higgins Archive – Lilleshall Company (National Railway Museum);

GWR, LNWR, LMSR and BR Working Timetables, 1898-1978 (National Railway Museum and author's collection);

Ordnance Survey Maps 1881 to 1975. 1:2500 series (Shropshire Records & Research); the correspondence files of the 3rd Duke of Sutherland (Stafford Record Office);

Agreement for restoration of working traffic on the Nantmawr branch between Cambrian Railways and John Parson Smith (RAIL252/278. PRO, Kew);

LNWR Diagrams of Private Sidings (RAIL410/996. PRO, Kew);

Ralph T. Russell Archive – Lilleshall Iron Company Locomotives (Courtesy Allan C. Baker);

Llay Hall Coal, Iron and Firebrick Co. Ltd. – Memorandum and Articles of Association dated 13 February, 1873 (Flintshire Record Office, Hawarden);

Llay Hall Colliery – Particulars of Sale on Wednesday, 26 October, 1881 (Flintshire Record Office); Locomotive Dimensions – NCB, West Midlands Division, No.2 Area (Engineering Dept., 3 April, 1964).

It is unclear as to whether this wagon has met with a nasty accident, or whether it was in the process of being scrapped. New Yard Works, 19 June 1954. [F. W. Shuttleworth]

INDEX

AG fuer Kohlendestillation	14
Albert, H. & E.	16
Bagnall, William G.	48
Bagueley, Ernest E.	48
Bell (Doncaster)	78
Benson, Moses George	98
Blockley, Benjamin P.	17
Birch, James	7
Bishton, James	7, 35
Blists Hill	
-Furnaces	12, 35
-Open Air Museum	81
Blount, William	8
Botfield, Thomas	35
Boulton, Matthew	7
Brassey, Thomas	40
Bridgwater, Duke of	7
British Wagon Co. Ltd.	126
Browne, Isaac	35
Cambrian Railways	92, 98
Canals	
-Bir'ham & L'pool Junction	35, 41
-Donnington Wood	7, 35, 37, 45
-Humber Arm	41, 42
-Lubstree Wharf	41, 43, 98
-Newport Branch	37, 41
-Shrewsbury	35, 37
-Shropshire	35, 37, 40, 84
-Shropshire Union	35, 41, 98
-Wombridge	35, 37
Cannock & Rugeley Colliery Comp	123
Cashmore, John	13
Chirk C'tle Lime & Stone Co. Ltd.	98
Church Aston quarries	97
Coalbrookdale Company	5
Coalport	35, 40, 89
Cook & Deans	122
Cowans Sheldon & Co. Ltd.	86
Darby, Abraham	5
Donnington	
-Barracks	18
-exchange sidings	41, 42, 79, 81, 86, 88, 90, 92, 102, 103, 107, 110, 114, 118, 128
-Ordnance Depot	81, 103
Donnington Wood	
-Brickworks	11, 21, 37, 45, 82
-Furnaces	7, 11
Dudley, Earl of (see Pensnett Railway)	
Eagle Ironworks	45
Thos. Edington & Sons	122
Fawcett, Preston & Co.	122
Fogerty, Joseph	40, 99
Fowler, John	40
France, Richard S.	98
Froghall quarries	98
Gilbert	
-John	7
-Thomas	7
-T. D.	8
Gilkes, Wilson & Co.	122
Gloucester Wagon Co. Ltd.	126
Gower	
-1st. Earl	5, 7
-2nd. Earl	7, 8, 35
Granville Country Park	11
Granville, Earl	6, 8
Great Central Railway	92
Great Northern Railway	123
Great Western Railway	79, 84, 86, 89, 90, 92, 98, 99, 123
Hadley Junction	88, 89, 92, 114
Highways Const'ion Ltd.	128
Hoffmann kiln	11, 46
Hoggins, Thomas	47, 48, 49, 130
Hollinswood	82, 86, 89, 90, 95, 99, 128
Hombersley, J.	8
Hope Paper Mills	17
Horton	
-John	18
-Robert H.	12
-Samuel	12
-T. E.	8
-William	8, 35
Humber Arm Railway	40, 41, 42, 43, 821, 98, 110
Humber Brook	41
Hurst, Neilson & Co. Ltd.	126
Ironbridge Power Station	85, 90, 117
Jerningham family	8, 18
Jones & Potts	122
Knowle Lime Ltd.	99
Lambs Lane	18
Leveson – Gower	
-Ed'wd Frederick	8
-Geo Granville	7, 10
-George William	47
-Granville	7, 8
Lilleshall	
-Cottage Hos'tal	18
-Quarry	97
-village	5, 97
Lilleshall Iron & Steel	8, 10, 92
Llanelly Dock & Rly Co	47
Llangollen Lime & Fluxing Stone Co. Ltd.	98
Llanymynech	98
Llay Hall Coal, Iron & Firebrick Co. Ltd.	17
Lloyd, John	47, 122
Lockwood, Sir G. H.	17
Locomotive sheds	27, 29, 41, 42, 43, 45, 82, 84
Lodge	
-Bank Coke Ovens	11, 27
-Furnaces	11, 12, 27, 35, 37, 41, 45, 78, 79, 81, 90, 98, 101, 102
-Tip	95, 104
INDEX (cont'd)	
LNWR	37, 41, 42, 79, 84, 88, 90, 92, 98, 122, 123, 124, 128
Lucena, Charles	8
Maddock & Son Co. Ltd., John	13, 84, 94
Madeley Wood Company	12
Malins Lee	18, 35
McConnell, James	8, 47
Meaford Pumping Sta	48
Midland Railway	48, 110
Midland Wagon Co. Ltd.	126
Murdock & Aitken	13

The former Granville Colliery brake van, restored to its former glory, at the Telford Steam Railway in 2002. The small panel on the lower left side, reading 'C.R.C. No.1' refers to its origins at the Cannock & Rugeley Collieries, from where it was transferred in the 1960s. [Author]

Nabb, The	11, 18, 37, 40, 82, 95
Nantmawr quarries	96, 98
Neilson & Mitchell	37, 67, 123
Nettlefold & Chamberlain	17
New Yard Engineering Works	14, 29, 37, 40, 42, 47, 48, 79, 82, 84, 86, 94, 95, 103, 113, 122
North Staffordshire Railway	92
Oakengates exchange sidings	79, 86, 88, 95, 128
Old Yard (Donnington Wood)	14
Onions, John	7, 35
Overend & Gurney	123
Pains Lane	18
Pave Lane	7, 35
Peel, Williams & Peel	122
Pensnett Railway	83
Philips, William	7
Phoenix Car & Wagon Wks Ltd.	122
Phoenix Foundry (see New Yard Works)	
Pierce Higgins, Selwyn H.	48, 123
Pitchcroft	35
Pits	
-Barnyard	19, 37, 45, 120
-Cockshutts	12, 16, 82, 120
-Dark Lane	20, 120
-Freehold	11, 22, 37, 81, 85, 104, 120
-Grange	16, 17, 23, 40, 46, 81, 93, 101, 113, 120
-Granville	16, 24, 40, 46, 81, 90, 93, 95, 101, 102, 103, 104, 105, 110, 113, 118, 120
-Hadley	7, 120
-Hope	17, 120
-Lawn	8, 16, 25, 35, 40, 92, 120
-Meadow	11, 16, 120
-Muxton Bridge	11, 16, 26, 37, 81, 104, 107, 120
-Stafford	8, 17, 32, 40, 90, 93, 120
-Waxhill Barracks	16, 33, 37, 81, 85, 120
-Woodhouse	8, 17, 34, 40, 46, 84, 93, 120
Potteries, Shrewsb'y & N. Wales Rlwy	98, 122
Presthope quarries	97, 98, 99
Price, Samuel T.	48
Priorslee	
-Asphalt Plant	16
-Distillation Plant	14, 84, 87
-Furnaces	13, 28, 45, 78, 84, 85, 95, 98, 103
-Hall	18
-Ironworks	13, 37, 40, 79, 82
-Signal Cabin	88
-Steelworks	13
W.R. Renshaw & Co. Ltd.	126
A. Roberts & Company	86
Rookery, The	102, 103
Russell, Ralph	48, 122, 131
Jos. Sankey & Son Ltd.	85, 92, 117
Severn Valley Railway	40, 90, 95
Shelton Bar Iron Company	8
W. Shepherd & Sons Ltd.	30, 104, 128
Shrewsbury	
-Coton Hill	114
-Harlescott	114
Shrewsbury & Birmingham Rlwy	37, 40, 95
Shrewsbury & Chester Railway	122
Shropshire & Mont'yshire Rlwy	98
Shropshire Associated Collieries	128
Shropshire Railway	98
Shropshire Union Railways & Canal Company	37, 42
Smith, John P.	98
Thos. Smith & Sons (Rodley) Ltd.	86
Snedshill	
-Brick and Tile Works	11, 31, 46, 84
-Concrete Works	14, 15, 31, 83, 84, 85, 87
-Forge	31, 84, 86
-Furnaces	12, 98
-Ironworks	7, 12, 35, 40, 79, 83, 128
-Steelworks	12
Southill Bank	35
Stafford	114, 117, 118
Stafford, Baron	8, 10
Stafford, Marquis of	7, 8, 10, 35
Steam cranes	85, 86
Stephens, Colonel H. F.	98
Stirling, James	123
Sutherland, Duke of	7, 8, 10, 42, 47
Tanat Valley Railway	98
Telford Horsehay Steam Railway	111
Uscocona	5
C. & W. Walker Ltd.	79, 103
Waxhill Barracks	18
Wellington	92, 99, 117
Wenlock Railway	40, 99
Wilkinson, John	12
John Hayes Wilson & Co. Ltd.	86
Wolverton Works	47
Wombridge	35
Wrekin Coal Company	11
Wrexham, Mold & Connah's Quay Railway	17
Wrockwardine Wood	
-Brickworks	11
-Furnaces	7, 11
Wyko plc	10

Tailpiece